THE TURNAROUND KID

THE TURNAROUND KID

What I Learned

Rescuing America's Most

Troubled Companies

Steve Miller

An Imprint of HarperCollinsPublishers

HarperCollins books may be purchased for educational, business, or sales promotional use. For information, please write: Special Markets Department, HarperCollins Publishers, 10 East 53rd Street, New York, NY 10022.

FIRST EDITION

Designed by Joseph Rutt

Printed on acid-free paper

Library of Congress Cataloging-in-Publication Data is available upon request.

ISBN-10: 0-06-125127-5
ISBN-13: 978-0-06-125127-6

08 09 10 11 12   OV/RRD   10 9 8 7 6 5 4 3 2 1

This book is dedicated
to the memory of
Maggie Miller
(1937–2006).

For forty years she was both my mentor and my tormentor.
At times she warmed my heart, and at times she gave me heartburn.
No one ever brought me more joy or more grief.

And if I had it to do all over again,
I'd do it all over again.

CONTENTS

PROLOGUE: AUGUST 11, 2006

It was past midnight as I drove through the deserted streets of suburban Detroit. My plane from New York had been delayed for hours by thunderstorms. I was exhausted from two long days of negotiations with lawyers and representatives of General Motors and the creditors and stockholders of the bankrupt Delphi Corporation. The latest in my string of complex industrial rescue missions, Delphi, a $27 billion global auto parts company with 180,000 workers, was my responsibility.

The talks had been torturous and frustrating. Normally, the details would be swimming in my head and I'd be eager to get home to share them with my wife, Maggie. Instead, nothing of what was discussed in New York was on my mind as I sped past darkened houses and commercial strips. I wasn't headed for home. I was driving to the sprawling complex of Beaumont Hospital, where Maggie lay dying of glioblastoma, an incurable brain cancer.

After parking my car in the hospital lot, I wound my way through the corridors and then took an elevator to the hospice floor. I pushed open the door to her room. The darkened space was washed with an eerie green glow from the lighting outside. There was no movement or sound. In the shadows I saw our eldest son, Chris, at Maggie's bedside, holding her hand as he had done all night, every night, for the past six days.

"SHE'S GONE," HE whispered.

She had stopped breathing twenty minutes before. The way she looked, lying still with her mouth open, made it seem that she was as surprised as I was by this turn of events.

Although I had known this moment was coming ever since Maggie's condition had been diagnosed in late May, I was stunned. As I sat down, I was flooded with emotions. I was angry, mostly with the weather gods who had denied me one last moment with Maggie while she still lived. I was also relieved that the nightmare of the past three months, watching her slip away, was finally over with. And I felt that strange, hollow sensation that comes with such an enormous loss. Maggie, who had been my mentor, and occasional tormentor, for as long as I could remember, was gone.

Chris got up and left us alone. I told Maggie I loved her and would miss her. I leaned over and kissed her and held her hand. She was still warm to the touch.

It was another ten minutes before a young doctor arrived and perfunctorily pronounced her deceased, and began filling out the paperwork. After the doctor came the chaplain, a cheerful and rotund fellow who said all the right things about life and love and family and death. Then he held hands with us in a circle next to the bed for a word of prayer.

At the nurses' station, they had all the paperwork ready to go. Two months earlier, Maggie, always the consummate planner, had insisted I go to a funeral home and get everything set. Also being a consummate skinflint in some ways, she had insisted on a simple cremation, no fancy casket, no memorial service. I had no intention of defying her last wishes in this regard, so I signed the papers, made sure Maggie's body was going to the right place, and then left with Chris.

———

CHRIS WOULD SPEND the next eighteen hours in his hotel room, recovering from near exhaustion. I returned to the apartment in Troy where Maggie and I had been living since I accepted the Delphi job a year earlier, in July 2005. I wandered around a bit and stared at all the touches—a picture here, a potted plant there—that she had added to make the sterile rooms our home away from home. Then, overwhelmed with fatigue, I crawled into our massive bed. Maggie had been my bed mate for more than forty years. We had held each other and cried in this bed after getting her prognosis. Now it felt like the emptiest place in the world.

After a few hours of sleep I arose and dressed and went to pick up our youngest son, Alexander, at a nearby hotel. Still in shock, and occasionally in tears, I was trying to grasp the notion of being a widower. Chris needed time to himself, so Alexander and I went to the funeral home as they were opening for the day and completed the arrangements for Maggie's cremation later that same afternoon.

Because I was the CEO of one of the nation's major corporations, one that was going through a widely publicized bankruptcy restructuring, Maggie's death would be news. At her insistence we had told almost no one of her condition, so her passing was going to come as a shock. I had a lot of calls to make, and I needed to take some time with details such as death notices and obituaries. I went into the office to work on these tasks, and was immediately and almost absurdly reminded that in the midst of my personal grief, which felt so enormous and all-consuming, the world continued to turn and the demands of my professional life were not going to let up.

For weeks a militant union group called Soldiers of Solidarity had been planning to picket Delphi headquarters, and this was the day. And so it was that on this brilliantly sunny morning scores of protesters from Delphi operations all over the state of Michigan arrived at the entry to our complex and rallied in full view from my office window to show their disgust at the company and at me personally. They chanted slogans, marched on the sidewalk, and carried placards saying things like:

REPLACE DELPHI BOARD OF DERELICTS
DELPHI COOKS THE BOOKS—WORKERS GET BURNED
SAVE PENSIONS—JAIL FRAUDS
READY TO STRIKE

My personal favorite was a sign belittling my decision to accept a salary of just one dollar a year during a restructuring that was going to cost thousands of workers their jobs. It read:

MILLER ISN'T WORTH A BUCK

Even in this dark hour, I could appreciate the life-goes-on irony of the moment and the wit behind the signs. Karen Healy, one of Delphi's top officers, wasn't so calm. She marched outside to confront the protesters and told them that they might want to reconsider their demonstration out of respect for Maggie's death. There was a moment of awkward silence, and then a sharp rebuttal. Workers die all the time, they said. The pickets stayed and were in full voice as I departed for the funeral home in midafternoon.

Alexander and I went to view Maggie prior to her cremation. (Chris was not ready to confront this kind of reality.) The viewing room was big enough for thirty or forty chairs, but Maggie was an intensely private person, and fittingly, Alexander and I were the only visitors. We each had a few minutes alone with Maggie, who looked peaceful in her favorite Lanz nightgown, the red-and-white one decorated with images of little dogs. She also wore her only watch, a twelve-dollar special with the Coos & Deschutes logo of our model railroad on its face. With her in the casket were an elaborate origami crane from our third son, Robin, and a handmade card from our only granddaughter, Weston.

As I stood beside Maggie I recalled that my father had said it was important to touch the dead so that we can absorb the finality of their passing. I leaned over to kiss her good-bye and touch her hand. She was cold and waxlike. My father was right. In this moment I knew she was really gone.

We followed the hearse that took her to the crematorium, a graceful white marble building in the middle of a beautiful cemetery. Once Maggie's casket was placed in the cremation oven, the attendant closed the huge and dignified brass doors that shut it off from view. Alexander went with the man in charge and personally activated the control to start the burning. We stayed for a while and talked about what was happening, but there wasn't anything further to see.

When I was back at my apartment, the phone rang. It was New York's governor, George Pataki, calling to express condolences. I thanked him and in the almost-awkward silence chatted a bit about work. I told him we were committed to keeping open our two big operations in New York, at Rochester and Buffalo. He thanked me for keeping jobs in his state, and sympathetically reminded me to take care of myself in the coming weeks and months.

That night Chris, Alexander, and I had dinner at a Japanese restaurant that had been one of Maggie's favorites. It seemed strange to be there without her. It seemed stranger still that on a day filled with so many varied and demanding experiences that I wouldn't be going home to talk them over with her. In the last twenty-four hours I had worked feverishly on the largest industrial bankruptcy in American history. I had come home to the death of my wife of four decades. I had been picketed at my office, kissed Maggie good-bye for the last time, and then chatted with the governor of New York, reassuring him about Delphi jobs in his state.

In the quiet when day was done, I realized how little I had ever reflected on the life I had lived at high speed for almost thirty years, moving from one corporate rescue to another. I was also struck by the fact that very few people, be they lawyers, stockholders, picketers, or politicians, ever seemed to understand that as we struggled to save big companies, they were dealing with a flesh-and-blood human being with compassion and emotion, not some one-dimensional caricature with a digital calculator for a heart.

As Maggie knew, I took every challenge personally, and from the beginning, with the Chrysler rescue, sought to lessen the pain while preserving what assets could be saved for workers, owners, debtors, and communities. These companies had never been mere numbers to me. They were always human endeavors, and the solutions I sought were based on rather idealistic values and what I understood of human nature. These were the things that Maggie and I discussed every evening.

Life's turning points invite us to take stock. I was confronted with one of these events in Maggie's passing, and it occurred at the intersection of controversies involving the fate of a major corporation, the anxiety of a workforce under duress, and a turning point of our global economy. These are more than enough impetus for this book, which I hope is something more than a business memoir. It is my attempt to understand, share, and explain a life spent performing rescue missions at the highest levels of corporate America, in partnership with many allies, including the one I lost on August 11, 2006.

THE TURNAROUND KID

One

FAMILY, VALUES, MAGGIE, AND ME

The sky was overcast and fog hung over the harbor, so even though it was ten o'clock on an August morning, the air was cool and the light was soft. Add the salty smell of the sea and the groan of the foghorn at the end of the nearby jetty, and this place—the small city of Bandon on the southern coast of Oregon—felt like home. I hadn't lived here in decades, but the connection was strong and I sensed it right down to my bones as I stood in front of the little house where I had spent many of my happiest days.

Painted gray with red trim, the two-bedroom cottage has been abandoned for years. Dust coated the siding. Dirt streaked the windows. I opened the door and saw the faded floral wallpaper that had been there since the 1940s. Inside I found a familiar green sofa. All the fixtures, from the kitchen sink to the ceiling lights and bathtub, were just as they were when I was six years old. The frame from my bed sat in the corner of the tiny room where I slept as a child.

In the stillness I recalled the sounds that greeted me from outside when I awakened on summer mornings. The sharpest of them all was the grinding whine of a huge band saw making the first cuts on a Douglas fir. It blended with steam whistles, the shouts of men, and the rumble of passing trucks to create a kind of industrial music. I also recalled certain scents—grease, sawdust, smoke, even exhaust fumes—that filled the air every day but Sunday.

All these sensations and images washed over me because this house, where I had gone to touch my roots and renew my confidence in the midst of crisis, once sat in the middle of a relentlessly busy industrial complex. Built atop a long wooden pier that jutted into the harbor, it included a huge sawmill circa 1910, shops and outbuildings, and a dock where coastal steamships were loaded with shipments for delivery to distant ports. It was called the Moore Mill & Lumber Company, and my grandfather, the manager and eventual owner, lived right in the center of it all.

Scenes from an old Oregon sawmill are not what most people find when they search their childhood memories, but I spent most of my preschool youth, my summers, and many school vacation days at the house on the pier in Bandon. As the first grandson of David and Emma Miller, I came in for extra attention (this was probably not fair to my siblings, David, Randy, and Barbara) and quickly came to love being with them. I took my first steps in their home and immediately began following my grandfather's lead.

"Let's go out to the mill and see if they're workin' or shootin' the breeze," he'd say to me in the morning. I'd scramble to get dressed— usually I wore a plaid lumberjack shirt, dungarees, and work shoes— and then tramp after Grampa as he made his rounds. I was fascinated by it all, but the sawyer who could turn a massive log into a stack of neat boards made an especially big impression. I could watch him for hours.

When I was old enough to avoid most of the dangers, I was allowed to roam free. I played in the corners of the mill complex and watched the endless parade of men, trucks, ships, and lumber. On one occasion, Grampa caught me riding the conveyor that hauled scrap wood and sawdust to the incinerator and gave me a stern lecture on safety. Sometimes I'd even clamber aboard the ships at the mill dock, and the crew would give me lunch. Without knowing it, in every moment I was absorbing vital lessons about the dignity of work and the rewards of honest enterprise.

In late summer 2006, as I walked to the little office building next to my grandfather's house, I felt the presence of the people of Moore Mill. Inside the abandoned office a half dozen swallows flitted around the ceiling lights in the rooms where bookkeepers, clerks, and salespeople once worked. Antiquated business forms filled the shelves in a back room. A mechanical adding machine gathered dust on the floor. Where Grampa's desk had stood, scraps of wood were piled three feet high. On a wall near the entrance, grime marked the place where the time clock and time cards were kept as workers checked in at the start of each shift.

Here, for generations, hundreds of men had started each workday. Management and labor formed a team to make not just two-by-fours but good lives for themselves and their families. The mill was the source of the money they needed to buy homes, feed and clothe their children, and save for the future. As an industry it was not an abstraction but rather the heart of the local economy. It turned the region's most valuable natural resource into a source of prosperity and pride. The mill's payroll fueled commerce. It paid taxes that kept the city going. It even sponsored the semipro baseball team, the Bandon Millers, who were the pride of the city every season.

My earliest memories of baseball involve Bandon Millers games, where I sometimes served as batboy. Even at the ballpark, Grampa wore his vested suit, tie, and fedora. A gold chain stretched across his belly, connecting the watch he kept in one vest pocket with the little knife hidden in the other. He was over six feet tall, a little bit stout, and his white hair gave him a sort of formal, distinguished look. He had an air about him that suggested a sense of purpose. His competitive spirit, whether it involved getting the best players for his semipro ball team or building his company by acquiring additional mills and timberland, was strong but tempered with the kind of realism expressed by so many people who had lived through the Great Depression.

Though always loving, even indulgent with me, at the mill Grampa was a serious manager who made sure things were done right. This was especially true when it came to safety. Sawmills are dangerous places, and though injuries were inevitable, he was a stickler about proper handling of tools and materials. He was also firm about production schedules. Customers depended on Moore Mill delivering on time, and he was determined that they be satisfied.

But while he was the boss, my grandfather was never a bully. Mutual respect governed his relationship with everyone at the mill, and I could see and feel in everything he did both his affection for the place and his sense of responsibility. He took all of it—the company, the workforce, Bandon—personally. My grandfather lived at the mill and worked every long day that it was open because he understood what it meant to real people. He had a feeling for the way that industries created opportunities for individuals. After all, he had been born into the working class. He had risen from the rough-and-tumble logging camps of British Columbia and the Pacific Northwest to mill manager and then finally—at the ripe old age of sixty-five—a mill owner, all without a high school diploma.

Grampa also knew how this operation, a simple lumber company, contributed to the well-being of the local community and a growing America. He had come to Bandon to run its biggest industry in the days following a great fire that had destroyed the entire city. The mill's success had financed the postfire recovery and lifted the people of Bandon out of their trauma. During World War II, Moore Mill aided the war effort with lumber to build bases and encampments. In the postwar years, the studs that steamed away in ships named the *Alvarado* and the *Oliver Olson* (among others) were used to build the suburbs of Los Angeles, San Diego, and many other cities.

There's something solid and essentially good in the history of the mill and Bandon. And I was lucky that when I returned to my mother and father in the not-so-big city of Portland, the virtues I had learned in Bandon were reinforced every day. Although he had joined the professional class, becoming a prominent lawyer, my father, Robert S. Miller, worked harder than anyone I have ever known, often donning his suit and tie and heading to the office on holidays and weekends, and even Christmas mornings.

As principal outside legal counsel, Dad was a key figure in transforming Georgia-Pacific Corporation from a small Southern plywood company into a huge global forest products conglomerate. He set the standards for ethics, character, and achievement that I would try to match in my own career. And it was G-P's founder and chairman, Owen Cheatham, who pushed me to add a business education to my law degree so that I would be properly prepared. He was right. I would forever be grateful for what I learned at Stanford Business School, which I attended after getting a law degree at Harvard.

But still, the important stuff about human character, values, and leadership I learned in Oregon. This education began with childhood observations, continued when I was given some work to do as an adolescent, and truly took hold when I was a young man. It was then that my father and Grampa sent me into the forest to labor as a real lumberjack. I did most of the jobs that were part of harvesting giant fir trees, including the dangerous work of breaking up logjams in local rivers. I can't say I was equal to the men who spent their lives in the forest. I wound up in the water almost every time I cleared a jam. But I loved the satisfying feeling that comes with giving your all, to the point of exhaustion, and then getting up to do it again the next day.

Besides offering me the chance to experience hard, satisfying work, my grandfather also introduced me to the world beyond Oregon. When I was eight he took me on my first trip east, to New York, for a World Series game. Everything I saw, from the stadium to the skyscrapers, opened my eyes to the possibilities in life. But nothing excited me more than the sight of Moore Mill lumber piled at the docks in Brooklyn. Here, thousands of miles from home, was evidence that what happened in Bandon mattered. Four years later, another trip east gave me further inspiration. Traveling this time with my father and brother David, I had lunch in the Capitol with Oregon's senator Wayne Morse. Somewhere between the famous bean soup and dessert, Senator Morse looked me in the eye and told me I should make sure to serve others, and the greater good, when I grew up. The message stuck.

Whether you consider life in the little gray cottage with red trim, the bustle of Moore Mill, and the wider world that Grampa and my father showed me, it's obvious that the family base in Oregon, and especially Bandon, formed my life's foundation. And though I'm in my sixties now, the place still pulled on me. There's no wondering why, in the waning days of summer 2006, when I faced two enormous challenges, I instinctively returned to walk the mill site, explore the nearby forest, and visit my family for inspiration.

———

ONE OF THESE challenges was very public because it involved my efforts on behalf of the huge Delphi Corporation, an auto parts and electronics supplier that had become an industrial basket case and was widely viewed as a bellwether for the entire U.S. auto industry. Spun off by General Motors in 1999, the company was losing about $1 billion per quarter on annual sales of roughly $28 billion.

Delphi had all the problems that afflict old-line heavy industries in America. Born as a spin-off from General Motors in 1999, it was saddled with labor costs equal to GM's but about triple the competitive labor contracts elsewhere in the supplier industry. They had been negotiated under conditions that had changed, and included retiree obligations that proved unsustainable. On top of this, many of the goods it made could now be manufactured much more cheaply abroad. Delphi's day of reckoning could no longer be put off, and to be realistic, its distress signaled just the start of what will be a painful but necessary restructuring of the entire American car and truck manufacturing industry, which people loosely call "Detroit."

The size of Delphi's problems, its status as a major industrial player, and a genuine belief that I could help led me to come out of retirement in June 2005 to accept the job as its chief executive officer. I had initially thought to refuse the job and remain in my comfortable retirement in central Oregon. But when I asked the recruiter why I should even consider undertaking such a stressful, arduous task, he simply replied, "Because your country needs you." It was the only thing he could have said that would have motivated me to accept.

———

BEGINNING WITH CHRYSLER in 1979–1980, I had helped about a dozen companies in similar straits with enough success that the *Wall Street Journal* had dubbed me "U.S. Industry's Mr. Fix It." (I take a less serious view, telling people they can find me in the yellow pages under "Flaming Disasters.") In Delphi's case, it seemed possible that I might help to salvage at least some of its jobs, assets, and intellectual capital for the good of everyone. Included in my concerns about the future of this Fortune 100 company were all the communities where it operated and the larger American economy, which would benefit if we could preserve at least some of the best parts of an important old-line industry. Equally important, a disastrous outcome for Delphi could take down General Motors and much of Detroit with it.

The tools at my disposal as I went to work at Delphi were limited and included, among others, the legal protection of a bankruptcy process to buy time, negotiations to reduce labor costs, and restructuring the company's domestic manufacturing operations. No matter what, the treatment for what ailed Delphi was going to hurt. Big cuts in jobs and manufacturing plants would be unavoidable. As the chief surgeon in this operation I wouldn't be doing the bleeding (not directly, anyway). But like many physicians faced with a desperate patient who waited too long to seek treatment, I would feel the pressure, hear the second-guessing, and receive much of the blame.

After a little more than a year on the job, we had made much progress toward saving most of the company's jobs and assets, in part by filing for bankruptcy. I had also become a piñata for militants in organized labor and demagogues unconcerned with complex realities. They attacked me with pickets, Internet blasts, and broadsides in the press. "They don't care about their shareholders; they don't care about their union contracts. It's all about them and all about corporate greed," said Ron Gettelfinger, president of the United Automobile Workers.

On the day when I traveled from Delphi's Detroit area headquarters to Oregon, the TV populist Lou Dobbs had muttered the word "disgusting" after a correspondent's one-sided report on Delphi and then growled, "The people who run that company should be embarrassed and apologize to the American people." I also received an e-mail message from a Delphi worker, who obviously agreed with Dobbs as he insisted that my own family must be ashamed of me. His note was a masterpiece of anger, but it's enough here to quote his closing: "Hoping You Burn In The Deepest Bowels Of Hell For All Of Eternity."

Though it was a little more harsh than usual, the stuff I was hearing from critics wasn't unexpected. I could handle the attacks. Painful as it was to quietly absorb the vicious verbal abuse, our executive team at Delphi had made a decision in late 2005 to stop talking to reporters—we didn't think the battle could be won in the media.

I also knew from experience, beginning in Bandon, how people and communities do struggle but eventually recover when industries leave. Opportunity breeds new companies, which grow and provide jobs and, eventually, a stronger, more diversified local economy. This had happened in Bandon when the Moore Mill reached the end of its useful life and closed. It could happen wherever Delphi might shut down factories. I empathized with workers and their families, but I also knew the process was inevitable, and I had confidence that things would work out all right in the end. The creativity and energy in our dynamic economic system inevitably lead us to adapt and improve, particularly when accompanied by the 'soft landings' (retirement or severance arrangements) that a revitalized Delphi could provide. Struggle is part of the equation, but whether it requires reeducation, reinvention, or relocating, Americans tend to find their way to a better life, and I was sure the people of Delphi, union and nonunion, could do it, too.

———

CONSIDERING THAT I had become a national scapegoat for what ails Detroit, you might assume that the overhaul I had agreed to perform for Delphi dominated my thoughts in the summer of 2006. In fact, it was the smaller of the two crises I faced that summer. The much bigger challenge of this season, perhaps the biggest in my life, had come when my wife, Margaret "Maggie" Kyger Miller, developed inoperable brain cancer.

In retrospect, there had been some early warning signs. In late 2005 Maggie had begun having trouble navigating the suburban Detroit neighborhood where we lived and said she got "nauseous" trying to figure out directions. This was despite the fact that she knew the area well, and it's laid out in such an orderly way, with major roads forming one-mile squares, that it's difficult to get lost.

At the start of 2006, Maggie had a few slipups while doing our household finances and bounced some checks. Though odd, these events were easy to ignore until May, when her occasional struggles to recall certain words, which is something we all experience with age, turned into a more stubborn speach impediment. When she was unable to communicate well enough to make an appointment, her doctor called me and insisted she go for tests immediately. Stroke was a real possibility. After a thirty-minute shouting match in which I threatened to pick her up and physically drag her to the car, Maggie finally relented. Later I realized that she had resisted so stubbornly because she sensed what was to come. The tests revealed the cancer. Only surgery, scheduled for the following week, would tell us how bad it was.

Maggie spent the time before the operation preparing for the worst. We talked about our sons, Chris, Robin, and Alexander, and what they should be told. She made sure I understood that if the issue arose, she didn't want extreme measures taken to keep her alive. No ventilators, defibrillators, tubes, and wires. If her time had come, she was ready to go. She cleaned everything in sight, even pulling beds away from the wall so she could chase down every last dust bunny.

On the morning of the surgery, the tension, and perhaps the tumor's effects on her brain, got to her. For some reason Maggie tried to wash a favorite old travel clock in the sink, with the result that you might expect—a ruined timepiece. "Everything is falling apart at the same time," she said through tears. "It's sending me a message that my time is up."

The surgery brought terrible news, which the doctor told me while Maggie was in the recovery room. The tumor was a glioblastoma, malignant and incurable. Half the people with this diagnosis die within six months, the rest within a year. I was devastated, and Maggie saw the truth on my face in the recovery room, even as I choked on the words. She was upset and cried, but only for a moment. Then she seemed determined to accept the verdict, saying that she was "grateful for the wonderful life" she had lived. She added, with her typical humor, that she was also happy that "I don't have to be worried about getting Alzheimer's."

People who knew Maggie as the strong, practical, and straightforward person she was won't be surprised to hear that she rejected every proposal I made to change our lives to accommodate her illness. Maggie was still her no-nonsense self. She always hated cut flowers because they wilt, and she wouldn't have them now. And she wouldn't even consider dropping everything and moving back to Oregon. There would be no retreat. "We came here to do a job, and it's not finished," she said.

In using the word "we," Maggie was correct. It's probably taboo for a CEO type to admit that his wife is his partner in business as well as marriage, but I have always been proud to claim Maggie as mine. I'm not talking about a typical corporate wife who supports her executive husband by taking care of home and family and social obligations, although Maggie did these things. I'm saying that she was deeply involved every time I decided to take a job, and her guidance was critically important. Once I agreed to an assignment and began work, she served as my daily debriefer, listening to my reports on various problems and challenges and helping me talk through strategies and solutions. She had a gift for evaluating people—she could go to the office Christmas party and by the end have figured out what made each person tick in a way that I couldn't in months of working together. Her ethical sense was always excellent, which helped me stay on course and in tune with my own values. (For example, when Delphi handed me a standard payment for moving expenses, it was Maggie who reminded me that the true cost of moving to a temporary apartment was near zero and I should simply return the check.)

So, as Maggie said, "we" had a job to do in Michigan, and true to our style, "we" were going to see it through. For the next few months she would insist that I meet my pressing obligations at Delphi. I put in long days at the office, flew to New York and elsewhere for vital meetings, and when necessary, fielded phone calls and e-mails when I was at home.

But as much as Maggie tried to keep things the same, this wasn't possible. I wanted to be with her, and made sure to get home early each day and devoted weekends to us. Sometimes we just lay in bed and listened to sentimental music, or laughed or cried together. We talked about everything. Did we do our best with our children? Of course we did. Were there regrets? None that mattered. But Maggie was sad that she would miss watching our grandchildren grow up, miss getting *really* old with me, and seeing the completion of the sprawling model train setup that we had spent years creating together in the basement of our home in Oregon.

The train layout had evolved into a miniature landscape of our shared dreams, experiences, and whimsy where shops and streets were named after children and grandchildren. It was a little world that we had built together, through countless hours of happy teamwork. Unfinished, it symbolized our future, and it was awful to imagine that

Maggie wouldn't spend more quiet hours on it with me in the years to come. I knew she felt the same way, but she moved quickly to acceptance.

"Your life will go on and I want you to be happy. You will find someone who will be perfect for you. She'll fill in the blanks, give you what I couldn't." I couldn't know it at the time, but she was right.

I didn't want to talk about the future without her. But she needed to discuss everything that lay ahead, even as she reviewed the life we had shared for almost four decades.

"I don't know how you stood living with me all these years," she said in a down moment.

"Yeah, you were a handful," I agreed, "but you were always worth it."

Ever practical, Maggie began cooking food that she could put in the freezer for me to eat sometime after her death. Accepting that it would never be finished, she closed the books on an extensive genealogy project that had become a bit of an obsession. She went through her belongings, the precious and the ordinary, and decided what would be done with everything. She tried to teach me everything I might need to know to live alone, including the recipe for the perfect popovers she made in a thirty-year-old cast-iron pan. (I had to produce a perfect batch before she would accept that I had learned her method.)

The markings on a calendar that Maggie kept showed the brief improvement her doctors predicted when she went on steroids to reduce the swelling in her head. Her speech got a little better, and her energy level rose to the point where she was able to exercise every morning. On June 25, her sixty-ninth birthday and four weeks after we got the terrible news, she wrote, "As good as it gets."

The way she seemed, I began to think Maggie might outlive the doctors' prognosis—six months or so—and I let myself hope she would be around for autumn and her beloved college football. In July I began to write this book, which is supposed to chronicle my life and experience as Mr. Fix-It for major corporations. I hesitated. Full of her usual strong opinions, she insisted I do it. She seemed like the Maggie of old.

Then the good effects of the steroids were overcome by the advancing cancer, and signs of trouble returned. She wrote "Downhill Slide" in her calendar. By the end of the month of July, the fatigue and speech problems were back. Having returned to the computer to resume her many e-mail correspondences, she suddenly found the mouse and keyboard too hard to handle. Talking again became a problem, with words and concepts becoming more elusive than butterflies. Maggie retreated, both psychologically and physically. She didn't want to see people or talk on the phone, even with our sons. She refused to leave the apartment and set up camp in a single, sunny little room where we installed a hospital bed and she pasted pictures of all the people and places she loved on the wall. Her decline was frustrating, terrifying, and exhausting. At a very low moment, she went into the kitchen and just pounded the hell out of the cabinet doors.

By August 1, Maggie's speech problems had grown much worse. Sometimes she just couldn't find the right words. In other moments she might grasp the vocabulary but fail to string together a sentence. Head shakes, nods, and other gestures became vital parts of our conversations. One morning I found her in the bathroom, staring at her toothbrush and the tube of paste. She knew they worked together somehow but just couldn't figure out how.

Two days later I came home in the evening and relieved a health aide who was with her during the day. I went to Maggie's room and offered a little menu of items for dinner, and she chose what she wanted. To pizza she said, "Too much!" But she nodded her approval for apple slices, grapes, bread, and soup. I put the soup in a cup, which I then put on the kitchen table, in front of her. She couldn't figure out what to do with it. A bowl didn't work either. She didn't recognize the spoon and instead put her finger in the soup and raised her hand to her face. She seemed puzzled that no soup had entered her mouth. I tried to help, but she wouldn't let me. In the end all she could manage was some fruit, and then she went back to bed.

The final crisis began about an hour after dinner. I went to her room and discovered her struggling to use her left hand to keep her right arm from flailing around. The muscles in her face twitched uncontrollably. "This is a short circuit of the brain's control panel," I thought to myself. In fact, it *was* a short circuit of a type. It was what's called a grand mal seizure.

Maggie shook her head to tell me that she wasn't in pain, but I knew she had to be frightened. I was. Over the phone her doctor said that if she didn't get better in an hour she should be taken to the hospital. When she didn't improve I knew I needed an ambulance but wasn't sure how to get one. I phoned Beverly Roberts, my calm-in-a-crisis executive assistant, and she told me who to call. The ambulance came immediately, and I followed as the medics took Maggie to the same hospital, Beaumont of Royal Oak, where she had worked as a volunteer and where our son Alexander had been born.

As an executive, I am decisive and sure-footed in emergencies. These are the qualities they pay me for. But as a husband following an ambulance taking his wife to the hospital, I was as distressed, anxious, and upset as anyone. I lost sight of the flashing lights and took a some-what longer route, but managed to park and then quickly locate Maggie in the emergency room. After they examined her and did some tests, the doctors told me that the tumor had grown and spread to cause the convulsion and put her into a light coma. The words that caught my ear were, "This could go slowly or fast."

"What are we talking about? Give me a range."

"We're talking days, not weeks."

In the brief moment that followed, I thought about Maggie's wish, that she be allowed to go without intervention. I remembered the distress I had seen in her eyes as her condition had grown worse in recent days. Now, at midnight, in the harsh light of the ER, I realized that this was actually good news. Maggie wasn't in pain. She would be spared the indignity of a long, drawn-out decline. I talked to the doctors about making sure she was comfortable and pain-free, accompa-nied her to a room on an upper floor of the hospital, and then went home for a few hours of sleep.

The next morning Maggie's care was managed by a young woman doctor from Romania who was warm, compassionate, and direct. She said that the parts of Maggie's brain that controlled breathing and heart function were being affected by the tumor's growth. Death would be painless, but it might come soon. Our three sons—Chris, Robin, and Alexander—should come right away, she added. "It's better that they come to say good-bye than to have regrets."

Nothing in life prepares you fully for these moments, but I knew Maggie well enough to be certain that she was ready to go. Two weeks earlier, when she could feed herself, read, and even write e-mails, she enjoyed at least parts of each day. But since then, her quality of life had been declining rapidly. I repeated Maggie's instructions to the doctors. She was to be kept comfortable, but they would spare her any interventions that would delay the inevitable.

Things were moving quickly. I called our sons, broke the news, and began making the arrangements to bring them to Detroit. A hospice specialist found me in a waiting area, and we began to arrange for Maggie's transfer to a special care group within the hospital. Difficult as all this was, I knew Maggie was going to leave us in the way she wanted, without a lot of drama and suffering. And at Beaumont I felt like she was going to get good, compassionate care. I liked it that one of the aides who had passed Maggie's bed took the time to pull the blanket over her exposed foot. And I thought it was a good sign that on all the hospital's computers the screen saver was a motto: "The patient is at the center of all we do."

Maybe it was the quality of care or the presence of her three sons, but after a couple of days, remarkably, Maggie woke up one last time. She recognized each one of us and seemed to understand what was going on. She smiled at jokes. She even reached out and straightened each of our shirt collars, after which she uttered perhaps the last word of her life: "Perfect!" This moment of grace lasted five hours. Then she went back to sleep, never to waken. She died a little after midnight on the morning of August 11.

When we were married, we had joked that we would give it a forty-year trial. We had been together for thirty-nine years, nine months, and two days.

———

THREE WEEKS AFTER Maggie died, I went back to Oregon, where my roots run deep, where we both felt at home, remembering how I had found in her reinforcement for the most important values I had acquired growing up. Although we had our ups and downs and some legendary blowups, we were never bored and never uncertain about what we stood for. As I thought about where life was going to take me without her, my mind was filled with memories of our past. And I realized how much Maggie and I had completed each other. Each one of us is broken in some way. If we are lucky, we find a partner whose strengths can fill in the cracks and missing pieces.

When we met, I was a twenty-four-year-old recovering straight-arrow nerd trying to have as much fun as possible while still grinding my way through Harvard Law. I had assumed that I would find a debutante/Wellesley type, marry her, and live a very conventional life. Then this beautiful woman, four years older than me, moved into the apartment across the hall with her seven-year-old son.

Beautiful, mysterious, and exciting, Maggie was a single mom who had come to Cambridge on her own from Hawaii so that Chris, her boy, would get a proper education. A free spirit, she dated regularly, even a law school classmate named David Rockefeller. Then one night she came to the apartment I shared with four other students and invited me back across the hall. On a mat on the floor of her living room, she led me into my first sexual encounter. There were only a couple months left before graduation, but we clandestinely repeated the experience numerous times thereafter. She made it clear that she loved me, and only me. I loved what Maggie stood for—honesty, hard work, fairness, integrity. These were the qualities I was raised to embrace, and she believed in them, deeply. And it didn't hurt that she had a romantic side that brought warmth to balance my very pragmatic approach. She expressed it in notes, drawings, and poems like this one:

> I think that I am very tired and sleepy
> and I think that I would like to have a nice
>   warm and comfortable Steven to
>   curl up against and close my
>   eyes and pretend that there
>   are no such things as
>   alarms that
>   ring at 5:00 AM
>   and I love
>   you very
>   much

In my entire life, before and since, I was never as conflicted as I was at the start with Maggie. We surely loved each other, but I was unable to openly challenge what I thought I was expected to do. This was a time before the sexual revolution had taken hold in middle-class

America. I was afraid to introduce Maggie—an older unmarried woman with a child—to my family and friends. Instead, I decided to let a pregnancy happen and used it to justify a sudden courthouse marriage. I then presented it as an unavoidable, shocking fait accompli.

It took me years to understand that the way I handled the most important personal decision of my life had been wrong. It went against everything that I had been taught growing up and everything that Maggie believed in. We prized openness, honesty, integrity, and fairness. But I hadn't acted according to these values. Instead I had underestimated everyone, including myself, and chose a path that I would regret ever after. The experience taught me many lessons, though. I learned to never abandon core values, that life doesn't unfold according to some script, and that the quick and easy way out often causes you long-term pain.

In time Maggie and I would build a life that was filled with more adventure than I ever expected. But at first we seemed destined to a slow-but-steady life of middle-class comfort. After business school I interviewed at several major companies, including banks in New York. I almost took a job with General Mills in Minneapolis, but after I noticed the Cheerios box on one executive's credenza I thought, "I can't get up every morning and make myself care about breakfast cereal."

Finally, Ford, which was considered one of the best-managed companies in the world, made an offer. We moved to the Detroit area, where I took a job in the finance department. In my first few weeks at Ford I got a glimpse of life at the top when the soon-to-retire company president, Arjay Miller (no relation), invited a bunch of us recent Stanford grads to lunch on the twelfth floor. Arjay was about to become dean of the Stanford Graduate School of Business, and he wanted to pick our brains. I remember the intense quiet, the private dining room, mahogany paneling, thick carpet, and Arjay's suit, which probably cost more than I was paid in a month.

At Ford I was trained in the ultramodern system for corporate finance developed by the so-called Whiz Kids hired from the air force by Henry Ford II when World War II ended. I also learned the difference between academic theory and real business, where I discovered that the reliability of the information I received was just as important as the sophisticated analytic calculations I would do with it. For example, one of my earliest assignments called for me to evaluate a proposed $100 million investment in a facility to make trucks powered by turbines. On paper, this was a clear winner of a project. Naturally, the engineering department had said they could solve problems with materials that caused the spinning turbines to break apart. We built the $100 million plant, but they never solved the problems; Ford never sold any turbine trucks, and the $100 million was a dead loss.

With such high stakes, it's easy to understand why the finance department labored over recommendations. Our standards were set by one of the Whiz Kids, J. Edward Lundy, whose rules guided everything down to how paper was properly punched. For a numbers guy, he was fanatical about the English language and always kept a copy of the classic Strunk and White guide to writing at hand. He issued to each new hire a sheet of regulations—we called them Lundyisms—designed to assure precise communication. For example, we were required to use the word *present* instead of *current* to describe a moment in time. Currents were found in rivers.

Lundy stressed precision in everything, right down to printed reports, and this could drive junior execs and their spouses a little crazy. In the days before photocopies were common, we used a reproduction machine called an Ozalid, which required carefully typed originals on onionskin paper, which you could edit by cutting out words with a razor knife and replacing them with the aid of transparent tape. This work was painfully slow, which meant many long nights of cutting and taping. I will forever recall one night when the last secretary had departed and a piece of tape got stuck in the machine. Our original was shredded. I wearily sat down to type a new page. The phone rang. Maggie was on the other end. "Do you know it's two A.M.?" she asked. Then she barked, "Well, don't bother coming home!" In fact, I didn't know just how late—or early—it was. But the tone of her voice helped me decide to just stay at work through the next day.

I could have remained in Detroit, mastering the Lundy way and coming home each night to Maggie, Chris, and soon a second child, named Alexander. The company was so big and stable that plenty of midlevel executives were like tenured professors comfortable in their routines and secure in their jobs. I was ambitious but realistic. Ford was hiring scores of bright executives every year. I wanted to go as high as I could go—vice president perhaps—but I looked at the odds and doubted I would make it. Then I was offered a chance to go to Mexico, where Ford had been making and selling cars and trucks since 1925.

Almost everyone I knew at company headquarters thought it was a bad career move that would put me "out of sight and out of mind" when the big bosses considered promotions. But I had been dealing with the Mexican subsidiary and was intrigued by the opportunity to get away from the paperwork in Dearborn and closer to the action of making and selling cars to customers. I had also enjoyed living abroad as a student at Stanford's outpost in Italy. But it was Maggie who was most thrilled by the prospect of a new country and culture. She had no doubts about the move.

Both of us bloomed in Mexico. I received a much broader and deeper exposure to business and got my start as a manager and boss. Among the expats and Mexican women Maggie met were many with a far more worldly and sophisticated point of view than she had discovered in suburban Detroit. Struck by the inequity in Mexican society, most especially the struggles of poor mothers, Maggie dove into volunteer work for a women's health organization and opened a charity bookstore, selling donated volumes for twenty-five cents apiece.

In her leisure time Maggie prowled shopping districts for arts and crafts pieces and began a lifetime pursuit of amateur archaeology. She started in the neighborhood where we lived, digging where crews had cleared land for a new home and uncovering artifacts from many different eras. It was exciting but also risky work. Our son Chris would forever recall the time he was buried when a hillside hole collapsed and he was rescued with a frantic pull on his legs. It was scary but it didn't stop the explorers. New opportunities arose every time local farmers plowed their fields. Maggie and the boys and a couple of neighborhood kids who became their helpers would race to sift the dirt and discover bits of pottery and relics that were as much as two thousand years old.

Mexico went so well that when the tour of duty ended and we returned to the United States, we felt bored. We jumped at the chance to go to Australia, where the company had a long history, including the first pickup-style utility vehicle, which the Aussies called a "ute" and founder Henry Ford had called "a kangaroo chaser." Ford was making a big push in the region. My new job, financial analysis manager for the far-flung Asia-Pacific group, which had five times the annual sales of the Mexico division, was a major step up. It also put me on the scene as the region's economy revved up for international competition. On trips to Japan, Korea, and other countries I could see that these countries would become major players in trade. Even though the American public still regarded "Made in Japan" as an epithet, the rumbling of Asian power in the global economy could be heard clearly.

In Australia we found a solid brick house in a pretty neighborhood where the boys could walk to the corner convenience store (called a milk bar) and the newsagent where Alexander checked every day for a new *Mad* magazine. The boys developed Aussie accents and a taste for cricket. I got to see the imperial side of the U.S. auto industry up close. It happened when Henry Ford II, a figure as mysterious to me as the emperor of Japan, announced that he would come for a visit. We dropped everything and began spiffing things up. The water tower at the factory, which sported the chief's name, got a fresh coat of paint and so did our offices. We also developed elaborate plans, including a night at the opera, a sail in the harbor, and a stay at a beach house.

This kind of preparation for a visiting mogul was not as unusual as you might expect and wasn't limited to Ford. People tend to overreact to the top bosses at the world's largest companies. At General Motors one bigwig announced that he wanted cold drinks and fixings for a ham sandwich in his hotel room. They knocked out a window and got a crane to lift a refrigerator into his suite. We didn't make any structural changes to buildings for Mr. Ford. However, as it turned out, our efforts came to naught. Right before he was supposed to leave Detroit he had a heart attack. He stayed in the States. In his stead came a cold fish, by-the-numbers finance guy named Phil Caldwell, who spent his visit poring over our books and critiquing our operations. I don't know if he ever even saw the water tower.

Imperial visits aside, Maggie and I both loved our time abroad. We relished the chance to learn about a new part of the world, and the company's generous vacation plan allowed us to stretch beyond our assigned post. Instead of taking our annual expenses-paid vacations in the United States, we took extended trips to Africa and the Middle East. Like my foreign assignments, these experiences gave us invaluable exposure to new cultures, people, and ideas. Whenever possible, I visited Ford facilities, like the assembly plant in Nazareth, Israel. Each of these encounters, like my boyhood visit to the Brooklyn pier where Moore Mill lumber was stacked on the docks, taught me that the world economy was becoming more interconnected every day and that the future for big industries would involve a global market. This truth was widely known at the time, of course, but seeing real people producing, selling, and competing all over the globe made a profound impression on me. I could see for myself that America faced a future of intense economic challenges from people who were bright, innovative, and in many cases, hungrier in every sense of the word.

The world would have served as our teacher for many years to come, if Maggie and I had followed the course we imagined for ourselves in the seventies. After Australia we went to Caracas, where I worked for Ford Motor de Venezuela, one of the company's busier foreign outposts. Here Mr. Ford actually did show up for a planned visit, which we had anticipated with so much care that a company plane had been sent to Aruba for cases of all his favorite spirits to ensure that every place he might go would be properly stocked. On the first evening as I escorted Mr. Ford to the restaurant bar, the bartender asked for his order, Mr. Ford requested ginger ale. The only thing we hadn't procured! The bartender shook his head no. I was sure my career was over. But did this prince of Detroit throw a tantrum? No, he had lemonade.

For the most part, our life in Caracas was agreeable. Although our oldest son, Chris, was at boarding school in Michigan, our home still bustled with Robin and Alexander and seven pets, including a Great Dane and a collection of chattering birds. The tropical setting, another friendly community of expatriates, and the delight of new experiences enchanted us. Where else could a summer vacation involve a trip into the jungle in a dugout canoe ending at Angel Falls, where the Auyan Tepui River plummets three thousand feet?

The Ford Foreign Legion, as I called it, was a great fit for the Millers. Robin and Alexander had become remarkably adaptable and happy in their life abroad. Maggie got to indulge her voracious intellectual appetite as she explored new cultures, territories, and societies. And for a still-young executive I had more freedom and could get involved in more vital areas of the business than would be possible back in Detroit. By November 1978, when I sat down to write my annual Christmastime letter to far-flung family and friends, we were truly happy and content with the life we had built.

> We are looking forward to another good year in 1979. Our plans for "home leave" are being set up for a trip to England in May to drive about the countryside and see whether we'd like to go on assignment there someday.

I didn't know at the time that my boss in Caracas, Gerald Greenwald, was being wooed by Lee Iacocca, the new boss at our competitor, Chrysler. Despite a remarkable record of success at Ford Motor Company, Iacocca had just been fired by Henry Ford II with the words "I just don't like you." The animosity was mutual. Lee considered Henry a bigot and "a real bastard." Ford had been so obsessed with Iacocca that he had ordered a sweeping secret investigation of his business activities and private life. As you might do in this atmosphere, once he was settled at Chrysler, Iacocca began raiding Ford's staff for talent.

Lee contacted Jerry and asked him to join his top executive team and help save the nation's number three carmaker from impending doom. Though he must have been flattered, Jerry was understandably wary. He took months to research Chrysler's prospects, consider his own options, and make a decision.

It was easy to understand why the competition had sought him out. Though hardly more colorful than a glass of water, Jerry was a true genius with numbers who could quickly digest a fifty-page report and offer an accurate analysis. Under his leadership Ford Motor de Venezuela had gained a larger market share than the company enjoyed anywhere outside North America. In his first year in Venezuela the division reported a record $100 million annual profit.

At the time, Chrysler desperately needed executives with Jerry's abilities. The company's problems were numerous and enormous.

First, it had a bizarre sales system that allowed factories to turn out thousands of cars that would be stockpiled until dealers requested them. At one point this inventory, called the "sales bank," exceeded one hundred thousand cars. Second, as turmoil in the Middle East was pushing gas prices skyward, the company had few efficient models to sell. Instead, dealer lots were filled with big cars. Finally, quality was so low that the company's share of the U.S. market had fallen to less than 13 percent, and it was spending $350 million per year on warranty repairs. Everyone knew the cars were troublesome. One cartoon I saw showed a salesman telling a customer that each Chrysler came with its own autoworker who would fix it. No wonder losses for the coming year were projected to total more than $1 billion, which *Time* magazine would call "the gaudiest splash of red ink in U.S. corporate history."

In the finance area, which was Jerry's specialty, Chrysler was similarly messed up. The company had almost no central system for borrowing or accounting. Managers relied on hundreds of small loans, each negotiated individually, and they paid bills through many different accounts and banks. Financial information was gathered catch-as-catch-can, and while the overall numbers were probably accurate, nobody could pinpoint sources of trouble.

Without good financial analysis, executives at Chrysler struggled to make decisions. If you wanted data, you needed first to invent the system for gathering it. All of this would be shocking for someone who had worked in finance at Ford, where precise systems controlled everything and analysts would prepare a thick binder filled with numbers, charts, and reports anytime a problem was identified or an important proposal was made.

Yet, with all its problems, Chrysler was still the tenth-biggest corporation in America and offered opportunity for a talented man like Jerry, who must have noticed, at age forty-four, that all the higher rungs at Ford were already crowded and the competition for space grew more cutthroat with every step. For this reason and others Jerry listened carefully when Iacocca offered him the controller's job and rapid advancement to the president's office if all went well. This route out of what he called the "bean counter" role appealed to Jerry because he had always wanted a broader mandate.

As Jerry weighed his options, he knew that on the plus side Chrysler had in Iacocca a charismatic executive whom Robert McNamara once described as "worth his weight in gold." Lee, who could fill a room with both his personality and the smoke from his Havana cigars, was a legendary figure in Detroit. He was widely credited with creating the Mustang—an achievement that put him on the covers of both *Time* and *Newsweek* the same week in 1964—and making Ford the hot brand of the 1960s.

Iacocca's appointment at Chrysler had made everyone from the executive suite to the production line more optimistic. He couldn't guarantee what the company would be like, or even if it would exist, over the long run. But he could promise Jerry a key role in one of the most exciting industrial dramas in American history.

On the negative side of the ledger Jerry had to consider that he was giving up a secure future at Ford. Chances were good that he would be viewed as disloyal and never be welcomed back. This was why he heard a lot of pessimism in the voices of those he consulted on a very private basis. At Chrysler the only thing that was certain was the challenge.

In the end, perhaps, it was the challenge that made him say yes. Anyone in Jerry's position might well tread water in the Ford bureaucracy until retirement. But for a smart, ambitious executive reaching his peak years, the opportunity posed by such a complex and intriguing challenge outweighed the risk. Jerry jumped in with both feet and refused to be lured back when both Bill Ford and Henry Ford II tried. He became the first member of what would be called Iacocca's "Gang of Ford" in the top rank at Chrysler. When he and Lee then targeted their next recruit, no one would be more surprised than me and, perhaps, Maggie.

Two

THE HARD PART STARTS NOW

In 1978 the U.S. auto industry was both a very a big and a very small community. It was big because counting suppliers, vendors, and dealers, it employed more than one million people and did more than $100 billion in business every year. It was small because managers were concentrated in one region and a relatively small number of key players—a few dozen, at most—called all the shots. Everyone tended to know everyone else, and thanks to a hyperactive grapevine and aggressive industry press, most of us understood who was up, who was down, and where the business as a whole was heading.

At the moment he took control of Chrysler, Lee Iacocca was the most visible automotive executive in America. He may have been the country's best-known businessman, period. Thanks to his personality and his success introducing the Mustang, the public recognized him as a dynamic and confident leader who was the youngest man ever to run the Ford division of the larger Ford Motor Company. And certainly everyone in the industry, from my outpost in Caracas to the General Motors boardroom, had an opinion about the man. He had turned himself into an actual celebrity, and this rubbed some traditionalists the wrong way. Others thought he had great instincts for the market and had reignited America's love affair with cars.

In my humble, midlevel executive's opinion, Iacocca was a superstar, one of the few people who understood every element of the industry from design to production to marketing. An engineer by training,

Lee was an earthy extrovert who had come up the ranks through the sales division and was a gifted communicator. He had a way of boiling down complex issues to a few basic facts. He was also the archetypal "buck smeller," a term he used himself to describe an executive who understood, on an instinctual level, how to meet the public's taste with cars that could be manufactured and sold at a profit.

Five years earlier, in 1973, the Arab oil embargo had produced gas shortages, a sudden demand for smaller cars, and a crisis for U.S. automakers who didn't have them to sell. Of course the problem wasn't just the price of gas. Oil shortages rippled through the economy, making people worry about the future, and when they are worried about the future, consumers delay nonessential purchases, like cars. This is why the auto industry suffers more than, say, agriculture when times are tough. You can't stop eating. But you can drive an old car for another year or two. This explains why Detroit sold 20 percent fewer cars during the 1973 oil embargo, while sales of small, economical foreign cars actually increased.

Iacocca had adjusted to the challenges of the 1970s. At Ford his team had built more fuel-efficient vehicles and begun to explore the future with designs for front-wheel-drive cars and minivans. Surely he would bring enthusiasm for innovations like these and his enormous competitive energy to the Chrysler cause. This energy would no doubt be amplified by the anger Lee felt about what happened to him at Ford. Always a man who took things to heart, he would pour himself into the job of rescuing Chrysler, if only to prove that conventional wisdom in Detroit, which held that the cause was already lost, was wrong.

Unlike others at Ford who may have resented Lee or were interested only in crushing the competition, I wanted to see him and Chrysler succeed. To me, Chrysler's survival seemed vital to the health of the domestic auto industry and the larger American economy. I believe in competition, and on that basis alone, it was better for everyone, including consumers, stockholders, and workers, to have a Big Three—General Motors, Ford, and Chrysler. It was better even for Ford to be second in a field of three than last in a field of two.

Besides my faith in the power of competition to produce better cars and better companies, I had a sentimental connection to Chrysler. In April 1979, when Lee drafted my boss, Jerry Greenwald, to become

Chrysler's controller, I knew that the turnaround campaign had a fighting chance for victory. More than most foreign divisions, Ford Venezuela was a car company in miniature with its own factories, suppliers, dealers, and finance arm. This setup meant that Jerry had received a top-to-bottom education in the car business. He wasn't a perfect leader in Venezuela. He made a big mistake when he ramped up production too quickly and overwhelmed our manufacturing capability. Nevertheless, during his three years in Caracas sales doubled and profits grew ten times. He also built morale and improved Ford's relationship with local government authorities. Since the U.S. government had begun to regulate the auto industry more heavily, and might play a major role in Chrysler's future, Jerry's entire skill set would be put to use.

Not that I gave Jerry's future much thought. In the months after he departed there was plenty to keep us busy in Venezuela, as we struggled with problems related to our rapid growth. Auditors from headquarters came for an extensive review, and we found we had to hire more than a hundred new people to improve management controls.

In September 1979 Maggie and I went to the annual convention of the Ford dealers of Venezuela, which was held in Rome. On the flight back we had a long heart-to-heart talk about our life in the Ford Foreign Legion. Maggie was already in her forties, I was getting close, and as much as we loved our life abroad, it was demanding. Ford required me to work long hours, days, and weeks. I didn't see as much of Maggie and the boys as I wanted to. She may have relished the exotic aspects in life in Caracas, but it was the kind of place where many Americans had to live behind security walls and faced the very real threat of kidnapping. William Niehaus, an American executive who had been abducted from a house in our neighborhood by leftist terrorists, had recently been freed after three and a half torturous years in captivity. Even though we tried to push the danger out of our minds, the stress was still there.

As we cruised across a peaceful sky, we noted that my experience in business was worth something, and also I owned both a law degree and a master's degree in business administration. We could return to the States, where I might move to a less demanding industry—no, not something as boring as cereal, just a less stressful business—and expect to make good money while enjoying more hours at home. It was a nice fantasy. It was not to be.

A week after the Rome convention, Jerry Greenwald called my office in Caracas. Guessing that he was likely inquiring about some old expense reports that hadn't been reconciled, I let him wait on hold while I went to get his file. When I finally picked up the phone, Jerry said he wasn't at all interested in expense accounts. He had news. John Riccardo, the chairman of the board at Chrysler, was retiring. Come January, Iacocca was rising to the role of chairman and chief executive officer. Jerry was going to be bumped up to executive vice president, and he was looking for troops.

Before he offered me a job, Jerry explained that the executive corps at Highland Park, where Chrysler was headquartered, had been gutted long before Lee got there. Talent was thin, and anyone with any ability would be drafted to perform the work of several people. "The good guys get sucked into the vacuum" was the way he put it. And, he added, he'd like me to leap into the vortex.

The position he offered, as an assistant controller for all of Chrysler, was so far above my current job that it might take me a decade to reach the same level at Ford. And the way Jerry described it, I would have a hell of a lot more responsibility than the title suggested. Chrysler was going to ask the federal government to provide guarantees for a massive refinancing plan that could involve hundreds of banks, insurance companies, and other lenders all over the world. The guarantee would mean that the Feds would pay off the loans if we couldn't. But it would be conditioned on every existing lender agreeing to certain modified terms.

The scope of the Chrysler reorganization was unprecedented, and much of the actual face-to-face work of negotiating each little piece of it would fall to me. This was hardly the peaceful, less hectic life that I imagined with Maggie on our flight home from Rome.

I didn't answer Jerry right away, and if anyone had walked into my office after I hung up the phone I would have said I was against the idea. But then I called Maggie at home. She said, "Well, of course, let's go." I blanched. "Not so fast," I said. "There are a lot of things for us to consider." For example, our home in suburban Detroit was leased out and had ten months to go before we might move back in.

But that's the way it was with Maggie. She made decisions in her gut or her heart and acted. And sure enough, we soon got a little support in the form of a telex from Detroit telling us that the tenant who had rented our house was breaking the lease and moving out ten months early.

Coming as it did on the very day that Jerry Greenwald made his offer, the telex seemed like a sign, but I wasn't going to heed it right away. Unlike Maggie, I liked to roll things around, list the pluses and minuses, and gather advice from people I trust before I make a big decision. In this case I turned to my sons Alexander and Robin, who were happy to help me fill in some columns on a notepad.

The list on the plus side was fairly short. It included the satisfaction of saving Chrysler for the good of the auto industry, its people, and ultimately the entire country. We also put down the possibility of future rewards—a higher post, better pay—should things work out. And we considered leaving Caracas, which was becoming more stressful every day, a plus, too.

On the minus side of the ledger we made a much longer list. First we noted that the job was going to be very demanding and pull me away from the family. Chrysler was cutting its international divisions, which meant no future posting to exciting locales. We had friends in the Ford family whom we might not get to see again. The salvage effort being mounted by Iacocca could fail, leaving me without a job. And finally, I would feel disloyal leaving a company that had done so much for me.

The minus list was long, but it didn't amount to a powerful argument. Yes, staying at Ford meant a certain level of security and comfort. But here was a chance to be part of one of the boldest business campaigns ever mounted. The challenge at Chrysler seemed too important to pass up. I took a risk and called a friend, Mike Hammes, who was president of Ford Mexico. After I blurted out the details, he offered a surprisingly bold response: "Take it."

Mike's words helped tip the scale, and I began to imagine a future at Chrysler that involved long, hard, but satisfying days spent on work that mattered. Senator Morse's words about public service echoed in my mind. A vital industry was at stake. Hundreds of thousands of families depended on Chrysler-related paychecks. The opportunity to play a key role in something so big and so important began to feel irresistible. Nevertheless, I left myself the option of saying no when I called Jerry Greenwald and said I was coming to Detroit to meet with him and Iacocca. I had one serious concern that needed to be addressed.

I tend to be a fairly doctrinaire, sink-or-swim capitalist. On principle I don't like government bailouts, handouts, or any easy outs for companies that have gotten themselves into trouble. But in this case, company executives had tried every way possible to find a private solution. Iacocca had entertained wealthy sheiks and foreign takeover bids, to no avail. Also, I could see how federal regulations had played a role in the company's troubles. Government-mandated equipment for pollution control, in particular, created a special burden for a lower-volume, cash-poor company like Chrysler. Why shouldn't the Feds help us out, given that burden and Chrysler's value to the national economy?

Still, I wanted to hear what Lee had to say about the loan guarantee proposal and how much federal oversight he would tolerate. If he anticipated a long-term relationship with government overseers who could challenge every decision we made, I wanted no part of it.

———

I FLEW INTO Detroit for the last weekend of September and ran over to Ann Arbor to see my son Chris, who was studying at the university there. On Monday, October 1, I drove to Highland Park, where, compared with the big glass box that was Ford's landmark headquarters building in suburban Dearborn, Chrysler's executive offices occupied rather dreary real estate. Highland Park had seen its best days in the 1920s, when it was home to the first Ford Model T plant, which was long closed. In 1979 its population was falling steadily, and urban decay—marked by boarded-up houses, closed businesses, and empty lots—was eating up the community, block by block. Chrysler's headquarters occupied an old factory, which stood forlornly against the tide of decline.

Fortunately, the setting did not dim Iacocca, a man whose body language and big smile always radiated confidence. He was optimistic and even a bit feisty when it came to my worries about federal interference. In the prior week some Treasury Department officials had tried to pressure him about future Chrysler products, and Lee had told them they could go straight to hell if they expected a loan guarantee would give them that kind of power. I told him I would be ready to start work in a week. And it was only after I left his office that I realized I hadn't even asked what I'd be paid.

Lee had that effect on people. His energy and sense of purpose made you feel like you were joining not just a company but an important cause. But while this emotion made it easier to sign up for something new, it didn't ease the pain of saying good-bye to people at Ford, where I had started my career and worked for more then ten years. On the day after my visit to Highland Park, I went to the glass box in Dearborn to see my bosses in the finance group. My voice cracked as I explained my decision, but to my relief everyone accepted it with grace. They even wished me good luck.

Six days later, after a frantic week of wrapping things up in Caracas, I joined the morning rush hour traffic in Detroit, pointing my car toward Highland Park. My picture had appeared in the morning paper next to a headline reading, "Chrysler Raids Ford Again for Financial Analyst." The news was also on the radio. This kind of publicity was a first for me, and it gave me a little kick. Other new experiences lay immediately ahead, and I quickly came to understand that I was no longer a "process" guy helping to run things day to day. I was becoming, instead, a more inventive problem-solver, a fixer you might say, who would have to create solutions on the fly as we dealt with a problem that no corporation had ever faced before.

Other companies, most notably Lockheed, had been rescued with federal loan guarantees. But none had ever needed to win union concessions and restructure more than $1 billion in debt from hundreds of banks in order to qualify. To make matters worse, we were getting killed by a recession that had reduced demand for new cars by more than 30 percent. All domestic manufacturers were in trouble. By 1980 more than half a million autoworkers would be laid off, and skyrocketing interest rates would make it very difficult for many potential buyers to finance a new car, even if they wanted one. It was worse for us because our market tended toward low-end, cheaper cars whose buyers were least qualified financially.

Chrysler's troubles were also made worse by the multiplier effect of poor sales at our dealerships. A hypothetical example explains this phenomenon. Imagine a dealer in Sheboygan who sells ten cars in a typical month and likes to keep double that number in inventory. In a normal month he'd have to order ten cars to replace the ones sold. But in a bad month, when an economic recession scares potential buyers, he sells only eight cars. Now he's got twelve cars on hand and starts to doubt he can move ten next month. A cautious sort, he orders only four new cars, so he can stock sixteen, which is still double last month's sales. He's acting rationally, but for the factory, a two-car sales drop in Sheboygan means a six-car drop in manufacturing for next month.

It gets worse. Take the trend in Sheboygan and stretch it across the country. Now orders are so low that there's hardly any work for the Chrysler factory. Losses at the company mount. Layoffs are announced. The nation's unemployment rises. The recession gets worse. Fewer people buy cars.

This is the vicious cycle that was at work when I joined Chrysler. In a year's time the company had had eliminated thirty thousand white- and blue-collar jobs. Iacocca had cut his salary to a symbolic one dollar, and other execs had accepted significant pay cuts. We were in a race to put all the pieces of a reorganization together and avoid bank-ruptcy, which would likely destroy the company.

Within days of my arrival at Highland Park I fell into the seven-day-a-week task of understanding our finances and plotting strategy. The first milestone was the development of a new five-year operating plan. (A previous one had been hastily drawn and then rejected by the Feds.) On my tenth day on the job, I produced a one hundred page plan called the 'green book.' This document would become the foundation of the Chrysler Corporation Loan Guarantee Act, and it would be revised almost continually as Lee and others negotiated with President Jimmy Carter's administration and members of Congress.

At the same time, the top management in the company still had to run a car company. They did their best to market Plymouths, Dodges, and Chryslers with rebates and celebrity spokesmen Joe Garagiola and Ricardo Montalban. But Chrysler didn't have the cars people wanted. The real key to our future involved developing new ones that would meet federal standards for safety, pollution controls, and gas mileage while demonstrating better design and quality for consumers. To reach this goal the company was tooling up to produce a new lineup, dubbed "K-cars," similar to a vehicle envisioned when its chief proponent, Hal Sperlich, had been at Ford. It was going to feature front-wheel drive and a gas-sipping four-cylinder engine, but carry six people.

While the K-cars represented the future, we still had to turn out cars in plants that were hardly state of the art. This task, when added to the reorganization effort and new product planning, practically overwhelmed our team, which had been cut to the bone to keep costs under control. The stress led to some surprises. At my first production planning meeting involving all of Chrysler's top executives, I followed one of our managers, Jerry York, to a conference room where he was going to present fifty pages of facts, figures, and analysis. Seated next to me, Jerry opened his report and started reading from the first page. Suddenly he stopped, turned to me, and said, "Why don't you take over?" Then he slumped over, unconscious.

For a brief moment some of us surely feared that this seemingly healthy guy had suddenly keeled over and perhaps died. But Jerry soon stirred and groggily came to. He had just fainted from sheer exhaustion. Medics took him out on a stretcher. When I was asked to take over the meeting, I just about wet my pants; I was pretty clueless about the subject matter. Jerry came back the next day, chagrined but ready to work.

In retrospect, it was probably inevitable that someone would collapse in the middle of all the frenzied work. Most of us ran on half rations of sleep and double helpings of coffee for months on end. But except for family and close friends, we kept the anxiety, frustration, and worry to ourselves. And because Lee was ultimately successful in getting Congress to approve the loan guarantees, many people wouldn't remember that he faced stiff opposition from many in politics and business. Editorial cartoonists also had a field day with Chrysler. One of my favorites showed two old tycoons at lunch. One says to the other:

My horoscope advises that I plunge ahead with reckless abandon and that wild success dominates my scenario. I think I'll buy some Chrysler stock!

The more biting cartoons compared Chrysler with bank robbers and welfare recipients. But even these barbs were easier to take than the attacks that came from business insiders. When the Business Roundtable, which spoke for many of the country's largest companies, publicly opposed federal help for Chrysler, Lee took it very personally. He wrote a stinging letter, pointing out that the group had not opposed similar help for steel companies, shipbuilders, and airlines, and he declined their invitation for Chrysler to join their group.

Other critics included former commerce secretary Peter G. Peterson, several prominent senators, and presidential hopeful Ronald Reagan. Even the *New York Times*, which could hardly be called a bastion of conservative economics, mocked the deal as a bailout "upholstered in rich Corinthian leather." Lee answered them, too, with a letter that argued that the government was not bailing out one company but preserving competition so the industry could develop the best cars for the future.

Fortunately for our side, Iacocca got help from union leaders, who controlled millions of votes in key districts, and from auto dealers around the country who flocked to Washington to lobby their representatives. These dealers, who came from every district in the nation, were generally conservative Republicans. They were the kind of people who contributed to campaigns and influenced others who supported candidates with cash. They were taken seriously when they spoke up.

With help from so many quarters, the legislation moved quickly. In its final form, the plan approved by Congress supplied federal guarantees for $1.5 billion worth of credit with private lenders. At the same time all the so-called stakeholders, including workers, stockholders, executives, suppliers, dealers, and others, would have to make sacrifices. The autoworkers' union was required to give up $462.5 million worth of pay and benefits, and banks would have to renegotiate old loans and add an additional $650 million in credit.

Knowing that hundreds of banks would have to be wrangled into new deals before Chrysler could find stable ground, I wasn't quite ready to celebrate when President Carter signed the guarantee act on January 7, 1980. Iacocca was at the White House for the event and even sat at the president's desk for photographers. But I had noticed that the banks weren't exactly opening their vaults to help us. In November, Walter Wriston of Citibank, one of our biggest lenders, publicly opposed the act and said his analysts doubted that Chrysler could pay its existing debts. At about the same time, John McGillicuddy of Manufacturers Hanover Trust Company said he couldn't imagine giving us new credit.

Citibank and Manny Hanny, as it was called, were two institutions that I would have to win over if the company was to be saved. No act of Congress was going to move them, and they certainly weren't going to respond to appeals from union workers and car dealers. Their judgments would be based on their cold assessment of Chrysler and its prospects. Perhaps this is why, after the president signed the bill and handed out souvenir pens, Iacocca told the press, "The hard part starts now."

Still naively assuming that I just had to dash around and collect signatures from lenders, I had no idea of just how hard things would get.

———————

AT THIS TIME, the banking industry was still largely a state-by-state business, with no bank fully national in scope. As a result, corporations with big credit needs tapped many different banks so they could make long-term investments and manage short-term cash flow. Chrysler had followed this process, and then added even more lenders to its roster by borrowing small amounts—$500,000 here, $1,000,000 there—from hometown banks in cities and towns where factories were located. This practice was a matter of building goodwill in local communities. Bankers liked to say, "I'm doing business with Chrysler," and the relationship might give us an ally if we ever needed one.

Of course now that we needed them, nearly all the bankers great and small were thinking about how to get the most out of Chrysler, even if that required scrambling ahead of the other lenders. Small banks worried that they were going to get trampled by the bigger institutions. The big banks could try to use their power to get us to grant them special terms. Some, who had lent funds to the comparatively healthy Chrysler Financial division, believed that they would get first crack at our assets if Chrysler went into bankruptcy. To accomplish this, they could drag their heels in the negotiations and make it impossible for us to utilize the federal loan guarantees before we ran out of money.

Our declining cash reserve and the bankruptcy threat set up a ticking clock scenario and explains why, as the rest of Detroit celebrated the loan guarantee act, I had spent the days between Christmas and New Year's Day in New York, talking to bankers. Things only got worse as time passed. Weekdays were spent on the road, mostly in New York, where the big banks were headquartered. Fridays found me back in the office in Detroit for strategy sessions. While I was at home for at least part of most weekends and tried to catch up with Maggie and the boys, the phone rarely stopped ringing. (Thankfully, in the age before cell phones we could just leave the house to escape the calls.) I operated on caffeine, adrenaline, and willpower. Rest was almost impossible. No matter where I lay down at night, numbers, arguments, and deadlines raced around in my head. I woke early every morning, with a vague feeling of dread and my mind revving.

Although I couldn't know it at the time, this frenzied process would teach me priceless lessons about corporate rescue operations. Perhaps the most important was that good solutions required us to operate with absolute integrity, which meant we had to be as open as possible and never make promises we couldn't keep. We also had to get everyone moving in the same direction, toward shared responsibility, shared sacrifice, and shared benefits, in the event that Chrysler emerged healthy and profitable.

Early in the negotiations we produced a legal analysis of the effect of a Chrysler bankruptcy that went a long way toward improving our chances. Thanks to a peculiar feature of the bankruptcy law, we were able to show that no one would enjoy favored status if the company were pushed into bankruptcy. Instead, all our bank creditors, whether they had given money to the car company or the finance arm, would have to accept a 6 percent interest rate at a time when short-term rates had gone over 20 percent. The banks would have to wait many years for payment, if it came at all.

The report allowed us to turn the tables. Bankruptcy was no longer such a threat to us. Instead it was a club we could brandish, if we chose, to persuade our lenders that it was in their interest to get a deal done. Ultimately, we would decide against making this threat because it was bad from a public relations standpoint and bad for morale. It could also scare away car buyers who might worry about resale values and getting repair parts for cars made by a bankrupt manufacturer.

As they got down to serious business, the bigger banks formed a negotiating committee to streamline our work. Even though the committee reduced the number of individuals I had to deal with, I still worked longer and harder each day than ever in my life, including the summers when I labored dawn to dusk in the Oregon forest. On a typical morning in New York I started with a six thirty strategy meeting with Ron Trost, a lawyer hired to be my key adviser in the early stages of this work. Next would come a breakfast session with some loan officer and a day full of face-to-face talks and telephone calls from bankers around the country and Europe. Nighttime brought business dinners, postdinner meetings, and telephone conferences with officials of Japanese banks or Chrysler's partner in Asia, Mitsubishi.

In most of these encounters I was alone with groups of executives representing the other side of a deal. This was probably the best approach, since I was able to keep things consistent as I moved from one encounter to the next. But the truth was, we didn't have the time or money to hire a cadre of negotiators, nor did we have the management team to supervise such a big group. If I needed help it was up to me to find it.

In mid-January of 1980, as I found myself struggling to keep up with calls from our Canadian banks, I happened to receive a visit from an old friend at Ford Venezuela who was passing through New York. Dario Verdugo was a sharp finance guy in the Ford mold whom I could trust to get things right from the start. In the middle of the night we knocked on the door of the hotel room where Chrysler vice president John Day was trying to get some sleep. He came to the door in his pajamas, talked with us for a few minutes, and we hired Dario on the spot.

This was one of the upsides you enjoy in a crisis. You get to make decisions without being hobbled by bureaucracy. In moments like these you are also free to try creative solutions when there's no time for the usual methods. And you can speak more bluntly than you might otherwise. For example, when German and Japanese bankers said they should be paid off by their American counterparts because it was "traditional" for the banks of the debtor's country to take care of foreign banks, I only had to say, essentially, "Sorry, none of the others will go along with this. It's not my decision, but theirs. You're all in the same boat."

For a few months it seemed like everybody was trying to get out of the boat and gain some sort of advantage. A group of Canadian banks tried to do this by holding on to $80 million that Chrysler of Canada had deposited in various accounts. They wanted to keep this money as a "setoff" to reduce the amount of debt we owed them. Haggling over this issue went on for about a month. Then our American bankers got wind of the issue and demanded to see me in a conference room at Manufacturers Hanover.

This encounter was like a scene from *The Matrix*, where a seemingly endless assault is carried out by countless unsmiling men in dark suits. The American bankers were angry at the Canadians, of course, because we were all supposed to be renegotiating Chrysler's existing credit on the same basis. But they were much more upset that I hadn't informed them about the issue. In fact, I hadn't even thought to discuss it with them because it seemed like a small problem that could be resolved fairly.

But that wasn't the point. They wanted me to be more open with them, and since my integrity was just about all I had to offer them, I took their complaint seriously and apologized. I was virtually in tears as I told them I had misjudged the situation. And I promised that from that moment forward I would make every effort to keep them all informed of even the smallest material fact. In business, people rarely admit mistakes in such an immediate and direct way. Ego precludes it. Afterward I heard that this approach, which seemed obvious to me, had earned me even greater trust.

I needed every bit of our bankers' confidence because, in the end, I was the voice of Chrysler for them. While Lee was acting as Mr. Outside, promoting the company's prospects (and cars) to the press and public, I was working as Mr. Inside to get the reorganization done. Only once in six months did Lee play a significant direct role in these negotiations, and then it was to urge me to press for more concessions. (It didn't work.) In the same period, the company's board of directors received monthly reports on our progress, but made no recommendations and set no policies related to the effort.

Having never even been close to a situation where so much responsibility fell on one person, I had nothing to compare with my experience, and in fact, I was too busy to stop long enough to get scared. Sure, the future of one of America's largest companies depended on what I was doing. Hell, you might say the immediate health of U.S. economy, already staggered by inflation and recession, depended in part on Chrysler's survival. But the enormity of it all didn't strike me until late March, when I prepared to bring forty lender representatives to New York, where we would meet in Chrysler's offices, which were in what was then called the Pan Am Building, at 200 Park Avenue.

On the last prep day my father came to town for a visit. Having done so many big deals to help Owen Cheatham put together the Georgia-Pacific Corporation, my father understood the pressure I was feeling. He joined me and a few friends to polish off a bottle of Jack Daniel's and tell war stories in my hotel room. Around midnight, I excused myself and said that I needed to get prepared for the big meeting the next morning. My father said, "Don't worry. You've been preparing for this meeting all your life."

The people who met me at the Pan Am Building on March 27 represented most of the banks and insurance companies who held loans with Chrysler. Because each loan had been negotiated separately, they were conditioned on widely differing interest rates and terms. Some were so short-term—ninety days—that we were already in default. Others wouldn't come due for a decade or more. The interest rates we paid ranged from under 9 percent to more than 17 percent. Obviously, if we were going to work out Chrysler's debt problem we had to find ways to consolidate these loans under some coherent scheme that would be fair to all the lenders when it came to them getting their capital back, with interest.

To make the deal more palatable, I agreed to give the lenders warrants allowing them to buy millions of shares of Chrysler stock at $13 anytime in the coming decade. (Should the stock climb higher, the warrants would have greater value.) Beyond these warrants, I had little to offer, and they knew it. Indeed, Chrysler's poverty was so well-known that even the local deli demanded cash up front before delivering sandwiches to the meeting. However, I still had a mom-and-apple-pie argument to make. I reminded the group that I represented one hundred thousand workers, and beyond them families, neighborhoods, cities, stockholders, suppliers, dealers, and others who would be devastated if we failed. There was far more at stake than interest payments.

For two days I stood virtually alone as Chrysler's debt holders argued. The Europeans put forward a proposal that was rejected, and they huffily threatened a boycott. Then news of a collapse in the silver market, where the famous Hunt brothers had been driving prices ever higher, sent a shudder through the room. I began to worry that if we failed, we might contribute to an actual stock market crash and a 1929-style depression.

Fortunately, I had an ally at that meeting in Fred Ferber of Prudential Insurance. With more than $250 million invested in Chrysler, Prudential was a major stakeholder, but Fred was willing to let most of the banks earn a higher rate of interest if it meant they would stop being so stubborn and agree to a deal. It was enough to get the process moving toward a resolution. By Friday afternoon I had distributed an outline of a deal that took into account Fred's proposal and other points raised within the group. We adjourned on an optimistic note, agreeing to gather again in three days and, I hoped, settle things for good. I went home.

Over the weekend, Chrysler continued to make news, confirming that loans from the state of Michigan and $100 million from French carmaker Peugeot, collateralized with Peugeot stock, had been arranged to help us continue to pay suppliers and workers. We also continued to cut costs, announcing that a sheet metal stamping plant in the Detroit area that employed more than one thousand people was to be closed. Clearly, we were doing all we could to keep operating.

On Monday night I was back in New York. I met two of our lawyers, Bill Matteson and Sally Neely, and our adviser Jim Wolfensohn of Salomon Brothers at the Peacock Alley restaurant in the Waldorf-Astoria hotel. Though no longer the city's social hub, the place retained the kind of beauty and elegance that helped you forget your troubles.

We expected to be joined by some European bankers, who never showed. But Jim made sure to entertain us in their absence. He told a long story about a lawsuit called *Kendrick v. Kendrick*, which came out of the Penn Central bankruptcy of 1970. In this case, Penn Central's treasurer had been sent to jail for failing to disclose that his father was director of a bank involved with the railroad. As I listened to this, my heart began to race. My own father was director of a bank in Oregon that had a small Chrysler loan. With panic in my voice, I pointed this out to Jim. He waited a moment, to let me suffer, and then began to grin as he explained that he had made the whole thing up. There was no case called *Kendrick v. Kendrick* and I didn't have to worry about taking a trip to the pokey.

The next morning I returned to the Pan Am Building to take one last shot at forging a framework for the refinancing. At ten o'clock, as I stood behind a lectern and waited for everyone's attention, I noticed with some relief that the Europeans who had stood us up at Peacock Alley were in attendance. When the crowd quieted, I adopted a very serious tone of voice and explained that the Chrysler board of directors had just finished an emergency meeting. They had considered the deteriorating economy, new gas shortage caused by the Iranian revolution, and rising interest rates. They also had talked at length about the bleak prospects for our refinancing deal. Considering all these factors, I announced, "The corporation has taken the extraordinary step of filing for bankruptcy."

I leaned away from the microphone to allow the words to sink in. In the silence that followed I heard a few audible gasps. Pencils dropped on the tables. Mouths fell open. Eyes opened wide in amazement. Then I cleared my throat, moved back to the microphone, and said, "April fool!"

A few seconds passed before the Americans in the room started to smile and breathed sighs of relief. It took a little longer for them to explain the April 1 tradition to the Europeans. Years later I don't know for certain whether they understood the joke, but it got everyone's attention so that we could reach a tentative agreement. It called for interest rate and payment schedule concessions worth more than $1 billion. New credit worth about $650 million would be made available to the company, which combined with help we were getting from suppliers, unions, and state and local governments, would bring us up to the levels required for us to qualify for the loan guarantees.

Much more work would have to be done before the agreement was completed and we could draw funds under the federal guarantee. Foreign officials, including some very stubborn Canadians, would have to sign on. At the same time, hundreds of smaller lenders would have to drop any notions they might have of demanding immediate payment and special treatment, to go along with arrangement we outlined. But we were all committed to solving this problem, and in some cases the major banks did the heavy lifting. For example, Manufacturers Hanover and Barclays negotiated with an Iranian bank that had lent Chrysler money before the shah was overthrown. This was all done very quietly, since the hostage crisis was under way and the Iranian bank's agent in Paris feared the ayatollah and being recalled to Tehran.

Though less fraught with risk, my negotiations with the small American banks were just as critical. The conditions set for the reorganization were based on the "all for one, one for all" principle. This meant that no one could expect special consideration, and even a small-town lender could bring down the entire house of cards by refusing to go along. This may sound strange to some people who might question how we could allow each and every banker such veto power. But ask yourself whether you would be part of a big concession plan if you thought someone else might get favored treatment. There's something deep inside each human soul that craves the basic fairness of evenly shared sacrifice and opportunities. This is a truth that helped me through the Chrysler reorganization and would help me in the future.

No one could say that we at Chrysler weren't willing to sacrifice, too. At the end of April, as we struggled to contain costs, we cut our white-collar staff by almost seven thousand people. These layoffs were on top of the more than fifty thousand imposed on factory and office staff in the previous year. Indeed, at the time only two groups of employees enjoyed any real job security in the company. The first included those who were preparing to produce the K-cars, which we hoped would carry us to the future. The second was comprised of all those, like me, who were working with lenders, suppliers, unions, and government agencies that were players in the drama.

Still trying to herd stray bankers, I went to Toronto to meet with a group of representatives from eight banks, who insisted I allow them to reach agreement among themselves on each point before moving forward. The Canadians resented being dictated to by Washington, which had set the parameters in the loan guarantee act and reserved final say once everything was worked out. But with the help of an extraordinary lawyer named George Lindsay, former New York mayor John Lindsay's brother, I left Toronto with all eight banks on board.

From Toronto I flew to New York, where the obligations of the Chrysler Financial Corporation were being restructured in the same way that the finances of the parent company had been fixed, with new terms for repayment. The meetings for this work were held on a couple of floors in our lawyers' offices on Park Avenue. I went from room to room for most of a long weekend, making decisions at a rate of about $50 million per hour. The only break I took was on Saturday afternoon, when I flew home to Detroit to fulfill a prior commitment—buying new bikes for my sons, Robin and Alexander.

The round-robin in New York was followed by a short hop to Washington to brief federal officials, and a big briefing session in Motor City, which I called the Detroit jamboree. This meeting, where we hoped to get all bankers great and small updated on the new financing plan, was held at the Renaissance Center. To add a little flash to the setting, we brought a K-car prototype into the meeting room so that everyone could see there was real steel behind Chrysler's plan for the future. Iacocca gave a rousing little speech, and so did John McGillicuddy of Manufacturers Hanover, who had become our biggest ally. In the little time left for me, I told the crowd they had a chance to do something good for themselves and for their country by helping us to avoid bankruptcy.

The jamboree went well, with almost everyone accepting it was better to let Chrysler live, and likely pay its loans in full, than die without enough assets to pay thirty cents on the dollar. But this was a three-party deal including the bankers, Chrysler, and the Feds, and although Congress and the president had given us what we needed, the arrangements still required the approval of a special board set up to monitor things on behalf of the American taxpayer.

Held in the ornate but acoustically dreadful Cash Room at the Treasury Building in Washington, the review by the loan guarantee board turned into a grueling ten-day marathon of meetings that often ran past midnight. The press covered the talks as if they were a horse race, with the headlines providing daily predictions of victory or defeat. Gradually the reports became more optimistic, and this was an accurate reflection of what was happening behind closed doors. We were making a good case. Outside the meetings, Iacocca continued to play supersalesman, selling both cars and our cause to the American people. "You'll be surprised what we do with the K-platform," he told the press, and then he added, "if we don't run out of money."

In fact, we were running out of money, fast. Accounting for the first quarter showed a loss of almost $450 million. It seemed as if every month we needed a miracle to keep operating, and one always occurred. This time a loan from the state of Michigan kept our doors open, but the money was not big enough to cover all of our operating costs, so we cut spending as much as possible and asked for more time to pay our bills. Even the lawyers who were helping us in New York had to wait for payment on the $500,000 they had earned so far.

Under great pressure to show the guarantee board our progress, Iacocca and Greenwald went to Toronto to spend an entire night haggling with the province of Ontario over preserving jobs. Lee was very effective in this role, bringing the power of his title and his genuine charisma to bear on a stubborn problem. But this kind of intervention works best when used sparingly. For the most part Iacocca stayed out of the negotiating. Concentrating on other aspects of our recovery, he made lots of key moves with government leaders and practiced public diplomacy with a real flair. One of his more successful strokes involved getting union chief Douglas Fraser to become a member of the Chrysler board of directors. For some time afterward, Fraser and the union were our real partners in saving the company.

Sometime in the early hours of May 10, Lee and Jerry promised the group in Toronto that 11 percent of Chrysler's workforce would be Canadian and that a new engineering center would be built in Ontario. This brought them into agreement on the whole rescue deal. Later that day in Washington, the five-member guarantee board announced they were satisfied. I watched the announcement on television during a brief stop at home. I never felt so relieved in all my life.

The decision freed up $500 million in loan guarantees, which Chrysler could, theoretically, tap by the end of the month. However, we still needed to complete the big refinancing agreement, and dozens of individual banks were still sitting on the sidelines. On a ten-day trip to Europe, where I was helped by Assistant Treasury Secretary Roger Altman and Jim Wolfensohn of Salomon Brothers, I told bankers in ten cities that the arrangement was take-it-or-leave-it and we had no fallback position. Roger and Jim assured them that both Wall Street and Washington were behind us. They also helped me knock down a *Financial Times* of London report that I had a secret plan to pay off recalcitrant lenders. There was no secret plan.

Hard as we labored, the European adventure was broken up by two musical side trips arranged by Wolfensohn, who never ceased to amaze me with his varied interests and connections. On a Friday he took me to a concert in Amsterdam that featured both a conductor and principal pianist who were his good, old friends. Though I was impressed that night when we went backstage for a visit, I was absolutely dazzled the next day when Jim took me to a Paris hotel, where we spent the afternoon with violinist Isaac Stern, who turned out to have a keen interest in international finance.

After the weekend we went from the sublime to the ridiculous as we turned to deal with a German bank that had gotten very creative in its attempt to get special treatment. Weeks before, Volkswagen had routed an $8 million payment to Chrysler through DG Bank of Frankfurt, which promptly snared the money and posted it against the debt it held with Chrysler. (Chrysler and VW were in business together in South America, and the payment was related to this operation.) The bank's move, which was unusual and perhaps illegal, was a way for them to get paid off immediately, while everyone else would have to wait for years.

When we talked, the people at DG Bank were hardly sympathetic. It seemed as though they couldn't believe that I was telling the truth about the all-or-nothing part of the deal. In the short time we had together I couldn't get them to reverse their decision and free the money. But I was able to warn them that political and financial leaders around the world were supporting Chrysler's rescue. If DG Bank proved to be the one institution that caused the deal to fail when we were so close to an arrangement that would save all the jobs, money, and industrial assets that were at stake, their reputation would be sorely affected.

And so it went as I visited one wary banker after another and added more flights to a log I had been keeping for the past six months. Before this odyssey was over, I would make 116 different trips to destinations all over the United States and Europe. Included were more than forty visits to New York, sixteen to Washington, six to Toronto, and five to Chicago. I was such a fixture on American Airlines service out of Detroit that the flight crews began to address me by name and brought me coffee fixed just the way I liked it without me ever having to ask.

While I was in motion, answering questions and cajoling nervous lenders so that Chrysler could draw on its credit, we had our lawyers draft the documents that we had to send to our four-hundred-plus lenders. After painstaking review the papers went to the kind of specialized printing companies that handle sensitive documents for major financial transactions. Accustomed to offering strict confidentiality and security, these places are not ordinary print shops. Even so, they confessed that it was the biggest job they had ever done. I was certainly taxed when I spent all of June 4 signing papers on Chrysler's behalf. I have always wondered if by signing my name five hundred times per hour for eight hours—four thousand signatures in all—I might have qualified for *Guinness World Records*.

On the fourth of June the best estimates had Chrysler running out of money in six days. We eagerly followed up on our mailings to urge quick action, and most people complied. Still, there were snags. A bank in Alaska put their package to us in regular mail, instead of using express service. We couldn't be sure the mail would reach us by our settlement date, so we sent them a second set and had them brought back to us by courier. We took similar action when a cleaning lady shredded the papers we provided to a bank in Minnesota. And when an airport strike made it impossible to ship a set from Lebanon, the American embassy in Beirut accepted the papers and sent official word that they were signed in good order.

June 10 arrived and as expected, the cash well ran dry. What happens when a major corporation is broke? It stops writing checks. In our case we asked twenty thousand suppliers, the companies that kept us stocked with everything from toilet paper to tailpipes, to let us run a tab. Some of these suppliers could have shut us down by simply refusing to ship parts, but to their credit, not one did. Instead they kept bravely shipping critical parts so that we could assemble cars and keep our hopes alive. "We'll ride with it," one steel company told the *Wall Street Journal*.

By June 12 we had whittled the number of holdout banks to just twenty. Most were still hoping they could get paid off by bigger players eager to close the deal. In Washington we distributed information on these banks to senators and representatives and asked them to help us with institutions in their districts. By this time we were so close to victory that it was easy for people to see we had done the hard part. One senator looked me square in the eye and asked, "Who do you want us to get?" I felt like a boy who just got a BB gun for his birthday along with permission to fire away.

Besides the power of Congress, we also had access to the press, which came in handy when a bank in our home state, Michigan National Bank, tried to break ranks. We didn't even have to contact the reporters ourselves. The other local banks did this job, so that on the morning we met with the bank's president, Bud Stoddard, the headline on the *Detroit Free Press* screamed, "Bank Seizes Chrysler Funds—Loan Guarantee Jeopardized" in big type. Stoddard took five hours of our time to complain about how his small bank was mistreated by Chrysler and the big banks. Then, after we agreed to let Stoddard write the press release and claim to be the hero, he gave us what we wanted.

In terms of attitude, many heads of the small banks who delayed our settlement, making Chrysler and thousands of suppliers sweat, displayed similar balance sheet envy toward the larger institutions. I certainly could see how a tiny bank might worry more about $1 million than Citibank would over $100 million. And I sometimes thought that there was something else getting in the way. In some cases it just seemed like an anti-big city thing. A Texas banker told me he held a grudge against certain New York banks and "they know who they are." With others I found that the problem was simply a single ornery personality.

The most ornery may have been David Knapp, president of a bank in the small city of Rockford, Illinois, where five thousand people depended on a Chrysler assembly plant for their jobs. With this kind of connection, you might expect that a sense of civic duty or human compassion would make Knapp want to help. We went to Rockford, where the mayor arranged for us to meet Knapp at City Hall. He was a very conservative, Iowa-born fellow about my age who wore oversize eyeglasses and listened impassively as we made our case. It was a bit awkward, talking for more than an hour without getting much of a response. Still, I hoped I was getting through to him. Then, when I finished, he said he hadn't heard anything new that would get him to go along with the restructuring. He then got up and left.

Outside, on the steps of City Hall, Knapp posed as a sober trustee of his bank's depositors and owners, telling a gaggle of reporters, "When we make a loan we expect it to be paid under its terms and conditions."

I was exhausted and frustrated. Days before, after a particularly frustrating private phone call, I had actually broken down and cried. But in Rockford I wasn't alone. Reporters were waiting, just in case I needed to vent, and I obliged them. With a Chrysler public relations man gasping at my side, I talked for twenty minutes about how this bank threatened every one of the five thousand jobs in Rockford and more than a hundred thousand nationwide that depended on Chrysler. Then I broke with policy and warned, out loud, that Knapp might push us into bankruptcy.

I thought I was talking just to a local reporter. In fact, my words wound up on the nightly network news and in many of the nation's major papers. Days later, as I traveled from St. Louis to New York and then Little Rock, I heard from a *Wall Street Journal* reporter that Knapp had capitulated. I was ecstatic for a moment. Then the reporter told me that Knapp had been subjected to bomb threats. He was worried about his family and employees. I felt bad about this and would eventually call Knapp to say that we had not encouraged that kind of behavior. He was no more receptive than he had been in the mayor's office. "Well," he said, "you people have your ways."

Again and again, people with the power to stop the biggest corporate rescue in history had demonstrated hostility and skepticism. More often than not, these attitudes came from bankers who had never been close to the major players in finance, and only imagined that bad things were afoot. It was a sobering thing to observe so much mistrust and fear. But our consistent approach—listening, explaining, and never granting exceptions—gradually won over even the most reticent.

Officials at the last American holdout, Twin City Bank of North Little Rock, Arkansas, started out saying the same things so many others voiced. Their bank is tiny and so is the loan in question. Why can't we just pay them off and walk away? "All they would have to do is buy us out," a bank director told the local paper.

Fortunately, once we got together and I explained that the deal was as much about fairness and integrity as cash, they agreed to the terms of our debt restructuring. It helped that the secretary of the treasury, Bill Miller, had called the bank chairman while I was there to tell him I wasn't fooling. Since even the Iranians had by now come through for us, this left only DG Bank of Frankfurt, Germany, outside the fold. I called them from Little Rock and, in one of the few hardball plays in this whole game, threatened to sue them and VW for conspiracy if they didn't give us the right answer by the time the company plane I had commandeered touched down back in Detroit.

I can't tell you what the people at DG Bank thought about my ultimatum, but my little team was so sure of success that during the flight we celebrated with a case of beer and a box of sandwiches. At touchdown I turned on the car radio and learned that the Germans had come around, and by nightfall word of our success, which meant that Chrysler would live, dominated the news on radio and television.

As I traveled home from the airport, I felt grateful for the support I had gotten from Maggie and our sons. When I got sight of our home, a pretty stone house cut into the side of a sloping hill, I was filled with both relief and a sense of triumph. For nine months we had all sacrificed. At times I'm sure Maggie felt like a single mother/laundress who had me around only long enough to empty my suitcase, wash its contents, and fill it up again.

That night we all went for a walk around the quiet neighborhood and shared the sense of victory. Afterward we went out for dinner at the type of restaurant the boys rarely saw. In cities across America, where Chrysler and its partners operated, people joined the celebration of a deal that would be good for everyone from Iacocca down to the manager at the Red Pump tavern, which served workers at one of our plants in Warren, Michigan.

"What does it mean to us?" said one worker in response to a reporter's question. "Only everything."

———————

IF YOU HAVE ever purchased a home with a mortgage, you know that the thrill of making the deal is followed by the drudgery of a closing, where buyer, seller, lender, and lawyers sit together to sign all the documents that make the sale a legal reality. Now imagine something similar, but multiply it by more than four hundred to represent all the lenders, and add the paperwork demanded by several layers of government.

The exact number was anyone's guess, but I estimated that roughly ten thousand documents would have to be signed before Chrysler received its first big check under the loan guarantee. This chore was to be handled much like a real estate closing, with representatives for all the parties coming together at the offices of our lawyers in New York, pens in hand. We picked a date, June 24, and began collecting the papers.

The rooms we would use were high in the Westvaco Building, a skyscraper on Park Avenue. On the evening before the closing I gave a *BusinessWeek* reporter a tour of the place, showing him all the neatly stacked documents and explaining the procedure we would follow. At about seven thirty we went to the cafeteria on the thirty-third floor, where a few dozen lawyers were going over their plans. As we left the room, I glanced out the window and saw some smoke. One of the neighborhood restaurants must be having a grease fire, I thought.

It wasn't a grease fire. No, it was a building fire, and the building in question was ours. Down on the twentieth floor, a small fire in a Bank of America office was feeding on computer paper and quickly becoming an inferno. Alarms began to sound. Some people got ready to evacuate, but I hesitated. What about our documents? What about our closing? Would all our hard work go up in smoke?

I gave serious thought to staying, but when security officers came through to demand we evacuate, I had no choice. I joined the stream of people who used the stairs to escape the smoke, which had already injured more than a hundred people. But while most of the others left the area as soon as they could, I stood on the sidewalk with a small cadre of lawyers and watched as flames leaped twenty feet out of broken windows. Park Avenue was filled with fire engines as the firemen skillfully doused the blaze and prevented it from spreading past the floor where it started.

"The banks are really holding our feet to the fire," joked one of the guys on the sidewalk.

"This is Rockford's revenge," said another.

Back in Detroit, Maggie and the kids watched with fascination the scenes from the fire on NBC *Nightly News*, completely unaware of the connection to me or to Chrysler.

Hours after the evacuation, as dawn approached, I was sure the documents had survived but worried that we might not have access to them for days. Sometime around 2:00 A.M. we managed to talk ourselves back into the building. A group of us seized a dozen big canvas mail carts and brought them up to the conference rooms. The smoke still hung in the air, so thick that you couldn't see across the floor. An oily ash was settling on desks and chairs. Working fast, we boxed our papers and loaded them into the carts. I was so nervous that my sense of humor departed. When I saw one of our group writing on a blackboard—"Neither rain, nor sleet, nor dark of night . . ."—I snapped at him to get back to work. Only later did I laugh.

In about a half hour we had all the documents loaded into mail carts. We then rolled them to the elevators, rode down to the street level, and paraded for six blocks up the middle of Park Avenue—traffic had been closed off—to the Citicorp Building, where another law firm had space available for the closing. At noon the next day, as other parties listened over the phone, one of our attorneys called a roll to ask if we were all ready. In the excitement of this moment I couldn't think of anything memorable to say when they called for Chrysler so instead when he said, "Chrysler ready?" I answered, "Aw shucks, I guess so."

When it was over I received a check for $486,750,000. After some handshakes and a phone call with Detroit I left the conference room and went directly to a Manufacturers Hanover bank, where Chrysler kept an account. I stood in line for a teller. When called to the window I then deposited the check with all the ceremony of a child making his weekly contribution to his first savings account. I probably felt a much bigger thrill, however, than most kids feel dropping off a share of their weekly allowance or paper route money.

———————

THE SATISFACTION THAT came with helping rescue Chrysler, and all that meant for so many people and our country, was deeper than I could have expected. The process had taught me much about finance, international affairs, politics, strategy, human nature, and myself.

Of course I noticed that the values of honesty and integrity practiced by my family, which I acquired back home in Oregon and were reinforced in my life with Maggie, were essential to my work on the reorganization. But I also saw how it was possible to apply them along with a negotiating strategy that converted an opponent's moves into an advantage for my cause, which in this case was the Chrysler rescue.

How did this work? The best example was the "all-for-one, one-for-all" tactic. I knew that bankers were morally and legally bound to get the most for their shareholders, and this meant that all of them would try to get an advantage. This issue was especially important for the smaller institutions, where officers had less leeway and might think they could get away with demanding they be paid off by one of the big guys with lots of available cash.

The solution, an all-or-nothing deal, may have seemed risky. In fact, it was the only way that I could engage in continuous talks with these banks. I wasn't the bad guy. It was those other bastards who were to blame. I was just their messenger, and they weren't going to make an exception for anyone.

The same dynamic—converting a threat into a tool—worked when it came to bankruptcy. At first some of the bigger banks who thought they had first dibs on our assets made noise about forcing us into bankruptcy so they could collect. With a little work we were able to show them that their assumptions were wrong. No one would get special treatment if we closed. Suddenly the talk of bankruptcy ended, and we knew that we had stolen the issue.

Fortunately, human nature leads most of us to seek harmony in shared sacrifice and fair dealing. I've always expected the best from others, and the Chrysler experience reinforced this attitude. Sure, you get disappointed sometimes, but you also get a lot more accomplished when you show people trust and confidence.

On a personal level, the Chrysler rescue confirmed for me that I prefer big-picture leadership roles over grinding away on details. Of course the chore of corralling four hundred lenders demanded I dwell on lots of details, and my notes from this era include pages and pages of lists and numbers. But I thrived when it came time to shaping the overall deal and selling it to the players. Performing in a room full of decision makers was actually fun for me. Plowing through documents was not.

Finally, the Chrysler crisis helped realize that I had been blessed with some personal traits that made it possible for me to meet this kind of challenge. First, I was able to work harder and longer than I ever thought I could. Second, I didn't take things personally in a way that kept me from making progress, even with the toughest customers. Third, I discovered that I had the ability to compartmentalize my life so that time at home refreshed me fully and strengthened my most important relationships. It was possible, I saw, to manage an intense corporate crisis and still be a human being.

Three

A RELUCTANT BEAN COUNTER

Anyone who has ever applied for a loan knows that it's much easier to get the money if you don't really need it. Got a rich portfolio of investments and big cash reserves on deposit? If so, your bank is going to offer you the best terms and throw in a toaster. In fact, just about everyone wants to get involved when you are doing well. Lenders know they can count on timely payments. Investors who purchase stock anticipate growth and dividends. And every schemer who ever wrote a letter or dialed a phone gets visions of big money and goes into action.

In Chrysler's case, the highly publicized triumph of our restructuring brought a flood of oddball financial offers, by phone and mail, which would go into my scrapbook for future amusement. Small towns in Texas were overrepresented, as letters with obscure Lone Star postmarks came offering loans worth up to $1 trillion, at 6 to 10 percent interest. A stranger phoned to say he could get us $7 billion from Mexico. A real estate agent in Covina, California, asked if we'd like to sell the entire company to one of her clients. The most straightforward communication came from a fellow in Saginaw, Michigan, whose stationery listed nonexistent offices worldwide. He wanted a $36,000 up-front payment to start things rolling.

None of the over-the-transom deals were legit, but the inquiries that came from the four corners of the earth reflected the public's confidence in Chrysler's turnaround. The sentiment was not misplaced. In the same way that the market economy grinds its way toward accurate prices and valuations, the public seems to inevitably sense the truth of a situation, whether it's a political battle, a pennant race, or a corporate recovery. In our case, people understood we were on our way back. What they couldn't know was how fast our recovery would be.

The Dodge Aries and Plymouth Reliant (our first K-cars) debuted for the 1982 model year. They were named Cars of the Year by *Motor Trend*, and despite a few early miscalculations—we built too many expensive ones loaded with options—we would sell more than three hundred thousand in the first year, and about two million by 1990. They were stingy with gas and, as promised, could carry six adults in relative comfort. (Competing Japanese models might haul five in a squeeze.) The K-cars didn't bring an instant cure, but gradually, as the overall economy improved and sales for all cars rebounded, so did Chrysler. At the same time our cost cutting and improved efficiency brought our break-even point down to 1.1 million vehicles per year. Previously we had to sell two million before we made a profit. By mid-1982 we were in the black, hiring more workers and expanding our dealer network. In 1983 we realized we could pay back all of the government-guaranteed loans—$1.2 billion—seven years *ahead* of schedule.

As chief financial officer I pushed especially hard to pay off the federally guaranteed loans because I considered government help a worst-case option from the beginning. We had done it to avoid bankruptcy, which in those days was a far more stigmatizing and destructive choice than it is today. By disengaging from the U.S. Treasury we could announce to the world that we were out of the hospital, so to speak, and strong enough to compete without any unfair advantages. Since the free market is like a religion to me, I was eager to get back in its good graces.

The stickiest part of the payoff decision had to do with a massive stock offering—the third largest in the history of Wall Street at the time—that would open the door to investors who wanted to jump on the bandwagon. The sale would raise scads of cash to repay the loans but also dilute the value of each old share, at least temporarily. Ironically, this move would hurt our leader Iacocca as much as anyone, because it would cut the value of the stock options he had accepted when he was hired in exchange for a symbolic $1 a year salary.

Although Lee later published an account omitting his initial objections to the early payoff and lauding the public relations value of the decision, when the possibility first arose he was very critical. His objections weren't all personal. He didn't want to hurt existing shareholders, who would see prices go down. And he thought we could use our cash profits in ways that could further strengthen the company.

Our big confrontation on the issue took place in Chrysler's New York office on the sixty-sixth floor of what was then the Pan Am Building. I was very firm, raising the specter of what was happening in Great Britain, where the government had tried for years to prop up an ailing auto business that sucked billions of pounds out of their economy. Government does not belong in business because it inevitably destroys initiative and creates dependency. I was not going to be a party to creating a welfare state mentality for the American auto industry.

The debate over this issue was fierce. At one point Lee actually started shouting, and I told him, "Lee, if you don't do this, I wish you well, but I could not be your CFO any longer."

I don't know if my threat made the difference, but Lee took the course I recommended. We did the stock offering and paid off the loans. What lesson did I take from this experience? First, I realized there are certain issues that are beyond compromise for me. Second, on reflection, I decided that I would think very carefully before laying my job on the line again. I respect the corporate hierarchy. The CEO gets paid to make the big decisions, and in Lee I had a boss who would hear me out beforehand. In the future we would have more big battles. I would oppose selling cars at a loss to rental fleets just to keep factories running, but Lee did it. I would object to using our capital to buy back shares. Lee did that, too. But in neither case would I feel that a matter of basic principle was at stake.

Looking back, I have to conclude that Lee actually showed restraint in his response to my challenge on the loan repayment. At that time no corporate officer in America, and perhaps the world, could match him in popularity and stature. During the restructuring he had spoken forcefully at congressional hearings, voicing the worries about global competition, especially from Japan, that millions of Americans shared. The press turned to him almost every day for comment and quotes, and Lee tended to oblige them with a feisty wit and intelligence. These public appearances raised his profile considerably even before he decided to become the face of Chrysler as its main pitchman.

After a slow start, Lee became a TV sensation with a bluntly delivered line—"If you can find a better car, buy it!"—that was his own invention. Though they would one day seem tame, even quaint, the Iacocca spots were revolutionary in their time. No one had ever put a real, tough-talking CEO in a car commercial before. How well they worked when it came to selling cars is anyone's guess. It's almost impossible to measure how a specific advertisement affects a product's sales. But I can say for certain that Lee's own image and ego were boosted by his frequent appearances in America's living rooms.

The Iacocca phenomenon only grew when he published an autobiography, which detailed his rise to power in the car business and the Chrysler recovery story. Released in October 1984, the cover of *Iacocca* featured a smiling Lee, pushed back from his desk, hands behind his head, smiling like the Cheshire cat. It became the nation's number-one selling book in three weeks. Within three months, more than one million copies were in print and *Iacocca* was on track to become one of the biggest selling books ever.

Many copies of *Iacocca* were sold on the basis of Lee's fame. He also benefited from a business book fad that had begun in 1982 with *In Search of Excellence* by Tom Peters and Robert Waterman. But *Iacocca* became a best seller because it was a very good book. As the *New York Times* noted in a review, every mother with a child "headed for a business career will want to give them *Iacocca* for Christmas."

Dedicated to his wife, Mary, who died just before it came out, Lee's book was filled with stories from his remarkable life, common sense, and business wisdom: You can learn from your competitors, including the Japanese. Companies should focus on what they do best. Top executives, especially CEOs, run the risk of falling in love with their own power and staying too long on the job.

They were fairly basic values. But living by them, while still being flexible and open to positive changes, is not easy. For Lee, the pressure to play superstar CEO was enormous. Everywhere he went people recognized him and treated him like a celebrity. On one trip I took with him to Asia, we had big police escorts from the moment we arrived at an airport until we flew away at the end of our visit. It was during that trip, by the way, that we began to move toward parts ventures in Korea, where it was clear that manufacturing was poised to take off. Soon we would have an office in Seoul and begin long-term relationships with suppliers whose prices and quality helped us compete in an ever-more-challenging market.

At home Lee was the subject of frequent rumors about a presidential bid. (Yes, I mean president of the United States.) It was never clear whether Lee was a Democrat or Republican, but it didn't much matter because he wasn't cut out for politics and knew it. Still, he allowed himself to daydream about the job. And in retrospect, the murmuring may have contributed to his gradual transformation into a rather imperial figure who would eventually lose his perspective on the middle-class experience he knew growing up in Allentown, Pennsylvania.

Inside Chrysler, we could all see the signs of Iacocca's tendency toward larger-than-life self-regard. He indulged his taste for luxury travel, at company expense, whenever possible and used more personal attendants and handlers, including a barber and a kind of social arranger, than a cabinet officer in Washington. Wes Small, a marketing guy at Ford, was brought over to be Lee's valet. He had some kind of title, but his job was basically was to take care of the CEO.

Taking care of Lee wasn't easy. Once, when I accompanied him over to Japan and Korea, we stopped in Hawaii for a brief rest at a hotel. When we finally got to Tokyo, we suddenly realized that Lee's suitcase was missing. Poor old Wes. The bag was his responsibility. Lee berated him and reminded us all that he was scheduled for dinner with the prime minister. Wes eventually figured out that the bag had been taken off the plane and delivered to Lee's hotel suite in Honolulu. This was a mistake. It wasn't supposed to come off the plane. We put a Hawaiian sales guy on the next plane to Tokyo to bring Lee's bag, so that Lee was dressed correctly for dinner with the prime minister. I suspect the incident aged Wes by about a dozen years

Occasional tantrums were expected and tolerated because Lee had become a prince of Detroit, if not the king. His status was quite apparent and accepted, especially at social events where executives and their spouses got together to mark a milestone or celebrate the achievement of some goal. Maggie had no patience for ladies' luncheons or similar stuffy affairs. Often she was so ambivalent about attending that she would back out at the last moment, a practice that made me tense up before every outing, given the possibility of an argument and canceled plans. This was a bigger problem than you might imagine, and it grew worse over time. Psychology is not one of my strong suits, and I couldn't tell if she suffered from a serious problem or was just being difficult. I did notice that her mood swings gradually grew more extreme and less predictable. Unable to explain it, I kept the situation more or less secret, and told myself and everyone else that she was a bit eccentric, one of a kind, and that was that.

When she did attend social events, Maggie refused to play the shy, retiring wife. If the men retired for cigars and conversation, she lit up a stogie and joined them instead of going with the women to another room. On the way home she'd offer me brutally candid and often spot-on assessments of my peers and associates. She was ambivalent about Iacocca, however. She admired his talent and intelligence but was annoyed by his royalist attitudes.

Most of all, Maggie wanted to make sure that I didn't allow myself to be seduced by the trappings of power and success. A good example of how she helped me to keep my ego in check can be seen in a little incident that took place at the annual Detroit Auto Show. Our Jeep brand had set up a kind of ride, like those at Disney World, where you climbed into a Jeep and were jostled as it simulated crossing some rugged terrain. When we went to the exhibit the staff recognized me and tried to whisk us ahead of everyone else in line. Maggie would have none of it. We went to the end of the line and waited. Minutes later Lee came by and without a thought, bypassed the queue. No one said a word about how rude this was, but we all noticed.

Maggie was right to see a problem in Lee's attitude—I certainly wouldn't have followed his lead—and as time passed his style would go out of style. But I can't say that at the time I worried about his foibles. They meant little to me in comparison with his success as a CEO who continued to make good things happen, which in my case included a seat on the Chrysler board at age forty-two, where I would get an even closer view of how a major company works.

———————

AT THE TOP of Chrysler I saw in Iacocca a man who operated much like a political leader, using his personality and values to inspire the ranks and the public. This is how leadership is practiced at a very large company. No one can know everything that's going on, much less control it. But a CEO can communicate his priorities and convey confidence, character, and integrity. Lee was so good at this that President Reagan tapped him to head the commission to restore the Statue of Liberty, and he accomplished this with such flair that the statue's centennial celebration went down in history as one of the nation's greatest ceremonial events. I haven't been to a more impressive event—a harbor packed with boats, Neil Diamond singing, "They're coming to America"—in my life.

One could say that the Statue of Liberty commission was a no-lose proposition, and so Lee had it easy. Combine the Chrysler hero and an icon of liberty, and you've got a hit. But what about when controversies arose? Here he was just as effective. In 1987 Chrysler would suffer a short-lived scandal when authorities discovered that odometers were disconnected on newly-built cars that assembly plant managers took home overnight. (This was both a perk and a way to check quality.) Other manufacturers did the same thing but notified customers who bought these cars. Chrysler did not, and critics had a field day with the news. Johnny Carson said he saw a bunch of Chrysler executives on the freeway. They were all driving backward.

Carson's joke was not the only funny thing about the scandal. I was secretly amused by how it was uncovered. It seems a couple of factory managers got caught speeding. They explained to the police that they were unaware of the speed, since they had disconnected the odometers. One thing led to another and suddenly we had national uproar on our hands with Chrysler being compared to unscrupulous used-car dealers. This chain of events is the kind of thing you expect to see in a TV sitcom, but it really did happen.

To his credit, Lee was smart enough about public imagery to resist getting defensive. While I would have likely raised a big argument in our defense, Lee went to the press and said that Chrysler had stopped the practice. "It went beyond dumb—all the way to stupid!" he proclaimed. End of story. It's hard for a top executive to do this. Natural instincts lead you to fight and get outraged. But a good leader understands how things look to others and gets control of a problem as quickly as possible. In this case Lee drove the story off the front page by simply agreeing with our critics.

Iacocca showed leadership in many other ways. He bet big on the development of a vehicle that our manufacturing people called the T115. The marketing people described it as the Magic Wagon, and as it was released in 1983–84 the world quickly dubbed it the minivan. Incredibly roomy and yet no longer or wider than a traditional station wagon, these Plymouth Voyagers and Dodge Caravans were snapped up by parents who appreciated how easy it was to load and unload their kids and all their gear. We sold more than 210,000 in the first year alone. GM and Ford would come late to the minivan party with their own products, but never caught up. Eventually, Chrysler would sell more than eleven million of these symbols of suburban ease.

The minivans helped Chrysler to a record annual profit of more than $2 billion. With so much cash on hand, and a steady flow projected for years to come, the siren song of acquisition and diversification began to echo through headquarters. It is a seductive melody that affects every business that is vulnerable to sharp swings in revenues and profits. Theoretically, you can make those swings less dramatic by getting into additional lines of business that either follow different cycles or, like the food industry, resist the highs and lows almost entirely. Wall Street tends to prefer diversified companies and rewards them with higher valuations.

Having seen debacles in other industries, we knew that we didn't want to stray too far afield in the quest for diversification. As Lee said, we would never buy the Burger King corporation because we didn't know a thing about hamburgers. But we knew transportation (and Lee liked their planes), so we bought the aircraft manufacturer Gulfstream for $637 million. This company was given its own division as part of a reorganization, which included making Chrysler Financial a semiautonomous unit, which I would lead as chairman.

Car companies had long been in the business of lending money to consumers who wanted to buy cars, as well as financing dealer operations. Staffed with smart finance people, these operations could become profit centers, and we saw the chance to make Chrysler Financial a much bigger source of revenue. We made an $83 million profit in 1984, which prompted Lee to ask us for $200 million per year in the future. In 1985 we very quickly began a real estate finance venture with GE Credit, bought a small business financing company from the old E. F. Hutton brokerage house, and acquired a consumer-lending business from Bank of America.

Since General Motors and Ford were making similar moves, there was an everybody's-doing-it enthusiasm for building our finance division, and nary a word of caution could be heard, except for an article in the *Economist*, which warned that lending can be tricky business. But with the media covering Chrysler's every move, this lone dissent was immediately drowned out by all the ballyhoo over our miraculous turnaround.

Although everyone says it's a mistake to believe your own press, it's hard to resist when they focus on you. In this period, *Ward's AutoWorld* described me as some kind of überexec whose résumé would make a headhunter "salivate like Pavlov's dog." *Detroit* magazine named me one of the industry movers and shakers, and many media outlets added my name to speculative stories about successors to Iacocca, who would turn sixty-five in three years. The others most often mentioned were Jerry Greenwald, who brought me to Chrysler, and Bob Lutz, a consummate car guy from Ford, who would join us in mid-1986.

Realistically speaking, Jerry had the inside track. He was the most experienced, and as early as 1983 he told me that Lee had promised he'd be CEO. Then, almost immediately after we repaid the loans, Lee began backpedaling on the matter of how long he'd stay around. This is a sure sign of what I came to call the CEO disease. The symptoms include overidentification with the company, fear that a successor will ruin what's been built, and an inability to set a retirement date. The closer Lee got to his sixty-fifth birthday, which would come in 1989, the less definite he was about his plans. In the meantime, we would all have to put our personal ambitions aside to pull off the one big acquisition Chrysler made in its core business, automobiles.

In 1986 the perennial also-ran of the U.S. auto industry, American Motors Corporation, was a money-losing manufacturer of quirky cars like the Gremlin and Pacer that had one product line that promised real value—Jeep. Born of the famous military vehicle, small Jeeps in the postwar era gradually moved from ranches to the suburbs and then grew into the earliest version of the sport utility vehicle. The big Wagoneers of the 1960s begat the nimbler Cherokees, which were prized by loyal drivers who preferred its rugged, Wild West image to the family sedan.

The passion people felt for Jeeps ran deep and foreshadowed the huge SUV market to come. It didn't matter that they were poorly built and prone to breakdowns. Even as they complained about repairs, loyalists bought their second and third Cherokees. Their loyalty impressed us, and so did their youth and wealth. At the time, the typical Chrysler buyer was a retiree on a limited income. The typical Jeep buyer was twenty years younger, better educated, and twice as wealthy. They were just the type of customers Chrysler needed to bring into its tent.

At the time, AMC's biggest shareholder was Renault. The French had bought into the company in 1979, hoping for leverage to manufacture and sell its own models in North America. The Renaults were fairly good cars, but they were, well, French, and they never gained popularity in the New World. In the meantime AMC's dilapidated factories, union contracts, pension obligations, and lawsuits related to rollover problems with smaller Jeeps became big headaches. It was safe to assume that after seven years of this, Renault had had enough.

At first, when Lee sent us on a quest to buy the Jeep nameplate, he insisted that we didn't want the rest of AMC. But as I shuttled back and forth to Paris (tough duty, but someone had to do it!) it became clear that Renault wouldn't separate the two. For the most part the talks were friendly but slow. Both sides were shocked in November 1986 when Renault's chairman, Georges Besse, was murdered by political radicals.

We got back together early the next year and moved toward an agreement that required us to take everything, including AMC's $800 million debt and part of its lawsuit liabilities. We also had to agree to continue selling the Renault-based cars for a number of years so their power train factories could stay open a while longer. The final negotiations for the deal were done in secret during an early March weekend in Paris. A big group of us spent forty-eight hours straight—two sunrises, two sunsets—in the Renault offices. We desperately wanted to finish so that the inevitable rumors could be headed off by the time the U.S. markets opened on Monday.

Try as I might, however, I couldn't get the French down to the price that Lee had told me he would accept. They weren't being unreasonable, so without real authority, I agreed to what they were asking for, which was roughly $1.5 billion in stock. Then I called Lee.

"Did you get that deal yet?" he asked.

"Yeah, we got a deal."

"Did you get it for what we talked about?"

"Lee, don't worry about it. It's a good deal. We're putting out the press release now. Trust me."

He did trust me. I confirmed the deal with Renault and went to my hotel to refresh myself while the papers were drawn. I drew a bath, plopped into it, and promptly fell asleep. I was awakened by a knock on the door and was so groggy I forgot to cover myself. The bellman didn't flinch as I appeared before him, soaking wet and naked. He handed me an envelope bearing the paperwork for one of the biggest deals in auto industry history. I closed the door and padded back to the bathroom in search of a towel.

Even with AMC's liabilities, we got positive cash flow out of the merger in the very first month. The Jeep brand turned out to be more powerful than we ever expected, and we sold more units than projected for years to come. But you didn't have to wait for annual sales figures to get a sense of the SUV's appeal. Sixty days after we acquired the company, almost every executive at Chrysler had replaced his car with a Jeep. The parking lot outside our office looked like a Jeep dealership.

At Chrysler headquarters the AMC deal was opposed by a few executives who thought we needed to invest more in our next generation of cars. They could say "I told you so" when the sales cycle turned down again at the end of the decade, and we had nothing to offer as competition to the blockbuster Ford Taurus and Toyota Camry. However, over the long haul Chrysler would sell more than two million

Jeeps, and a sizeable proportion of them were loaded with high-profit options. With this record, it's difficult to count the AMC deal as a mistake, which is not to say we were perfect. We made lots of errors. And the biggest was not a matter of money but intellectual focus.

———————

By the mid-1980s, the U.S. auto industry had had more than a decade to contemplate the powerful challenge coming from Japanese companies that were making steady gains in our market. These manufacturers, especially Toyota and Honda, offered smaller, more fuel-efficient cars than the Big Three generally sold.

Federal regulators had tried to push American manufacturers toward efficiency by requiring an average 27.5 miles per gallon for new vehicles. By the mid-1980s Chrysler reached this goal, closing the gap with the Japanese. Ford and GM did not match us, but in the end it didn't matter. Despite our objections—I spoke out strongly on the matter—the Reagan administration noted lower gas prices and eased the standards. This move changed the rules of the game as Chrysler crossed the goal line. I'm no fan of regulation, but easing the standard was obviously unfair to us, and it took the steam out of our nation's progress toward energy independence. As with health care and pension costs, the day of reckoning with foreign oil was pushed into the future.

In the moment when fuel standards were eased, lower gas prices made mile-per-gallon less important to consumers, yet they were still buying more and more Japanese cars. The trend continued because the public sensed that the Japanese cars were built better than ours, and soon independent sources like the J. D. Power ratings organization confirmed it. Civics and Camrys, to name just two, were small and light on luxuries, but they ran forever and rarely broke down.

Worse for Detroit was that our competition was able to turn out these small cars so efficiently that they could pay the freight to land them on our shores and still make a profit on each one. What was their secret? It wasn't a superior work ethic. Their guys couldn't screw on more lug nuts in an hour than ours. The difference was deeper and broader, and it had to do with how Japanese companies managed every aspect of their businesses.

Iacocca's response to the Japanese had been mainly political, as he attacked them for unfair trade practices and pushed successfully for quotas on their exports to America. Some of the rhetoric he used in this campaign bordered on racism and confounded executives at Mitsubishi, who were supplying us small cars like the Plymouth Colt. To my mind, protectionism ran against America's free market ideals and wouldn't shield Detroit forever. Eventually we would have to improve ourselves and beat them in the marketplace. I was reminded of this point when I gave a talk at the University of Wisconsin and was approached afterward by a young Japanese American woman.

Reiko McKendry told me she had been distressed by Iacocca's speeches and recent anti-Japanese incidents that seemed to be linked to resentment about trade. (In one instance an Asian American man was beaten to death.) She was a loyal, patriotic citizen of the United States and told me she wanted to come work for Chrysler to help us in the global competition. I was impressed. She gave me her résumé. I passed it to our human resources department, and soon she was hired and put to work in the bowels of the organization.

Though she was a tiny woman, Reiko had big ideas and the energy to match. She organized a group of young people, newcomers in management, who spent their lunch hours, nights, and weekends gathering and analyzing information about one of the premier Japanese car companies—Honda—and their methods of design, manufacturing, and marketing. They discovered a streamlined bureaucracy organized to discover consumer desires, match them with new products, and bring them to dealer showrooms with far less time, money, and effort than required in Detroit. The core of this process was the "platform team," a group of experts from manufacturing, engineering, finance, procurement, design, and sales who worked together continuously, with the authority to produce a new vehicle that fit the needs of every department and, ultimately, car buyers. The spirit of this process was reflected in Honda's use of fieldwork to observe people and their cars and discover how they used them, and in the big open spaces where teams worked in a warm, informal atmosphere.

In contrast, the Detroit way involved designers who loved cars consulting small focus groups of consumers and working in isolation on plans for a vehicle they considered attractive, even artful. (Think of the kid in sixth grade who always doodles pictures of cool cars, and you have the idea.) They eventually presented the design to the engineering department, where infeasible designs might become a nightmare. Then on to a manufacturing group, who then reacted with a list of changes to accommodate the assembly line. The sales and marketing people wouldn't be asked to weigh in until late in the game, and they often howled about being forced to sell cars that were too big, too small, too round, too square, or otherwise didn't suit demand. Conflicts would bubble up to the top level of management, where big shots had to settle the differences. The process wasted significant amounts of time and money.

Of course the Japanese had other advantages. Our union contracts were laden with costly and arcane work rules. We paid much higher rates for wages and benefits. And the Japanese had newer plants and equipment. But Reiko and her group rightly saw that we could learn immediately from the Japanese development process and use some of their methods to improve quality, cut costs, and get closer to the sweet spot with consumers.

Not surprisingly, the Honda study made slow progress up the chain of command at Chrysler. But eventually someone brought Reiko and her team to present it to Iacocca, Greenwald, and me. When they were through, they recommended a few big moves that might change the culture of Chrysler for the better. First, they wanted to deemphasize quarterly profits and focus the company on long-term goals of quality and customer satisfaction, and reward every employee who did this—not just executives—with bonuses. Second, they wanted Honda-style teams, utilizing people from all different departments, working together in big open spaces. Finally, they wanted to pay professionals and managers based on their performance and contribution to the company, not on how many people reported to them.

All of these were Honda ideas and they worked well in Japan. The platform team concept was embraced by Chrysler in the early 1990s with the development of a new line of family sedans, and that in turn helped Chrysler become the nimblest, hottest car company throughout the mid-1990s. But at Chrysler, much of the culture change of the kind Reiko proposed was considered but was slow to be adopted. It was an old-line, industrial company governed by the kind of hierarchy found in the military. Iacocca was comfortable as the commander-in-chief, and he wasn't going to cede any of his power. In the ranks below, managers would follow his example.

For a moment we did, however, flirt with openness in the managerial ranks. Groups were brought to seminars—informally called "truth weeks"—where participants were coached to speak honestly. People actually admitted to fears about the quality of our cars, our financial strength, and many other issues. We also listened to some insightful talks on group dynamics, including a fanciful story about the members of a big Texas family who all agree to go on a miserable outing to Abilene because Grandpa suggests it. In truth, nobody, not even Grandpa, really wants to go, but out of respect and fear of speaking up, they do it anyway. At Chrysler, we made a lot of trips to Abilene.

At the final truth week, Iacocca arrived at the end and listened to a summation of the lessons learned. Then, like Grandpa, he ordered us all to work with more openness and collaboration. There it was, word from on high. And everyone immediately went back to the old way of doing things.

Why did we not change? One reason was that Lee was an old dog whose tricks had always worked in the past. He was not eager to learn new ones, and we all knew it. But there were also a host of other reasons. We operated not in Japan but in America, where Wall Street demands short-term success and punishes those who fail. Bucking the system is nearly impossible. Most of all, we were not in the kind of crisis that demanded radical change. As I would come to learn and relearn, there is something in human nature that makes us wait until a situation becomes extreme, and then wait some more, before we'll try a new approach. At Chrysler in the mid-1980s we were doing much too well, and crisis seemed so far away, that we couldn't adopt new ways.

———

A CRISIS, AS the Chinese character for the word indicates, presents both danger and opportunity. Many of us reflexively fear crises and are so concerned about the danger they pose that we may have trouble responding in a creative way. But for a few people, moments of crisis cause feelings of excitement and inspiration. They recognize that when things start falling apart, they have the option of picking up the pieces and putting them together again in a new and possibly better way. Think of the guy who loses his job but responds by opening a successful business, or the homeowner who loses her house to a fire but builds a new one that is safer and stronger. These people know how to handle crisis.

In my years at Chrysler after the restructuring, where I worked one rung below the CEO, we would not face another genuine crisis. There were exciting challenges. The AMC deal gave me the chance to throw myself into a job and feel the satisfaction of success after making a maximum effort. The talks were a grind, and I worked myself dizzy with fatigue. But I loved it. I also enjoyed building Chrysler Financial and other elements of the business.

At the same time I noticed that I felt a little uneasy, if not bored, with the daily routine of managing a bureaucracy, which is what a big corporation can be. In the mid-1980s *Automotive News* published an article about me, titled, "The Long Arm of the Bean Counter." It was a very complimentary piece highlighting my successful effort to grow revenues and profits. But the bean counter role was feeling less and less comfortable to me. I'm not suited to nitpicking columns of numbers, and I get antsy reading through long financial reports. It's not that I don't value these skills or recognize that they are essential. I do. But I get no kick from ledgers and reports.

My preferences were obvious to those who were closest to me. Maggie could see that I thrived under pressure and loved finding unconventional solutions to business problems. A good example arose during Chrysler's strong days in the 1980s. We were selling so many vehicles that our factories couldn't meet the demand. Years before, when they were doing much better in North America, Volkswagen had bought a plant that had formerly been used by Chrysler to make Redstone rockets for the U.S. Army. The place was located twenty miles north of Detroit and had over two million square feet of floor space, ideal for making cars. They planned to make a car called the Rabbit there, but VW sales began falling and they never cranked it up.

With Chrysler straining to meet the demand for its suddenly popular vehicles, it didn't take a Redstone rocket scientist to see the possibility for a win-win deal. Iacocca talked to VW chief Carl Hahn and said, "You don't need this capacity. We'd like to buy it. Do you want to sell it?" Hahn answered, "Ja," and they agreed to have their finance experts work out the particulars.

The chief financial officer for VW of North America met me at a cheap motel near the town of Sterling Heights, where the plant was located. Ian Anderson wanted to keep our talks secret until they were concluded because any news about a factory changing hands would have an immediate effect on Wall Street. Since our bosses had agreed to make a deal but had not discussed price, we had to come up with some sort of figure on our own. I started the process, giving a lowball figure since the plant had little value now for VW.

"It's worth $100 million more than that," answered Ian, "and you really need it."

In fact, Chrysler was hungry for manufacturing capacity, and the Detroit region with its big pool of experienced autoworkers was an attractive location. But there were other options around the country, and we knew we would have to put at least $150 million into machinery before producing a single vehicle. I explained all this and raised my offer by $25 million.

The talks took several hours, but eventually Ian and I got close to the point where we were $5 million apart. After hours and hours I finally said, "I'll flip you for it." He gave me a look that said, "You're kidding," and I gave him one that said, "No I'm not." He took the challenge, and I pulled a quarter out of my pocket. He flipped and I called heads. The coin landed with George Washington's profile facing the sky and Chrysler saved $5 million. Ian kept the quarter.

Was the coin flip a fair move? I think so. It brought us to a price we were headed for anyway, and it added a dash of fun to our negotiations at a moment when we needed it. Would our bosses have approved? I never asked.

Unfortunately, $5 million bets were rarities, and everyday office intrigue was not nearly so stimulating for me. I wasn't the best at deciphering conversations and analyzing people. Maggie did what she could to help me in this tricky territory. And on her own she enjoyed occasionally yanking chains and shaking people up. At parties she would take a cigar and stand with the men instead of accompanying the other wives to a room where the air was clean. In conversations with vice presidents and top managers she asked blunt questions and teased those who could take it with a barrage of zingers.

One of Maggie's favorite targets was a colorful old Ford hand named Fred Zuckerman, who came to Chrysler to work with me in finance. A New Yorker, Fred was outgoing and funny and extremely well-liked. He was honest to a fault, which made him popular in finance circles, where integrity is everything. He dressed flamboyantly, wore a rather ill-fitting toupee, and was happy to trade barbs—"busting chops," as he called it—with anyone. Maggie teased him about his weight, which was always high, and his hairpiece, which was often askew. She was signaling, in her own way, that "we're all just people here, so don't take yourself so seriously." Fred got the message, and since it came from someone he liked, he took it in stride. So did I.

Maggie's effort to keep me level-headed produced results that one might not expect. Take the whole matter of telephone etiquette. In the executive realm, people often engage in a strange dance of power around the issue of who gets on the phone first. Those who are determined to win have an assistant place a call and ask for me to come to the phone. If I get on the line and have to wait even for a moment until the other person comes on, then he (it's almost always a he) has shown that he is more powerful.

You would not believe how much time and effort is expended by executive assistants playing the telephone game. I refuse to do it. If I want to speak with someone, whatever the rank, I call and wait for the person to get on the phone. The same is true with face-to-face meetings. In my experience a great many executives, including Iacocca, simply say, "I want to meet with so-and-so. Get him in here as soon as possible." I do not do this. If I want to meet with someone to do business, we talk over the arrangements, and as often as not I leave my office to visit the other person, regardless of level.

My way of handling calls and meetings has become an ingrained habit, and it's effective for several reasons. First, it saves time. Second, it communicates sincerity. Third, it enhances rapport. Whom would you rather work with to solve a problem, a guy who always has to play for the upper hand or someone who comes across as a human being who offers respect?

A DOWN-TO-EARTH STYLE fit me, the product of an Oregon lumber family, as comfortably as an old Pendleton shirt. And if Maggie didn't reinforce the basic values behind my style, I could still find reminders and inspiration during regular visits home to be with my family in Portland and Bandon. The things that happen in our families matter the most and, if you pay attention, help you maintain proper perspective and priorities.

In the mid-1980s, our Moore Mill and Lumber Co. was evolving into a forest management operation. Our old sawmills were shut down, and the last, the big old one in Bandon, finally ceased operations in 1986.

In the summer of 1987 a happy family event promised to lift our spirits. Our son Chris, who was not my biological child, got married in Oregon to Barbara Beale, who was my sister's adopted daughter. (I know it sounds unusual for "cousins" to marry, and it is, but they were, in fact, not related by blood.) We were all happy for them, and Chris and Missy would go on to have a very successful marriage and a house full of five children.

During that trip home, when we also celebrated my dad's fiftieth anniversary at his law firm, a few of us went down to Bandon to catch some sea air and visit. I took a few folks who had never been there, and decided to start our tour with a moment at the family plot in the cemetery that overlooks the harbor and the Moore mill from an elevation of perhaps fifty feet.

We rolled into the cemetery and paid our respects to my grandparents. Then, as a group, we walked to the edge of the cliff, where we expected a spectacular view of the mill and the water. The harbor was there, in its choppy, steel gray beauty, but where the mill was supposed to be we saw the charred remains of its massive wooden beams and joists and the pilings of the pier that supported it. A few firefighters stood by with a fire truck, as sentinels against the return of the flames.

The mill had burned during the night while we all celebrated Chris and Missy's marriage. An investigation would eventually conclude that a worker dismantling equipment with a blowtorch had accidentally set a tiny fire that he didn't even notice. Years of grease spills and sawdust combined with the tinder-dry lumber used to frame and sheath the building to make the ideal fuel for a fast-burning fire. High winds fanned the flames into such a ferocious blaze that fire companies didn't have a chance against it. They spent the entire night protecting nearby buildings and brush from flying embers and watching the mill, once the heart of the local economy, go up in smoke.

Since the mill was closed and we were already engaged in transforming our family firm into a forest management company, the effect of the fire was more symbolic than financial. But still the sight was a shock, and the smoldering wreckage spoke to the vagaries of life. Nothing, other than our values and character, is permanent. Change is inevitable. The mark you leave on this earth depends more on what you do for others than what you accomplish for yourself.

Long after the remains of the Moore mill were carted away, people would recall how the jobs it provided kept families going. They would remember relationships, baseball games, and the satisfaction of helping to build America. In a column published in the local paper after the fire, one writer explained that the mill gave workers a way to pay the bills with a job that let them catch a few salmon after work and save enough to buy a new car at the end of the year.

Within a year's time, my father's brother Walt died in a tragic accident when the boat carrying him back from a fishing trip was swamped, capsized, and sank near the treacherous Bandon Bar. My brother David, who was also onboard, survived. But he and my uncle were very close, and David and his wife took the loss hard.

A few months later my father would become ill, move to Bandon to convalesce, but then succumb to multiple organ failure. His death came, ironically, on my own forty-seventh birthday. Dad's obituary, published in the Portland paper, noted his extensive service to others, including his work on behalf of education in Oregon. His passing, and the example he set, was another reminder. Our time on earth is short, and the opportunity to serve is a great gift.

———

PART OF ME was looking for a meaningful challenge, something beyond bean counting, and it came at the time when my father was growing sicker and his life's example was fresh in my mind. One summer Sunday in 1988 three of the Detroit area's civic leaders came to see me at the new home Maggie and I had built to live in as our boys moved out to start their own lives.

Alan Schwartz was a senior partner at a big law firm.

Al Glancy was head of Michigan Consolidated Gas, the big utility in town.

Federal judge Damon Keith was one of the most prominent African American leaders in the region. I knew they were all on the board of the Detroit Symphony Orchestra, but was shocked when they asked me to take over as chairman of the DSO. The orchestra was a basket case suffering from the dual trends of rising debts and declining audience.

Although Maggie and I attended concerts occasionally, my idea of classical music leaned more toward Elvis than Amadeus. But as my three visitors said, the job was about leadership, not making music myself. The orchestra faced a budget deficit of nearly $5 million, and management had been bickering with labor for years. The fighting had led to a musicians' strike that had ended only recently. Worse than that, the orchestra had been playing to an audience crowded with too many red coats, which was their term for the empty red seats in the hall. This was bad, not just for the DSO but for the city of Detroit, which was already in decline. A successful orchestra would draw people to town and boost its economy and reputation. Its failure would be another blight on the community.

The DSO's situation was complicated by the fact that it got more than $2 million per year from the state of Michigan and was therefore subject to political pressure. At the moment I was offered the chairman's job, the orchestra was being criticized as an all-white enclave in the middle of Detroit. Since tryouts were conducted on a blind basis—musicians played behind screens and judges didn't know their identities—this was a tough problem. However, the legislators who demanded change represented constituents who couldn't see why their community should pay for an all-white orchestra that played for an audience that was practically all white on any given night.

Because an orchestra is more a cultural asset than a business, I accepted that government would be a partner, at least for the time being. But I was also intrigued by the idea of making the DSO less dependent and more self-reliant. This challenge was appealing, and Maggie was all for me accepting as a matter of public service. But before I decided, I wanted to consult with an expert whose opinion I could trust—my son Alexander.

Alexander had taken up the oboe in school and excelled to the point where he was accepted to study at the Juilliard School after high school. In the summer of 1988 he was at a music festival in Aspen. Already scheduled for a trip to the West Coast, I stopped to see him the week after the DSO trio visit to my home. Alexander was thrilled by the idea, especially since it meant I could learn about his world. He also thought that the DSO was well worth saving. For a time, when Mischa Mischakoff was concertmaster, it was one of the premier orchestras in America, if not the world, and it still had the potential to be great. However, Alexander did warn me that union musicians would be no easier to bargain with than union autoworkers. And on some issues, they might even be tougher.

I took the job and immediately discovered that the DSO was in worse shape than I had been told. (This is a rule for organizations that seek out a savior. Things are *always* worse than they tell you.) In fact, the orchestra was broke and was losing key people. Günther Herbig, the music director, didn't see the orchestra going anywhere, was fed up with the Detroit scene, and was soon leaving for a new job in Toronto. The executive director, who was in charge of all the operational matters, had made some offensive statements that had angered the community and been dismissed. There was a nice guy as a temporary fill-in, but we needed to find a permanent replacement, quick.

Personnel decisions would play a big role in the DSO's future, but it was easy to see that some basic reorganization was needed, too. They had, literally, more than two hundred people named as board members. It would be impossible to manage anything with so many, so we quickly restructured to create a smaller group of decision makers who could move nimbly and had access to people who might make substantial donations to keep the orchestra alive.

At the same time we had to build a bigger audience. The problem here wasn't the music. It was first-rate. However, many people didn't want to come into downtown Detroit at night to hear a concert. Also, the DSO's home, the Ford Auditorium, was too big and lacked proper acoustics. Fortunately, a community group had begun working on the restoration of Detroit's old Orchestra Hall, a gem built in 1919 but vacated in 1958. Local activists had saved it from the wrecking ball but were struggling to complete a renovation.

It seemed obvious that Orchestra Hall was the facility that the DSO needed and that the orchestra, with its vastly superior network of contacts, could help finish the restoration. Together I figured the two operations needed about $10 million annually. Clearly, it would be easier for one combined group to raise this money with one fundraising campaign. Otherwise you would have two different pleas going out to the same basic group of potential donors. That's not only inefficient, it's annoying.

Unfortunately, the obvious isn't always easy to accomplish. The two groups came from distinctly different perspectives. Poor as it was, the DSO represented the old money elite: ladies in diamonds, gentlemen in tuxedos. The Orchestra Hall folks were the types who didn't mind getting plaster dust in their hair and were suspicious of the rich and powerful. Nevertheless, I was determined to broker some sort of deal that would benefit us all.

On my first day as DSO chairman, I went to their place to meet with Orchestra Hall's chairman, Frank Stella, and their executive committee. "It's nonsense for the two of us to continue as separate institutions," I said. "We need each other." Stella and his group were understandably reluctant to give up their baby. They had worked against great odds to bring the theater back to life. What if DSO folks dominate the board of a merged organization? they asked. Will our vision and our values get trampled?

The answer lay in power sharing. Frank and I could be cochairmen of a board that was drawn on a fifty-fifty basis from the two organizations. After a little back and forth, they seemed to warm up to the idea. Like a business merger, the deal would cut certain costs. Instead of two executive directors, we could have one. The same would be true for other positions and even some facilities. I was able to add a little energy to get the deal moving by imposing a deadline. If the DSO was going to switch venues for the next season, which would begin September 15, 1989, the decision would have to be made by the first of November.

Although a deadline and a reorganization scheme would make anyone nervous, it also created some excitement. Whatever problems existed, our work was ultimately about the music and serving the public, and this was a special kind of motivation. The people I dealt with were highly creative and sensitive. I liked their company and I think they liked mine. I certainly felt appreciated as I worked to make the DSO more secure and supported Orchestra Hall's greater ambitions, with included constructing an arts complex that could become a big cultural asset for all of Metro Detroit. Gradually, I think they came to believe that a guy who made key moves to save Chrysler might help them reach big goals, too.

Remarkably, the merger decision came in less than two weeks, with both sides agreeing to make the deal. The news came in time for Maggie and me to celebrate at the DSO's first concert of the year. In seasons to come, Maggie would get more involved in the Detroit social scene, hosting parties for the symphony and helping me to squire around influential people we invited to be our guests at concerts followed by dinners.

Over time, our efforts would bring new supporters to the symphony and Orchestra Hall, but in the short term, we still had to cope with revenue shortfalls that were going to get worse before they got better.

The people who worried most about our finances were the musicians who depended on their paychecks to pay rent and feed their families. Soon after I was made chairman I went to rehearsal and talked with them about the state of affairs. The musicians had union leaders who were in many ways like other union leaders. They thought they were owed enough money to make them happy, and they weren't about to give up any of their privileges, including the lifetime tenure that came with their jobs.

But while they could be militant, the members of the orchestra wanted to see the DSO survive and thrive. When we missed a payroll, they could have stopped playing. But when I asked them to go on and give me time to fix things, they agreed. As my part of this deal, I worked with the National Bank of Detroit to secure some loans, which I personally guaranteed. When one of the bank's officers asked, "Steve, do you know what you are doing?" I told him I believed in the orchestra's mission and its people, and I knew we would succeed. I said the same thing to Iacocca when I hit Chrysler up for a $1 million donation. Actually, I said, "Lee, I'm knee deep in this thing and I need $1 million to keep it going." He approved the donation but had to deliver a dig—"Take the money, but now get back to work, Miller"—along with it. (GM and Ford soon made significant donations, too.)

I meant what I said about the people who were the DSO. An orchestra is only as good as its musicians and leaders, and based on everything I heard from those who knew, we had great people who could perform brilliantly. The people part got even better as we filled vacant leadership posts. First came Deborah Borda, who left her post as head of the Saint Paul Chamber Orchestra to manage both the orchestra and the hall. A thirty-nine-year-old with lots of energy and enthusiasm, she would be the first woman at the top of one of the nation's top ten orchestras. (Deborah later assumed the top post at the New York Philharmonic, and then the LA Philharmonic.)

With Deborah's appointment we had only one major post to fill— music director—but that would take much more time. Because their talent and personalities determine an orchestra's success or failure, real maestros are rare birds and difficult to capture. Many enjoy extraordinary job security and status, and become so much a part of high society in the communities that they cannot imagine leaving. When they do consider it, great efforts are made to prevent them from leaving. We were going to have to be smart and maybe lucky to get the right person.

In the meantime, we had to deal with the kind of challenge that usually doesn't affect a real business. In early 1989 half the cash the state paid the DSO as a subsidy, more than $1.2 million, was withheld at the insistence of state lawmakers who demanded we immediately hire at least one black musician to add to the one we had. The two Detroit democrats, Morris Hood and David Holmes, had been pressing their demand for affirmative action for more than a decade. With the orchestra on the ropes, they timed their move to have maximum effect.

I went to the state capital, Lansing, and to these lawmakers' local offices, to work on this problem. The response I got—wary and watchful—made me realize for the first time in my life that I was the Man to some people. They couldn't know that I approach everyone know-

ing there are things they can do and that they know that are beyond
my frame of reference. My hope, always, is that we can eventually
celebrate together when a problem is resolved. But you cannot tell
people you have good intentions and expect them to accept it. You
have to prove yourself, over time.

In those meetings I made it clear that I was not going to promote
an orchestra that offended a large segment of the community. "I want
to keep it alive to help Detroit," I said, "and I think that if you care
about the city you'd want that, too. But if you really want me to shut it
down, I'll let it go."

Despite their often heated rhetoric, Representative Hood and Senator Holmes didn't want to see the DSO disappear, but they were ada-
mant about adding black musicians and saw quotas as the way to do
it. To me, the concept seemed insulting to both the orchestra and
those musicians who would be hired in the future. Who in the highly
competitive world of classical music would want to get a job based on
racial preferences instead of merit? And who among the musicians already employed would think it fair that a newcomer hadn't earned his
or her way in blind auditions?

I could see how someone might look at the two sides in this debate
and figure it's a puzzle without a solution. But I had learned a few
things in my business life. One of the most important was that creative solutions can often be found outside the nonnegotiables. In this
case, the DSO would ask union members to suspend the formal rules
and allow us to hire an exceptional black musician, renowned bassist
Richard Robinson, as an apprentice immediately. Afterward, blind auditions would be the rule. But we would mount a campaign to recruit
black musicians to compete for slots and offer coaching in advance of
the competition. The coaching would make up for the disadvantages
black musicians may have experienced in the past, but on the day of
the auditions, merit would still rule.

The orchestra was in the middle of a very successful European
tour—standing ovations, rave reviews—when they gathered in Madrid
to vote on the exemption. Noting it was a one-time, nonprecedent
move, they approved the idea and Robinson was hired. Holmes and
Hood released their hold on our state grant. When the homecoming
orchestra landed at the Detroit airport, I was standing near the jetway,

holding a sign, reading, "Welcome Home DSO, Conquering Heroes. Detroit Loves You!"

The exemption sparked some criticism in the arts world, where even some black musicians criticized us for seeming to cave in to outside pressure. But we were in an extraordinary position with our future at stake and a record of failing to address the diversity issue. Further progress on this front would be very slow because hardly anyone ever left the orchestra. We did, however, make sure to hire a diverse group when adding musicians for particular concerts and developed an apprenticeship program that allowed us to bring many minority musicians into the DSO community.

But it was not enough to begin to change the makeup of the group on the stage. If we wanted to raise revenues and be relevant to the community we served, we also had to build a bigger and hopefully more diverse audience. New programs like an African American composers' forum and a Classical Roots performance series helped. But we didn't confine the work of black composers to special nights. They were added to our regular events, too, and we did see greater diversity, and greater numbers, in our audiences.

When the immediate funding crisis eased, I could focus on somewhat longer-range plans and fundraising to benefit the DSO and its new home. Unlike other turnarounds, this one involved lots of social events and concerts, and Maggie and I hosted several of these. Given her lifelong love for classical music and the meaningful contribution she could make—not just lunching with the ladies—Maggie happily threw herself into the assignment. An early computer whiz—she worked one with abandon, while I moved with painstaking care—Maggie crunched lists of donors and volunteers into workable databases that let us target fundraising and other activities with much greater efficiency. And since she had a purpose beyond mere chitchat, she devoted herself to DSO social events with an enthusiasm she never showed for the dinners and parties that were business obligations.

It was one of the happier times in Maggie's life. Every week or so, we invited a different couple to dinner and a concert in hopes that they would become DSO patrons. We also held fundraisers at home, where we got to hear the strains of a woodwind ensemble echo from our foyer. At these parties, guests were enchanted by Maggie's collection of art and archaeological artifacts and by the elaborate gingerbread village—so large it needed a room of its own—that she kept on display year-round.

The gingerbread creation, which included scores of buildings, figurines from around the world, and even a little model railroad, had grown from a tabletop display Maggie had first made almost a decade earlier. Once, when we lived in Venezuela, rats got into a shed and gnawed her sugar-and-spice creation to bits while it was in summer storage. In Michigan I had protected the gingerbread from predators with a rope and pulley system that let me hoist it up near the ceiling of our garage. The system was foolproof until the season when a certain fool lost control of the rope and the whole thing came crashing down, bounced off Maggie's head, and landed, like a piece of buttered toast, upside down on the garage floor. Fortunately, Maggie wasn't injured in any serious way, we salvaged some of the village people figurines, and the gingerbread village soon got a room of its own.

With Maggie guiding the social side of things, I worked with others at the DSO to produce a long-term plan to raise almost $20 million in capital. The same proposal postponed salary increases, cut costs by canceling a domestic tour, and projected 12 percent annual gains in audience through better promotion and marketing. These were the same methods a company might use in a turnaround and would eliminate our operating deficit in three years. We had to get the union to understand we were serious, and when a cash flow crisis forced us to miss a payroll they saw that we were and agreed to deferrals of raises in salaries and benefits.

Deborah Borda, who often worked into the early morning hours to save the DSO, deserves much of the credit for the plan. A great communicator, she also showed deep appreciation for our players as people and artists. Together we developed a one-for-all attitude, and that goodwill could be heard in the music. Deborah led the hiring of a new music director, Neeme Järvi. After a hard-driving, technically obsessed conductor like Günther Herbig, Neeme's softly creative style was just what the orchestra needed. With him conducting, the orchestra produced wonderful new recordings. Their success proved an old axiom in business that suggests that organizations that alternate disciplined leadership with creative excellence get the best results. Järvi also had the kind of charm and talent that would draw audiences and donations. With him in place, ticket sales jumped 25 percent. Eighteen months after the judge, the lawyer, and the utility executive had come to my house to ask for my help, the tools used for corporate rescues—cost cutting, improved product, and better management—had put both the DSO and Orchestra Hall on sound footing.

I wouldn't stay involved long enough to see it, but over time the merged organizations would reach new heights. In 2004 they opened a $60 million center for music education that includes a new 450-seat theater. The Orchestra Hall complex was joined the next year by a new high school and public television facility devoted to broadcast education and production. This big complex would bring life back to a part of downtown Detroit that would stand as a symbol of hope for a city that had struggled too long.

For me, the DSO rescue had been a chance to explore the world of classical music, which I knew only through my son Alexander, and an opportunity to practice meaningful public service by putting my skills and contacts to work for a good cause. The excitement around the symphony project also reminded me that I loved the creative work of saving and rebuilding big enterprises (and I could tell I was getting pretty good at it). I wasn't quite through with the climb up the corporate ladder. In fact, I had one more exciting Chrysler drama in my future.

Always ready to say things that other people only thought, Maggie foreshadowed the turmoil to come at a company dinner gathering where I took the lectern to talk to several hundred of our top management group and then invited questions. I was stunned when Maggie's hand was raised with the first question, a very treacherous one. She stood up from the table and asked what I'd do differently if I were head of the company instead of Iacocca. Without missing a beat I answered, "The first thing I'd do is forbid spouses from attending meetings."

Four

___

THE BLACK LETTER

___

In cyclical businesses like real estate, agriculture, and yes, cars, it's easy to become obsessed with finding ways to counter the drop in revenues and profits that come when the industry sags. Diversification can seem like a good choice, but it's hard to manage. Similarly, it's wise to pile up cash for rainy days, but when you make cars and spend millions of dollars a day doing so, it's almost impossible tell when you've saved up enough. Besides, some of your profits must be poured into the costly job of developing new and better products or the market will pass you by.

Since there is no panacea, smart auto execs fight the cycles with a combination of diversification, cash reserves, and vehicle development. They also maximize efficiency and thereby reduce the number of cars that must be sold each year to keep the company going. This was how the best Japanese companies managed their affairs. They were lean. They saved cash when they could, and they never stopped researching consumer preferences and developing cars to meet future demand.

With our K-cars, minivans, and SUVs courtesy of Jeep, Chrysler had the new models it needed through the mid-1980s. But the car lineup was growing stale when 1990 brought a down year, and we were behind in developing new models. New ventures acquired during our salad days, including Gulfstream, weren't producing the kind of profits we desired. We had several billion dollars in the bank, but the funds wouldn't last forever when withdrawals were made at a rate of millions per day. Worst of all, prosperity had brought the inevitable flabbiness, and our costs had risen to the point where our break-even point—once 1.1 million units—was again approaching two million vehicles per year.

An important part of the problem was due to Iacocca's emphasis on market share rather than profitability. Lee wanted us to sell every car we could make, even if the profit was negligible. With his focus on market share competition with Ford and GM, he continually pushed for higher volume, as if we were in a sort of three-way game and the only score that mattered was the raw number of sales. To boost this number we acquired several car rental companies, which took on many of the cars we made that dealers didn't want to buy. The problem was that we cut these companies such a great deal that we made almost nothing on these sales. We then guaranteed to buy the cars back in three months. The "used" cars went to dealers, who were able to make more profit on them than they could by selling a brand-new, zero mileage car.

Think about it. You are about to buy a new $12,000 car, which the dealer paid $10,000 to acquire. He then says, "Oh, by the way, we have the same car, a former rental car with two thousand miles on it, on our used lot for $9,500." What he doesn't say is he paid Chrysler only $7,000 to get it. You save a bundle, he gets more profit, and the car is practically brand-new.

With this scheme, we ended up on some product lines selling *more than half* our production into short-term rental fleet deals. This madness, which my Chrysler colleague Bob Lutz called "manufacturing used cars," upped sales totals but actually reduced our profits. Lee didn't care. If we could make $1 over variable cost on a car he said, "Ship it." But Lutz and I preferred gearing our factories for leaner operation and higher per-car profits on less volume.

The rental car deals and the push for market share reflected an old-fashioned approach to the business, which was understandable given that Lee cut his teeth in the 1950s and would turn sixty-five in the fall of 1990. He was also behind the times when it came to automotive style and design. Lutz, who once worked for BMW, understood that cars have to be built from the chassis up, with the emphasis on performance. He made this point when he unveiled his first new design. We all gathered around a pedestal draped with a canvas. When it was removed we saw not a model of a car, but a chassis with its power train and wheels but no body. Styling was the easy part, he explained, and secondary to performance. Lee, on the other hand, emphasized a car's exterior appearance and believed that quality was measured simply in the number of defects found in new vehicles rather than in the features that delight the consumer. Our troubles were not all Lee's fault. Like all big bureaucracies, auto companies suffer from inertia, and the people who run them can become so isolated they don't see changes in the market. As part of our planning, for example, we considered projections for the growth of the national economy, and then projected that the demand for passenger cars would at least match it. We didn't take into account that the boom in truck, minivan, and SUV sales was eroding demand for cars. We planned production the old way and got it wrong year after year.

But if we all suffered from a bit of rigid thinking, perhaps the least flexible member of the key executive group was our chief, and his problem was caused by factors that were almost beyond his control: ego and time. Lee was famous in a way few people ever experience. His face, voice, and name were instantly recognizable. Reporters followed him like puppies. He was an *entire category*, not just a question, on *Jeopardy!* Only Mother Teresa could endure the fawning attention Lee received without losing perspective. Similarly, time was affecting him in its inevitable ways. We all find it harder to keep up with modern trends as we reach our midsixties. Chief executives also tend to lose touch with ground-floor essentials after they've been at the helm for more than five or six years. This is why turnover is fairly common at the top—fresh faces are valued—and boards tend to expect a CEO to retire at about age sixty-five.

But in1990, the usual rules didn't apply to Lee Iacocca. With him acting more and more like a king, the board of directors behaved more and more like his court. Despite Chrysler's down year in 1989, they raised his salary 15 percent, gave him almost two hundred thousand shares of stock, and actually bought his two homes (one in Michigan and another in Boca Raton) at above-market prices to spare him the inconvenience of selling them himself. All this was done at a time when execs at the other two major car companies were accepting pay cuts and the nation as a whole was sliding toward the worst recession since World War II.

Although the rewards lavished on Lee were excessive, they might have been considered appropriate as parting gifts for a hero CEO on his way out. Jerry Greenwald certainly hoped they were. Having been assured he was next in line, he had served for years as the consummate number two, carrying out Lee's policies and decisions without ever letting anyone know if he agreed or disagreed. Scrupulously honest, Jerry was a master of finance who grasped every detail of our business, but he did not fit the CEO image that had been set by Iacocca. He grew up poor in St. Louis and retained a soft-spoken, humble kind of presence. He couldn't tell a joke to save his life.

Jerry's modesty and decency did not mean he had endless patience. As time passed, and Lee had pushed his estimated retirement date further into the future, Jerry worried his time would never come. Finally, in May 1990 Lee told some reporters in Los Angeles that he planned to stay on through age sixty-seven, and perhaps even longer if Chrysler's new cars took off. "If this stuff starts to sell," he said, "I might want to sit around a while and enjoy it."

Clearly, Iacocca didn't intend to leave soon. And if he wasn't leaving, then Jerry would. Before the month was up, insiders were gossiping about employees at United Airlines recruiting him to lead a buyout of the airline. On May 31 he took the job, which put him in line to become CEO if the takeover succeeded. Since the position came with a long-term contract and a big pay increase, it was easy for everyone, except Lee, to see why Jerry took the offer. Lee saw it as a betrayal. Within hours, Jerry's name was immediately removed from every bit of stationery and every document. His responsibilities were carved up and distributed to the remaining executives, and his name was no longer mentioned in meetings that Lee attended.

As he took off, Jerry created a vacuum that seemed to suck me and Bob Lutz closer to the top job. In stories about post-Iacocca succession our names led the list of CEO candidates followed by Jerry York, another finance guy, and Tom Denomme, who was VP for a host of corporate functions, including quality, productivity, labor relations, and strategy. In time the names Ross Perot and Roger Penske would also float in trial balloons, and rumors flew about a couple of big shots at GM who might be willing to defect. Iacocca was determined that someone he favored, someone who would protect his legacy, would get the job. His commitment was so strong that he even rebuffed the Pennsylvania governor's effort to appoint him to the late John Heinz's seat in the United States Senate after Heinz was killed in a plane crash. It was a rare gift—free admission to the most exclusive club in the world—but Lee was so concerned about guiding the choice of the new CEO that he turned it down.

Among the leading candidates I had ample experience, status as an insider, and Lee regarded me as no real threat to his image and legacy. For the first time, I felt that it might be my destiny to land in the top job. I wasn't sure that I deserved it as much as, say, Lutz, who was far more passionate about cars. But I also understood that if you are a solid team player and don't focus too much on who gets credit for what, the ball will eventually bounce your way. For example, during the big turnaround, when Lee became a superstar, others did most of the grunt work. But ultimately a lot of glory was passed around and I got my share.

The lesson of Chrysler's salvation, and its effect on my career, became the basis of my approach to so-called office politics. When young managers ask me to describe it I tell them: You are never as good as they say you are when things go well, and you are never as bad as they say you are when things are in the dumper. Don't worry about credit. Your boss may take credit for things you did. But people aren't dumb. People know. They figure it out. Also, the more you let others take credit, the more they come to rely on you and share ideas, and those things enhance your value. Ultimately you will be rewarded.

I thought that I wanted the reward of taking the top spot. But when feeling gave way to reason I saw a better option—joint leadership with Lutz. No one had more raw automotive sex appeal than Lutz, who was a fast-driving former Marine Corps fighter pilot who spoke several languages and helped develop BMW's enduring reputation for performance cars. He would be the perfect public face for the company. I possessed what he lacked in financial management expertise and connections. When we talked about the idea, we agreed that together we could match or even surpass King Iacocca.

We took the idea of a Lutz-Miller team for a test drive when *Forbes* magazine sent writer Jerry Flint to do a piece on Chrysler's future. He came out to our styling center, viewed a few upcoming models, and interviewed us at length. Bob and I also agreed to be photographed sitting in a convertible Viper V10—him behind the wheel, me in shades in the passenger seat—looking for all the world like a couple of supremely confident car guys.

The article gave us a chance to boost the company's image, and it did leave readers with a sense that the future was bright. I got to say, "Having $4 billion in the bank means never having to say you're sorry." Lutz got to talk about how we could develop new cars and bring them to market much faster and at much less expense than our competitors in Detroit. And, oh yes, we did allow ourselves to chat about how we could run the company together, as a team.

Although *Forbes* did print our optimistic statements about Chrysler's operations and its future, the magazine naturally focused on the human drama of succession and made much of our statements about what we would do should Lee, as I put it so indelicately, be "run over by a truck." You can imagine his reaction to what we said, and you would be right. He was furious. But he was even more upset about the picture. For ten years Lee had been, literally, the face of Chrysler. Now we show up in a major business magazine seated in a flashy muscle car looking like we're ready to take over the company.

The boss was already wary of Lutz. He resented Bob's image as a swashbuckling fighter pilot–sophisticate and knew that Lutz ridiculed his taste in cars and penchant for salesmanship. Now he saw me as a potential usurper, and I was added to his unofficial enemies list. If he was going to be true to the tradition of imperial CEOs, this meant he would try to undermine me. It happens all the time. Rulers can't seem to resist the urge to destroy potential successors. It's almost an unconscious thing, based on some primal instinct for dominance and survival. In the days before reforms made directors more independent, many CEOs wielded extraordinary influence over company boards. Directors were beholden to the chiefs for information and rarely met without them. In the entire time I had been at Chrysler, until Lutz and I appeared in *Forbes*, the board had never met without Lee present.

In the run-up to the succession struggle Lee demanded that the board be reduced in size "to make it more efficient," but since most of those who were forced to depart were inclined to be independent, the remaining smaller group was more deferential to Lee. Still, they couldn't avoid the work of planning for a new leader, and they began by asking for input from five insiders who were considered contenders. Flexing his muscles, Lee got in the middle of this process, instructing us to submit letters to him dealing with three issues—Chrysler's current problems, priorities for the future, and who should take the reins. He said he would report our comments to the board. (Note I didn't say he would pass the letters along to them.)

My letter was blunt. I wrote that the company had followed a myopic product strategy, devoting too much capacity to cars and thereby refusing to recognize the strength of the minivan, truck, and SUV lines. My list of future priorities was extensive. I said we should focus on the strong vehicle lines with an emphasis on safety, fuel-efficiency, and eco-friendly technologies. These products would allow us to market Chrysler as a brand of excellence, not the brand you turn to when you can't afford something better. Looking ahead to global competition, I saw that we had to somehow get more production out of our workforce. We had to ask the same from our executives, which meant flattening the pay scale at the top and making sure that no one, not even the CEO, was viewed as royalty. And who should be that CEO? I suggested that Lutz and I split the titles of CEO and president. It didn't matter to me who got which job.

Fifteen years later, when I look at a copy of the letter I sent Lee, I am happy to see some firmly stated ideas and a bit surprised by how candidly I expressed them. At the time, Maggie warned me that I was heading into treacherous waters, but I still trusted that my views would be transmitted without too much filtering to the board. This did not happen. As a member of the board myself, I soon realized that very little of what I gave to Lee had been passed along, and the same was true for the other candidates.

If Chrysler wasn't drifting downward, and if Lee seemed the right man to halt the slide, I might not have gone around the blockade he had established to keep my ideas from the board. But the company clearly needed change, and I was ultimately responsible to the board, not the CEO. When several board members asked to meet with me privately, I drafted a new letter and flew to New York, where a group of three was supposed to receive it. The flight was on a company jet, which also carried Bob Lutz and Jerry York (by now Lee's favorite successor candidate), who had other business in Manhattan. In a fit of candor designed so I could see their reactions, I gave them copies to read. Lutz said he liked it. Jerry wouldn't commit and said only, "You've got balls."

In New York I was met by five directors, not three, and the group included Joe Califano, the former Carter cabinet member who was one of Lee's most powerful supporters. Like York's, his eyes bugged out as he read my letter, and he offered only a cryptic response—"This is significant"—when he finished. Eventually I would conclude that it was probably Califano who told Lee about the letter. For all I know he helped coin the title Lee would use for it ever after: the Black Letter.

Though overly dramatic, Lee's response is easy to understand, since the first couple of pages (out of seven total) urged the board to take control of the succession issue out of his hands and end the tension and infighting caused by his meddling with the process. I wrote about how hard it would be for Lee to give up his CEO perks, including "limos waiting at the steps of the G-IV jet wherever in the world it happens to touch down," and I argued that he should leave his post completely, without taking the kind of ongoing "nonexecutive chairman" role he seemed to desire.

"I do not believe that Lee's continuing guidance is essential to the success of the Company," I wrote. "In fact, I would say the opposite."

While giving Lee proper credit for all he had done in his early years at the helm, I had to add to the ledger all the mistakes—"blunders," I called them—committed since the middle of the 1980s. Among his biggest mistakes were the rental car arrangement, money-losing joint ventures with Maserati and Renault, and a failure to recapitalize the company when times were good that left us dangerously overleveraged. More generally, Lee terrorized the ranks with a management style that was erratic, contradictory, and intimidating and "leaves our people cowering in fear for their jobs."

Bad as things were inside the company, Lee's standing with the outside world was worse. His tirades against Japan and U.S. trade policies had convinced our partners at Mitsubishi that he should leave and had alienated the administration in Washington. At the same time Lee seemed to avoid making any serious attack on the big problems affecting industries like ours.

The media had picked up on Lee's failure to grapple with important issues and on his hostile political tone. *Business Month* magazine had recently published seven pages "deconstructing the myth" of Iacocca that suggested his fame had become a liability. Some of our biggest dealers told me privately, "Lee has got to go." Similarly, the financial community seemed to have lost confidence in him. Our most important bankers were telling me that they would not make any more deals with us until the CEO had been replaced.

Most of these problems, from Lee's politics to his declining reputation in the financial world, found their way into my report to the board. I concluded with a strong pitch for a Lutz-Miller team to replace the legendary Iacocca, who cast such a big shadow that he should not be permitted to hang around even as a member of the board. In making this argument I took another swipe at Lee, who had recently begun a campaign to discredit Bob Lutz.

> Of considerable distress to me lately is what I'd call a deliberate campaign by Lee of character assassination aimed at Lutz. Lee has identified a number of people at all levels of the Company with whom he is carrying out a quiet "witch hunt" to seek out any dirt about Lutz. If nothing else, this has terrorized people into fearing they will end up on the wrong side. There is also a whisper campaign of sorts impugning Lutz's "integrity." (Lee has even expressed this to me in private.) I for one am mystified by this. I have no evidence of any reason to question Lutz's business ethics (whereas I cannot make the same comments about Lee) and I have not known Bob to consort with any sleaze balls. . .

The line about sleaze balls was a bit harsh, but Lee's taste in friends had brought him close to a number of questionable characters. I didn't think Iacocca was himself involved in anything unsavory, but his friendships with certain people indicated a lack of good judgment and concern about his public image. It might be fun to create your own personal Rat Pack and pal around with them in Manhattan, but when the leader of a company as big as Chrysler does it, you have to wonder if he has become overwhelmed by the CEO syndrome.

———————

ON THE DAY after delivering the Black Letter I returned to my office in Detroit and was summoned to Lee's lair. He knew I had met with Califano and the others. I was sure he either possessed a copy of my letter or had been briefed on its contents. But at this stage of the drama he couldn't acknowledge this fact, so he went through the exercise of asking me what I had said in New York. I told him my message was similar to the one I had written for him, but which he failed to pass along, months before.

"Did you give them anything in writing?"

"Yes, I did."

"I'd like a copy of what you gave them."

"Okay, but you won't like it."

I went back to my office, retrieved a copy of the letter, and brought it back to him. He put it in his briefcase and said he'd read it over the weekend. I understood that whatever remaining bond we had would be broken as he read the letter. His anger would be justified, in his mind, by the fact that I ranked below him and owed him loyalty for bringing me to Chrysler in the first place and backing my advancement. He wouldn't reflect much on the fact that I was also vice chairman of the board and owed a higher duty to the directors and our shareholders. They were a higher authority.

———————

I THOUGHT LEE was going to rip me apart, and the next Monday he called me into his office to fulfill my expectation with an angry tirade. He said that he had talked to Jean de Grandpré, a Chrysler board member who was also chairman of Bell Canada. They had agreed that I had "wandered off the reservation" and was "blinded by ambition." I was a traitor, said Iacocca, and I was wrong about him, his decisions, and the state of Chrysler.

I was shaking as I listened to Lee's rant. Later he would tell people that I actually shed a tear during this meeting. I don't recall that happening, but I wouldn't be embarrassed if it did. It was a highly emotional moment. The guy who had brought me out of obscurity, trusted me, and shared with me the glory of Chrysler's rescue was now branding me an outcast. I felt a twinge of guilt. And when he accused me of acting out of my own personal ambition, I couldn't say he was all wrong. I *was* making a move for at least a piece of his job. But his anger didn't erase the fact that Lee had stayed in the game too long. I was just a younger player vying for the starting position that he would inevitably have to vacate.

With our conflict out in the open, we both moved quickly. Lee gave my letter to our top human resources executive, Glenn White, with the order to develop a response to the board refuting each of my points. Glenn was the man Lee used to handle difficult personnel problems and would be the best choice for the assignment. But if he ever completed the document he was sent to write, I never saw it.

I knew I might have some allies on the board and was pleased when Bob Lanigan, of Owens-Illinois, called to tell me the Chrysler directors would protect me. He said that they knew about Lee's shortcomings and were prepare to replace him. They didn't want me to leave in a huff at a moment when my expertise would be needed, and perhaps they feared I might do significant damage if I went to another company. Lanigan invited me to come see him at his office in Toledo, Ohio. I agreed to meet the next day.

That night, as usual, I replayed the day's events for Maggie, and she helped me sort out the psychology at work. "Lee's a bully," she said. "You kicked him in the shins, and now he's going to come after you."

She was right, and if I had been completely dependent on Chrysler I would have been more worried. Fortunately, I did have my share of the Miller family wealth, built by three generations, which served as a real bulwark. This support meant that I could do what was right—act on my conscience—with a little less fear. This independence was the best thing about my inherited wealth, and I always regarded it as the main difference between me and colleagues who were working without such a safety net.

My family's wealth had a much different effect on Maggie, by the way. She was conflicted about it and never wanted to claim it as her own, outright. In fact, every once in a while when she was overwhelmed by insecurity and said we ought to split up because she was somehow unworthy, she'd start talking about how she wouldn't take a cent from me. "I arrived in this marriage without a penny, and I'll leave without a penny," she would declare.

At these moments, when Maggie seemed to be fighting inner demons that were born during her very insecure childhood, there was little I could do but let things run their course. She would get tearfully worked up and announce with all seriousness that our marriage was breaking apart. The timing of these outbursts was confusing and somewhat mysterious to me, at first. But eventually I realized that they seemed to occur at times of stress. Holidays often brought them on. Sometimes she would go so far as to leave the house and check into a hotel for a day or two. But she would always come back and we'd pick up where we had left off.

Several of these crises arose at the time of the Chrysler CEO shake-up. Maggie would start talking about how her outspokenness might cost me the top spot at the company. She also knew that if I got the job she might be dragged into the limelight, and she dreaded the scrutiny that would come with being one of the Big Three's first ladies. All of these worries and fears came boiling out of her as the succession battle raged, so in the midst of working on my own agenda, I also had to struggle to reassure her that we were in it together for the duration and she couldn't possibly be responsible for my ultimate fate. This was at times a very difficult job as Maggie's emotions often ran wild and she would convince herself that she and I should break up because she was holding me down.

On the evening after my highly charged Black Letter session with Lee, Maggie announced a few dozen reasons why she didn't deserve to be my partner. She even talked about how she should leave me, hole up in some dive, and support herself as a maid somewhere. This was a recurring theme for her, one that was probably based on deep-seated fears and insecurities, but I didn't understand it. My response, as always, was to try to reassure her, and argue with her until she eventually agreed to stay home, and stay married to me. Someone else might have become so frustrated he would have agreed to break up the marriage. Another man might have pushed Maggie to get professional help. Neither of these options fit me. I didn't know enough about mental health problems or treatments to imagine what was possible for Maggie, and as long as I could talk things through with her, which I did that night, my values dictated we stay together.

The next morning I took off for Toledo, using the travel time to shift my focus from my personal crisis to my professional one. At Owens-Illinois headquarters Bob Lanigan welcomed me into his office, and we began a very warm conversation. He wanted to let me know that the board was aware of the need for new leadership and that the Lutz-Miller team enjoyed support. He even invited me to stay in his office when Iacocca happened to call on the phone, and then briefed me on what was said during their chat. I left feeling as if I was on the offensive in my chess match with the king. But fortunes shift quickly, and less than a month later I got a different response from Lanigan when I called him on some routine matter. Instead of warm and friendly I got cool and professional. I would never discover what changed things. Perhaps this time Lee was sitting in his office when I called.

A street fighter who no longer felt any gratitude for my long service, Iacocca was going to use whatever means necessary to prevent me and Lutz from assuming control of a company that was both a reflection and a total expression of his identity. Iacocca was Chrysler. Chrysler was Iacocca.

Toward the end of the year, the board seemed to be drifting sideways. We got together in Detroit to take up the issue again. This time we would meet on the top floor of the American Center, a forty-story building in suburban Southfield that had been acquired as part of the AMC-Jeep deal. Plans called for top management to occupy this new space, but the move was only half completed. The place had the look and feel of one of those instant spaces people rent in office parks—bare bones, sterile, and much too quiet.

Lee and I were asked to leave when the board reached the point on the agenda when the succession issue was to be discussed. He reacted as if was the first time he had ever been kicked out of any boardroom. It certainly was the first time that *his* board ever got together without him. In the large waiting area outside we found separate corners and plunked ourselves down. Some of the other CEO candidates were also there. I asked Tom Denomme what he thought. He glanced over at Lee, who was still fuming, and said, "Steve, the chance of you becoming CEO is remote."

It was like a splash of cold water on my face. He was right. I wasn't going to be CEO. And much to my surprise, I was not very upset. I had taken my shot because I thought I might team with Lutz to do the job right. But I was never the kind of political animal who had to win every time. Besides, I wasn't so sure that I would be happy running a company on a day-to-day basis. In the back of my mind I still wondered if I preferred the firefighter role of corporate crisis intervention.

Before I had time to think it all through, I was called to the phone. It was Jim Wolfensohn, an old friend who had played a key role as our adviser from Salomon Brothers during the Chrysler rescue. A former Olympic athlete and jet fighter pilot for the Australian air force, Jim was one of those people who would qualify as a "most unforgettable character" in *Reader's Digest*. Shortly after Chrysler was settled he opened his own firm—James D. Wolfensohn, Inc.—and turned it into a consulting powerhouse for the world's premier companies and deal makers. (While generally called "bankers," the Wolfensohn group would best be described as advisers who aid companies with financial needs.) He said, "Steve, we need to talk. Come see me."

Although nothing was settled on that December day at the American Center, I realized that I probably wasn't going to get the top job at Chrysler. Lee was not going to permit it. I went to New York a few times in January and February to see Wolfensohn and his partners, including Paul Volcker. The work they described was exciting, if a little beyond my experience. I had helped save one big company and an orchestra. I wasn't at all sure about translating that experience to the broad range of clients Wolfensohn served. I told them that I wouldn't bring a Rolodex full of big connections or a salesman's flair for lassoing new customers. They didn't care. They pushed me to take their offer and were soon joined by an enthusiastic ally they couldn't have recruited—my wife.

As much as I fretted about living in noisy Manhattan, Maggie relished the prospect. This was the early 1990s, and Rudy Giuliani had yet to be elected mayor and begin the great quality-of-life campaign that made the city much more livable. In 1992 menacing squeegee men still worked a number of intersections, and so many panhandlers crowded some sidewalks that you needed a roll of dollar bills to walk a few blocks. The subway resembled one of Dante's circles of hell, and it seemed like joggers put their lives at risk anytime they passed through Central Park.

None of the dangers, inconveniences, noises, or even smells bothered Maggie a bit. Instead she felt completely invigorated in Manhattan, more alive than she felt anywhere else, and though she found it exhaustingly stimulating, she loved "the daily struggle for survival." Add the special extras that make New York alluring even in bad times—operas, museums, galleries, music, etc. Add the chance to socialize with some of the most interesting people in the world, and Maggie had her ideal home. In part because of her enthusiasm, and as a reward for all the sacrifices she had made—lonely nights, disrupted weekends, boring corporate social functions—I said yes.

In February 1992 I announced my departure from Chrysler, clearing the way for whoever became the new CEO to hire his own team. Maggie and I went to Manhattan and bought a most unusual and expensive bit of real estate—the entire tenth floor of a small apartment building with 180-degree views of the East River with its barge and boat traffic and the Queensboro Bridge. It was comfortable but in need of some renovation. We found a wonderful decorator and began imagining the kind of urban homestead that would make any boy from Oregon a little wary, but which absolutely thrilled Maggie.

With such a big personal transition approaching and the clock winding down at Chrysler, more than a few of my colleagues expected me to take it easy until I could just slide out the door. I couldn't do it. Like the lumbermen in Bandon I had a deep need to give an hour of real work for every hour's pay I was going to receive. As my quit date approached, I took on the task of negotiating one last agreement, with our partners at Mitsubishi at their headquarters in Japan. Before leaving I briefed the man who had been tapped to replace Lee, a well-liked GM executive named Bob Eaton, who had most recently headed their European operations. I gave him two pieces of advice. First, I urged him to value Lutz and let him have his share of the credit for the new products that were coming out. I explained that Lutz was a proud man and would thrive on the recognition. Second, I warned him that every five or ten years Chrysler runs out of money. They get into a financial crisis and then sacrifice long-term product development to cut costs. I suggested he use the times ahead to beef up the balance sheet so he would not have to cancel work on the next generation of vehicles just to meet payroll.

With my duty to the new guy satisfied, I flew off to Japan and immersed myself in the work of a financing deal that involved some of Chrysler's holdings. The work wasn't especially demanding, but it went slowly because even those Japanese who spoke English well insisted on translation, just to be sure. I expected to wrap things up, take a flight back home, and enjoy two weeks of vacation before showing up at Wolfensohn's offices in Manhattan. The plan held until my last day in Tokyo. In the morning Maggie had faxed me some papers on the sale of our home in Michigan. (The buyers were, poetically enough, named Robert and Margaret.) I was busy reviewing and signing them when the phone rang.

"Mr. Miller, this is Paul Reichmann. I have a small family real estate business, and we are having some cash flow problems. I'm wondering if in your new capacity as an investment banker you might be able to help us."

Five

I'M A NEW YORK BANKER, SORT OF, BRIEFLY

If the Reichmann family business—called Olympia & York Developments Ltd.—was a small real estate development company, then McDonald's is just a hamburger shop. In reality, O&Y was the largest urban commercial property company in the world, and at one time the wealth of the reclusive Reichmann family was widely estimated to be second only to the riches held by the British royal family.

In our first phone conversation Paul Reichmann, his calm voice crackling over many thousands of miles, explained that someone in his company knew of my work on the Chrysler rescue and had noticed a press report about my move to Wolfensohn's firm. Even though my real estate expertise didn't go much beyond buying and selling my own homes, he was certain that I could help him. I explained that I was about to start a two-week vacation. He asked if I would forgo my vacation, put off my orientation period in New York, and start work at his headquarters in Toronto the next day.

With all the pride and confidence of a cavalry officer summoned to the rescue, I said, "I'll be there." When he asked me about a fee I had no idea what my employer might expect but nevertheless confidently told him the price was $2 million up front followed by $100,000 per month. In the next breath he agreed to pay it.

A quick call to New York brought congratulations from Jim Wolfensohn, who must have thought I possessed some magic power to attract new clients willing to pay well for our advice. He faxed me a sheaf of news clippings about Olympia & York's troubles, so I could at least see the outlines of the crisis. The clippings were almost all that was available since the firm was privately held and produced none of the reports required of public companies. The articles were nevertheless eye-opening. They showed a once-invulnerable empire crippled by a worldwide collapse in the real estate market and costly delays in promised public infrastructure development at its most ambitious project ever, the $6 billion Canary Wharf office and retail development on the southeast side of London.

Every day Canary Wharf sucked buckets of cash out of O&Y's otherwise profitable businesses in such cities as Toronto, Calgary, San Francisco, and New York. The project's main problem was a faltering government effort to extend subway service along a route called the Jubilee Line to the new development. Although Olympia & York was contributing hundreds of millions of dollars to the extension project and had already built a station, it was far behind schedule. Without it, transportation to Canary Wharf was so poor that potential tenants wouldn't leave other locations—even the decrepit quarters common in the city's financial district—for the wharf's beautiful, modern facilities.

Under normal conditions O&Y's far-flung holdings, which produced steady revenues on rents, would have been able to sustain Canary Wharf until the Jubilee Line was finished. I liken managing money this way to the cash-strapped truck operator who carefully drains the fuller gas tanks in his fleet of diesels to provide fuel for the empty ones. Over the short term, you can use this method to keep everything moving even though you don't have the money to buy more fuel. But the strategy can buy you only so much time. And God help you if some of the tanks develop leaks.

Unfortunately, by 1991 O&Y's tanks had sprung some leaks. After years of frenzied construction and rising rents, every major city in the world was suddenly overbuilt and the commercial real estate business plunged into a recession. Vacancies in office and industrial buildings skyrocketed, and obeying the laws of supply and demand, rents plummeted. Where they could, developers halted planned projects. But at sites like Canary Wharf, where the cranes were in place and buildings were already rising, there was no option but to finish and try to lure tenants who would start paying rent.

Many knowledgeable people assumed that the Reichmanns had assets enough to mortgage for cash to pay the bills in London for many years. Throughout the 1970s and '80s they had acquired or built hundreds of top-quality properties—including the massive landmark World Financial Center in lower Manhattan—that had escalated in value. To take one example, a set of eight New York skyscrapers they bought with a cash outlay of $46 million had reached $3 billion in value ten years later. With this kind of record, banks had willingly lent the Reichmanns more than $18 billion without requiring the usual documentation and security. In most cases a simple promise from Mr. Paul, as he was called, was enough to seal a deal.

Success had built on success until outward signs of serious trouble, the first ever for the storied Reichmann empire, appeared in late 1991 and early 1992. In December the company refused to purchase a completed $241 million building at Canary Wharf, which it had promised to buy from the Morgan Stanley financial group. Morgan Stanley soon filed a lawsuit, demanding its money. Around the same time, to raise cash the Reichmanns began massive borrowings against their stock holdings—they held controlling interests in Gulf Canada and the forest products giant Abitibi-Price—and backed down on plans to build the tallest structure in Moscow, a sixty-story office tower.

By the time he called me, Paul Reichmann had discovered that his word was no longer gold and that even when he offered his properties as collateral, the banks were not interested in helping him refinance. He was desperately trying, and failing, to get extensions on loans held by a consortium led by Canadian Imperial Bank of Commerce. O&Y was in similar trouble in Europe, where it was unable to make a $62 million interest payment to bondholders. Among his lenders, especially the Canadian and American banks who were his major backers, anxiety was about to turn into panic.

I digested all the available facts about O&Y on the long flight from Tokyo to Toronto. I landed with the happy feeling that my new job was never going to bore me.

————

HIGH IN THE Bank of Montreal building in Toronto, which he had built and still owned, Paul Reichmann's office was a classic example of the hushed, wood-paneled space that communicates wealth and power. Its occupant was a rather short, bearded, sixty-year-old man who always wore a yarmulke and dressed in a plain black suit to show his devotion to Orthodox Judaism. The clothes, like so much about Paul Reichmann, signified spiritual humility and fealty to Jewish law. He ate only glatt kosher food. He wouldn't shake a woman's hand. And he always stopped work and got home before sundown on the Sabbath and the Jewish holidays. He even required that all his employees, Jewish or not, cease work on those same days.

Reichmann's way of life would be considered unusual in many business circles, and his reserved demeanor could be misinterpreted as mysterious or rejecting. Some people saw him that way. But when he came to greet me, Paul was anything but aloof. He was warm, open, and completely calm. He apologized for asking me to wait while he finished some other business, and when he returned he seemed genuinely sorry that I had been left alone for more than an hour.

When we were alone, Reichmann revealed Olympia & York's trouble as only he could. As a family business, O&Y didn't generate the kind of data you might expect from similar firms with outside stockholders. Instead, Mr. Paul held every important fact in his head. Employees were informed on a need-to-know basis, and worked solely in response to his personal orders, which meant that information was very compartmentalized. People did not discuss their work openly, share ideas, or exchange data. Odd as it was, this way of doing business had allowed him to build one of the greatest companies in history. And until this moment, it had never failed him.

As we discussed his predicament—vast obligations and dwindling cash flow—I realized how Reichmann's bankers felt. Over time they had set aside many of their usual cautions, accepting minimal documentation and collateral to lend O&Y billions of dollars. Now their longstanding trust seemed misplaced. They feared huge defaults and recriminations from their own directors and stockholders, who would want to know why they had offered the Reichmanns such special treatment. Desperate for reassurance, the big lenders had insisted that Reichmann name a former New York banker from Manufacturers Hanover, Tom Johnson, as president of O&Y. He was to be their inside man, peering over Mr. Paul's shoulder.

You can imagine how Tom Johnson's presence affected a proud man like Paul Reichmann and was resisted by loyal staffers, who had never responded to orders from anyone else. They were most upset when Tom put himself between them and Mr. Paul, requiring they clear with him first any responses to requests from Reichmann. Johnson, who was working without a formal contract, was so wary of the company's finances that he had demanded that a substantial sum be set aside to protect his salary. When this request wasn't met he turned it into an ultimatum. "It's Friday afternoon," he announced the week I arrived. "I'm going to New York for the weekend. If my salary isn't secured by Monday, I won't come back."

Paul Reichmann asked me about Tom's demand, and I explained that the banks had no right to foist Johnson on him in the first place. In my mind, Mr. Paul was the genius who had built the assets of Olympia & York, and he was the only guy who could possibly figure out how to fix things. My advice was to let Tom go. It was the answer Reichmann wanted, and he showed his appreciation by asking me to take over as O&Y president.

Since I hadn't even settled into my office at Wolfensohn and was practically winging it in Toronto, I thought I'd better call Jim in New York before responding to Reichmann's offer. He brought me back down to earth fast. "We're not operating an employment agency," he barked. I agreed, turned down the offer, and then counseled Mr. Paul to give the post to Jerry Greenwald, who had been my comrade in crisis in Detroit. The Persian Gulf War had temporarily wrecked Jerry's efforts to take over the top job at United Airlines, and he was both willing and available to help us.

Jerry took the job but couldn't come immediately. This left me and Mr. Paul with the task of assembling a restructuring program and fending off demands from lenders. Over the next two weeks banks and other creditors continually requested information, but O&Y didn't have the financial information systems to create the reports they requested. Still, we tried.

As I wandered from office to office, picking up bits of data, I also served as a kind of grief counselor, listening and empathizing as people struggled to adjust to O&Y's decline. The entire staff suffered from a certain sense of denial about their predicament. They had been so successful for so long that the idea that they were truly vulnerable didn't get through to them immediately. They had trouble understanding why their once-friendly bankers had become cold and demanding. Many uttered bitter epithets about lenders who had suddenly turned into idiots who didn't know what they were doing.

The denial and bitterness were sometimes voiced by Mr. Paul, who for the first time ever, was having trouble getting his telephone calls returned by his banks. Worse, whenever he did hear back, he was forced to deal with lower-ranking executives, who ran so-called workout departments devoted to bad loans. This happens to every distressed borrower, by the way. When you are doing well the bank sends you the smiling guys with firm handshakes to lend you money. When you are failing you have to deal with the cold analytical types who only want to know how much meat is left on the bones. Not only are the nice guys nowhere to be found, they won't even come to the phone.

Not surprisingly, Mr. Paul resented his bankers for turning him down in a moment of need and was certain they were ruining a workable plan to save O&Y for everyone's benefit. I tried to explain to him that these last-gasp rejections were not the precipitating event for his crisis. "It's like the Confederates firing on Fort Sumter," I said. "Technically, those shots started the American Civil War, but a great many things happened before that moment that were much more important."

Fortunately, Mr. Paul wasn't the type to dwell for long on problems he couldn't solve. Instead we focused on developing the argument that might persuade our wary lenders to keep us going. By the way, I used the words "us" and "we" almost reflexively from the moment I agreed to help O&Y because I felt personally attached to the cause, like a member of the team. My associate from the Wolfensohn office, Maureen Healy, counseled me to put a little distance between myself and our client, to speak about "the company" and "Mr. Reichmann" so I might show a more professional "banker's perspective." Years later I would conclude that she was right. I *was* a consultant, not an employee, and a little separation might have been reassuring to the banks, reinforcing my image as an honest broker. But at the time I was just two weeks away from my career as a loyal corporate executive, and I hadn't changed my self-image. I had made a commitment to

Paul Reichmann, and I wanted to put everything, including my name, reputation, and heart into the cause.

The first product of my commitment was the package of documents that made up our plan for recovery. Though less comprehensive than the Chrysler plan sent to Congress, the restructuring plan for O&Y was, nevertheless, 270 pages long and included a big collection of charts, graphs, and financial assessments. Much of this material would be disseminated for the first time at an upcoming conference with our creditors, and this made some people think we were about to pull back the curtain on the Wizard of Oz. As the moment for presenting the case to the bankers approached, reporters flew in from all over the world and staked out the hotel where the meeting would take place.

On a mid-April morning we lugged the whole lot of books, files, slides, and charts to the Sheraton Centre, where more than a hundred lender representatives waited to hear us. Interest in this meeting and the famously secretive Reichmanns was so high that one journalist actually dressed as a hotel waiter to sneak into the room. Fortunately, he was discovered and expelled before he could hear anything of a confidential nature.

When the meeting began, I presented the plan while Mr. Paul watched from a seat at a table facing the crowd. In the darkened ballroom I ran through a series of slides that hit the high points of our request for lower rates on some loans, interest-only payments in the upcoming months, and a new line of credit worth $260 million to see us through the Canary Wharf crisis. To support this request, I offered estimates on the value of our holdings, which were based on the assumption that markets would stabilize and improve. Because real estate values are changeable and not pegged to an active market like the one for stocks, our assessments were somewhat less than scientific. However, they were not completely unrealistic, and they showed that with a little more time we might repay everything that was owed.

"Your choice," I concluded, "is to feed this horse so that it can run again, or kill it and divide up the meat."

Every financial crisis comes down to this kind of choice. Do you keep extending credit, and thus time, and hope that a valuable enterprise can recover? Or do you withdraw your support and carve up the assets at the very moment when they may hold their lowest value? The decision can depend on the size of the debt involved. Ironically, because they have more to lose, bankers may be more willing to extend help to companies with enormous debts. In these cases the stricken companies are sometimes described as "too big to fail," and they are kept alive at almost any cost because their failure might imperil the bank itself. As they say, "A rolling loan gathers no loss"!

In reality, no banker will put so many eggs into one borrower's basket that a bankruptcy will ruin his bank. Therefore, no company is too big to fail. Still, some are so big and valuable that they merit extra effort. I believed this was true for O&Y. There was great value in Mr. Paul's real estate acumen and the team he assembled to manage and build properties. Canary Wharf was obviously destined to be a great success, just as soon as the public transport issue was resolved. Finally, we knew that the real estate business, which cycles as regularly as the seasons, was going to recover. Olympia & York's buildings were the best in the world and would eventually gush with rent payments.

If I had made the same pitch—don't break us into pieces now—on behalf of a car company, I would have had a more receptive audience. Everyone knows that a plant that makes transmissions for Chryslers would have very little value if it were seized by a lender. How much of a market would they find if they tried to sell it? But an office building in San Francisco or Calgary or Montreal is worth pretty much the same whether it's owned by a big international firm or a local landlord. Our bankers understood this truth and found the notion of claiming O&Y's buildings, one by one, extremely attractive. Later I would also realize other important differences between a Chrysler-style crisis and the O&Y situation. Unlike Chrysler, O&Y employed few people, enjoyed no political support, and its collapse posed little danger to local communities. In short, the company had no natural allies.

Still, after the briefing at the Sheraton we saw signs that the uproar over O&Y had been calmed at least a bit. Banks that held major loans saw the prices for their stocks stabilize—one even rose on the Toronto exchange—and lenders suspended their demands for more information during the few days they required to study all the material we had handed them. For a moment it seemed we might avoid the worst-case scenario, a true panic among bankers who, terrified that someone else would get in line first, might move to foreclose on our assets.

THE PRESS COVERAGE of our campaign to save O&Y generally acknowledged the psychology at work. We had to build confidence in our effort, and that required us to balance honest reports on our predicament with confidence about the future. I sought to do this by speaking as plainly as possible and using common, upbeat terms like "no-brainer" to explain why everyone should support Mr. Paul. As a result, I was generally described as "folksy" or "down to earth" in the media accounts of our efforts.

I was happy about these portrayals, both because they were accurate and because I am a bit of a ham. I admit it. I like the limelight. It makes my work more fun. But my interest in publicity is not all about ego. When handled correctly, press coverage can also build public support for troubled companies. I learned this lesson from Iacocca. Chrysler certainly benefited from reports that emphasized his determined leadership and the company's importance to millions of people. I'm sure that officials in Washington, for example, knew how their constituents—workers, local dealers, and stockholders—felt about our plight.

Unfortunately, the greater public had little reason to root in a similar way for Olympia & York. Except perhaps for some construction workers, no one outside the company and its lenders would be affected if the Reichmanns lost control of O&Y. Their buildings would remain, serving tenants who would simply make out their rent checks to a different landlord. The Canary Wharf project would no doubt be completed by some other developer. And even though the economy depends on them, lenders are widely regarded as faceless and heartless institutions. No one really cared if they lost out. This may explain why the press, especially in London, seemed to treat the O&Y story more like a Hollywood scandal than a serious business crisis.

Some people even seemed to take perverse pleasure in seeing the Reichmanns fall. Their troubles entertained those British snobs who agreed when Prince Charles declared Canary Wharf an architectural monstrosity. Similarly, some members of the clubby business community in London, where the Reichmanns were considered outsiders, no doubt preferred to see them fail. And though I hate to say it, a grotesque cartoon in a Fleet Street paper that depicted Mr. Paul as a caricature of a Jewish businessman/King Kong under attack made me wonder if anti-Semitism fueled some of the public's interest.

Whatever its true sources, Britain's almost morbid fascination with the Canary Wharf saga was made obvious to me when I went to London and was literally chased down the street by reporters and cameramen. During one week in May, as I participated in long, hard, and ultimately fruitless negotiations with lenders, my picture appeared in the British papers almost every day. When we finally offered to make O&Y a public company and turn our lenders into shareholders, the *Times* of London filled most of its lead business page with articles about the move. As they reported, we proposed to give the banks that supported Canary Wharf part ownership of the vast development as well as shares in the parent company. In exchange, they would back off their demands for prompt payment on our debts.

For a proud family that had owned Olympia & York outright for thirty years, the equity offer was a sign of desperation. It came only after the company had failed to make a payment due on $200 million from the Bank of Nova Scotia and another lender, Royal Trust, threatened to seize First Canadian Place in Toronto, which was the tallest building in the Reichmanns' home country. In a last-ditch effort, Mr. Paul had all but circled the globe in search of new financing. This campaign had produced just a single $8 million "keep the lights on" loan from Hongkong and Shanghai Bank Corporation. As the name suggested, it was intended to pay for the basic services—for example, electricity to run the pumps that kept basements dry—to maintain Canary Wharf.

The "lights on" loan was necessary because Mr. Paul had finally drained all the fuel from O&Y's tanks. Unfortunately, the loan sent a signal to the financial world that said we were practically bankrupt. No one was impressed by our equity offer, and a week later a British court found that O&Y did indeed owe Morgan Stanley $241 million for the purchase of one of the Canary Wharf buildings. The issue that had announced the company's crisis back in December had returned to mark its demise.

On May 14, 1992, Olympic & York and nearly thirty subsidiary Reichmann firms filed for bankruptcy in Canada. At about the same time, the entity that owned Canary Wharf sought equivalent protection in the United Kingdom. Although I tried to put a positive spin on things, telling the press that we were simply "opening an umbrella" so we could continue to walk through a rainstorm, I knew we were through. This was especially true in London, where I quickly learned the difference between the laws in North America, where generally as the debtor you can manage your company after filing bankruptcy, and the laws in Great Britain, where they literally take away your keys to the office.

Courts in America and Canada allow for "debtor in possession" because they assume that the people who have built a major enterprise possess valuable knowledge and expertise and are best positioned to help it recover. The British courts assume you are incompetent and that only hard assets—land, buildings, machinery, inventory, etc.— have any real value. Much like a sheriff who throws out a deadbeat renter and lets the landlord keep his belongings, the British bankruptcy system moves quickly to turn the physical remains of a company into cash for creditors.

In the Canary Wharf case a man from the Coopers & Lybrand accounting firm became the sole authority for the company. On the morning he took over we held a meeting for workers in a big auditorium and explained the changes. I thought they'd all be scared about their jobs. Yet when we called for questions, the first that came from the back of the room caught me by surprise. "Excuse me," said a man in overalls, "but are we still going to get Jewish holidays off?"

I don't recall Mr. Coopers & Lybrand's reply to that question, but I did follow the fate of Canary Wharf closely, even after it passed out of our hands. While the banks in North America took pieces of the bankrupt Reichmann firms and went their separate ways, the lenders for Canary Wharf decided to manage its continued construction and operation as one big entity. As the real estate market recovered and the Jubilee Line was built, they were able to find plenty of new tenants. Soon enough, investors around the world saw great value in the property. A host of bids were made. In October 1996 the lenders who had foreclosed on O&Y accepted an offer put together by none other than

Paul Reichmann, who had mortgaged his own home to get back into business. Although he held only a 5 percent stake, he would manage the project and see it fulfill his original vision. Today it is fully rented and stands as one of Europe's premier business addresses.

I WISH THAT I had been involved, somehow, in Mr. Paul's return to real estate as a less powerful but nonetheless formidable figure. I believed that he was a genius of a developer. He was right about Canary Wharf, and but for market forces beyond his control—and a slowpoke mass transit bureaucracy—he would have succeeded. The project's ultimate success proved that there was never anything wrong with his vision of a new London skyline.

In my work with Mr. Paul I learned important truths about entrepreneurs. Entrepreneurs build value with their ideas, energy, vision, and expertise. They believe in the future. This is why the Reichmanns insisted on valuing their assets based on projections for the coming year or two. They knew, in their hearts and minds, that the market was going to recover and their holdings would be worth billions of dollars more than they might fetch in a fire sale.

When times were good, Paul Reichmann was able to get bankers to see his vision for new projects. Since his track record was spotless, they wanted to believe in his stories and cheerfully gave him the money to make them come true. Think of the song "Fidelity Fiduciary Bank" in the musical *Mary Poppins*. The lyric describes in excited terms how the bank plays a vital role creating such wonders as "Railways through Africa!" and "Dams across the Nile!" The people who make loans really do get excited about being part of big, successful projects and feel proud of helping to create businesses or real estate developments that might stand for generations or even centuries.

But the minute an entrepreneur gets into trouble, the lending executives are replaced by collections specialists, who are blind to the exciting vision he holds for the future. Instead of regarding the entrepreneur as a visionary, they consider him a fabulist who must be treated with intense skepticism. Suddenly faithless, they withdraw credit—the term itself is based on the Latin word for *belief*—and move quickly to recover as much of their investment as possible. This starts the equivalent of a panic run on a bank, with creditors rushing to demand repayment and the entrepreneur being forced into bankruptcy.

As you can see, the process is as much psychological as financial, a matter of belief as well as facts. Since no normal company is rich enough to repay all its debts at once, it takes just a small number of unbelievers demanding their money back to ruin everything. Ironically, in many cases you could argue that time will tell that it's the sky-is-falling deserters who spin the wrong story about the future. In Mr. Paul's case that certainly was true. From Canary Wharf to America's West Coast, O&Y's properties returned to profitability in a few short years. Those who sold off the company's assets at steep discounts missed gains that would have made them whole in the end.

Unfortunately, by the time I arrived on the scene, nothing I said would have calmed the creditors. Instead of mounting a series of skirmishes to win a big war, we staged strategic retreats that ended with a quiet surrender. When it was over, I concluded that I had provided just one significantly valuable bit of guidance for Mr. Paul. As the banks took over O&Y they needed a very clever structure to avoid some nasty tax issues. But they couldn't make it happen without his cooperation. In a letter I told him he was the most imaginative developer in the world and could get back into the game and succeed. But before he could do so, he needed to make a clean break. I counseled him to help the banks and demand in return signed releases that freed him from any future litigation related to his old companies and properties. With the calendar adding to the pressure, the banks agreed. It was a victory of sorts, but it was hardly enough to make me feel like less of a failure.

My colleague Maureen, who understood the consulting banker's role, would have seen things differently. Looking at the situation as a detached outsider, she would have recognized that the Reichmanns were responsible for Olympic & York's demise. We worked for Wolfensohn, earned fees for our own firm, and would move on to the next assignment. As a matter of business, this view was correct, but emotionally I had trouble accepting the outcome.

IN MY MIND, the fall of Olympia & York was a personal failure, and my batting average had slipped precipitously from 1,000 after Chrysler to .500. As much as this result depressed me, no one else saw things this way. At the office everyone focused on the next project. At home Maggie was mostly happy to have me around so I could help her with the apartment renovation and join her as she explored the city. The project at the apartment had become much bigger than I had expected and more ambitious than I would have deemed necessary. Instead of moving a few walls and upgrading fixtures, we decided to gut the place entirely and make it over completely. Was this necessary? Given that the apartment had recently been featured as the cover photo in *Architectural Digest* I had my doubts. But this was Maggie's big chance to make the home she wanted in a place she loved, and I couldn't argue with that.

Maggie's love affair with Manhattan was genuine. She haunted the museums, especially the Metropolitan Museum of Art and the Museum of Modern Art, each of which held more art than anyone could absorb. Even though only cheap seats were available, we were enthralled by *Madama Butterfly* at Lincoln Center's Metropolitan Opera House. On warm days we walked in Central Park or toured the Bronx Zoo. In the evenings we tested recommended restaurants all over the city and were rarely disappointed. At night we slept in a hastily arranged rental—our temporary home during the renovation—and Maggie basked in the street sounds made by noisy garbage trucks, emergency vehicles, and honking cabs. Being more fond of foghorns, I felt more enervated than enlivened, but I did take pleasure in seeing how Maggie enjoyed it all.

At the Wolfensohn office I worked with people who were similarly energized by the challenge of advising a varied group of clients on intricate financial deals. The firm specialized in high-stakes confidential projects that required sensitive negotiations and creative approaches to raising funds. Wolfensohn himself was a master of this art. His contacts in government, finance and various industries spanned the globe, and his capacity to absorb and then analyze the facts of a business problem were truly astounding.

Jim Wolfensohn's brilliance shone when we worked together with the New York Times Company. The Times was working on an offer to buy the *Boston Globe* from its owners, the Taylor family. I needed to labor over the details and put in an all-nighter to prepare for a key meeting with the Times Company's board of directors. Jim had only to scan the report to grasp it. He then got up in front of the board and delivered a speech on the state of the deal that blew my socks off. He knew every key issue, from the advantages of scale that would come from a merger to the market dominance the *Times* would gain, and he was able to discuss them in a way that made perfect sense.

Every meeting went the same way, with Wolfensohn speaking in a firm, confident, but deferential style. He never raised his voice and always seemed to understand his client's point of view. In meetings where I would want to scream, "You're being an idiot!" Jim was able to make the same point in a low-key way. "You're right," he would say, "those other guys *are* being unreasonable. But now you have a choice to make. We would suggest path A, which would allow the company to prosper. You might also choose B, and it could result in the collapse of the company. It's your choice."

In other settings, I watched with genuine amazement as Jim moved from discussions of geopolitics to music and then finance with seamless perfection. He was the type of man who could, and did, go out to court the powerful on Wall Street, return to the office to change into black tie, and then go schmooze with royals from Europe at a Carnegie Hall concert marking his own birthday.

As strange as it might sound coming from someone with my range of experience, I was a little in awe of Wolfensohn, and I tried hard to live up to his example. (Like Iacocca before him, he was a role model.) But I didn't have his temperament. For example, during the *Times-Globe* talks—I got frustrated when I met with the Taylors in Boston and they seemed shocked to learn that once they sold out, they would no longer have ultimate control of the management, the labor relations, or even the editorial content of the paper. Wolfensohn would take this in stride. I was appalled.

Similarly, I found it hard to match Jim's enthusiasm for esoteric financial arrangements. I understood the world of stocks, bonds, mergers, acquisitions, restructurings, and workouts, but I couldn't say that I got much pleasure out of shaving interest rates or putting together a consortium. I was still, deep inside, the boy who was fascinated by the mill in

Bandon where strong people ran a heavy industry that made a vital, tangible product. There's romance in a business that requires a little sweat—like cutting lumber or making cars—and while I didn't need to experience it every day, I did like to know it was part of my world.

The somewhat removed quality of my work as an adviser made the job a less-than-perfect fit. I was also a bit annoyed by that fact that New York State expected me to pass its broker/dealer test in order to continue to serve clients after my probationary period. The same test required of every new stock salesperson hardly related to my training or my actual job. I hadn't taken an actual test since my days in school. I resented being forced into it at age fifty, so I kept putting it off. Then when I tried to study pretest materials, my eyes glazed over and I had trouble staying awake.

By December 1992 I was discouraged. Maggie loved New York but I did not. Wolfensohn was a great place to make money, but as the long grinding hours of work led to ambiguous outcomes, it was not a good fit for me. The state of New York was bearing down on me like a schoolmarm armed with a ruler, and the renovation of our fancy apartment was starting to resemble the plot of the movie *The Money Pit*. Not surprisingly, I found myself slipping into a dark mood. The wind that whistled through the city's concrete canyons seemed unbearably cold. After it snowed it seemed that every time I went out I stepped into a slush puddle deeper than the top of my boots.

Unable to deny my unhappiness, I sought out Ray Golden, who was a senior partner of the firm and a calm, wise friend of Jim's, for a little advice. During lunch in a small conference room I told him how I felt, even explaining that the O&Y affair had been downright depressing for me, like watching the *Titanic* sink. I didn't think I would ever feel comfortable in New York. And the more I heard from my brothers in Oregon, who were spending much of their time on golf courses and ski slopes, the idea of early retirement, or perhaps semiretirement, sounded very good.

As we chatted, it became obvious to Ray that I was not very happy trying to turn myself into a globetrotting financial facilitator. Something I said, perhaps about how much I admired Jim, caused him to interrupt and issue a firm judgment. "Steve," he told me bluntly, "you are no Jim Wolfensohn and you never will be."

I almost felt relieved to hear this truth. Just as I would never become a copy of Lee Iacocca when I worked in Detroit, I wasn't ever going to match my role model as a banking consultant. This didn't mean there was anything wrong with me. It just meant that I wasn't anyone's clone. I had my own particular strengths, including the ability to drop into a crisis and spark a burst of activity that might revive a failing organization. Something about the way that I'm wired makes me love this kind of action, but I also grow impatient and may even become less effective after my first sixty or ninety days on the job.

I'm not saying that I understood everything about my own strengths and weaknesses when Ray Golden and I met. It would take me years to settle all those issues. But I knew for certain that he was basically right, and that I was feeling pretty close to miserable. I thought it over a bit more and decided that I needed to retire from the daily grind. Several interesting companies had approached me about serving as a director, so I figured I'd accept some of these posts as a way to stay engaged in business. But what I really wanted was to go home to Sunriver, Oregon, ski a bit on nearby Mount Bachelor, soak in the hot tub, and go to sleep to the sound of . . . nothing.

Admitting these truths to myself was difficult, and so was sharing them with Maggie. On a cold, dark night when I worked late and then met her at the gutted apartment, we sat on a dusty wooden crate in the middle of the debris and I explained it to her. At the time I didn't grasp just how much she loved New York. She must have felt all of it start to disappear, as if she was waking from a pleasant dream, as I said, "I can't stand this. I have to have a change." Later, as I came to understand it more fully, her reaction seemed all the more generous. After listening, she asked a few probing questions to make sure this wasn't just temporary dissatisfaction, and then agreed to go.

At the office Jim Wolfensohn asked me to stay, and some of his partners joined a little chorus that urged me to reconsider. But I had made up my mind. I did, however, agree to make a detour to Washington when Deputy Treasury Secretary Roger Altman asked if I'd consider heading the Resolution Trust Corporation, the government agency which was sorting out the savings and loan crisis. I went down and met with him and Secretary of the Treasury Lloyd Bentsen, who was a refreshingly candid man, for a politician, and remarkably pro-business, for a Democrat. He joked that in bringing me on board the Clinton administration would satisfy its affirmative action policy by hiring "an out-of-work Republican." Nice as he was, I stuck with my plan and turned down the job. Working twice as hard for one-tenth the pay, and having to deal with the Alice-in-Wonderland aspects of Beltway realities was beyond me. My batteries were worn out. I had to put my feet up for awhile.

————

ALL THAT WAS left was for us to sell our apartment, pack, and go. During the second week of February movers collected the stuff we had in a storage facility and began trucking westward. Maggie and I were supposed to depart together, but at the very last minute the board at our apartment building required one of us to stay for some meeting related to the sale of our place. She went ahead by herself, arriving in Oregon just in time for Valentine's Day. There she was, all alone in the stillness and the deep snows of Sunriver, where in winter the population dwindles to about eighteen hundred. In time, I hoped, we would create a happier life there. Meanwhile, I would have to just accept that every once in a while Maggie would feel compelled to tell whomever we met the story of how "Steven took away my dream when he made me give up New York."

Six

MATCHMAKER

Having given up her big dream in New York, Maggie found some pretty good substitutes back in Oregon. Truly convinced we were entering semiretirement—my objective was to serve on a few corporate boards—we decided that we would split our time between the coast and the mountains, and embarked on bit of a building spree. Maggie served as artistic authority and design director as one house went up on a treed lot in Sunriver and the other rose on the beach in Bandon. And just for fun, we set to work together on a sprawling model train layout that would become a perfect American community in miniature.

Whether we were making plaster of paris landscapes or sitting side by side, painting tiny figures and buildings, Maggie and I found it easy to lose ourselves in this hobby. Sometimes we'd chat. Sometimes we'd focus intently on the work. Time flew and we were having fun. Sure, there were moments when I felt restless and wondered about going back to work. But I am not the kind of person who has trouble filling his time. I taught myself how to make documentaries in the style of Ken Burns, starting with a video history about the Moore Mill and my family, and then branching out to make playful pieces for friends. I spent more time with family and more time on myself. In general, I felt so engaged in life that I stopped having my usual predinner glass of beer or wine (a habit born in more stressful times) because I wanted to be sharp to return to my hobby projects in the evening.

Although I wouldn't recognize it until years later, while I was busily occupying myself with hobbies, activities, and board meetings, Maggie was becoming more withdrawn. While I have always been outgoing and sought out new people and places, she had always been ambivalent and even reluctant when it came to social events or travel. But in this time period the tendency became more pronounced. Maggie could go for weeks without going anywhere or seeing anyone but me, and at times, I think, even my presence was too much.

I didn't realize how little I knew about Maggie's attitudes toward our retirement until March 1995, when a phone call interrupted our model railroad work. I took the call in another room and returned to tell Maggie that it was a fellow named Steve Hanks at a company called Morrison Knudsen, which was on the brink of collapse. Accountants at Deloitte & Touche who knew me in the Chrysler days had persuaded the leaders of MK that I could help. I told him I was happily semiretired but would take a day to think about it. I picked up a little figure of a railroad worker and a paintbrush.

"Call him back now," said Maggie.

"What?"

"I'm tired of fixing your lunch."

The crack about lunch was a joke, mostly, but Maggie was very serious about me responding to the overture. She knew that MK was one of the world's biggest and most capable construction companies with a huge pool of talented people and a truly glorious history. After several years of optimistic reports and predictions about new business and growth, the company had posted a huge surprise loss—$310 million— for 1994 and fired its imperial chief executive officer, William Agee. Big projects were in trouble, promising further losses, and the stock, which had been worth over $30 a year earlier, was trading below $6.

It was just my kind of company, said Maggie, a down-and-almost- out wreck that nevertheless mattered greatly to many thousands of people, including everyone who lived in MK's hometown of Boise. All she had to add was something about how "you've been fortunate in life and should give back when you can," and I was back on the phone with Hanks, agreeing to meet with members of the MK board.

Time was critical, and I left almost immediately for New York, where the board members and I talked over lunch in a dining room atop the MetLife Building. Together we planned for me to work intently on restructuring the company with the idea of turning the reins over to Robert Tinstman, head of their mining operations, in three or four months. My title would be chairman, not chief executive officer, and I insisted that my salary be set below the very top executive level, so that everyone would understand that any sacrifice required to save the company would be shared fairly.

Then, as always, people tended to attach great symbolic meaning to executive salary levels, and while I am a free marketeer on this issue, I have never made money the issue in deciding on a new job. I am turned on by challenges and the opportunity to do something meaningful, and if I can make a positive statement as I handle the compensation issue, I'll do it. At Morrison Knudsen one of the big statements made by my modest salary was: "I'm not Bill Agee."

———————

FOR SEVEN YEARS, the people of MK and Boise had endured a roller-coaster relationship with CEO William J. Agee, who was one of the most controversial executives in the country. Once a wunderkind, Agee had left his first high-ranking position, at Boise Cascade, just prior to that company posting a huge and unexpected loss. In 1976 he became one of the youngest CEOs of a major company when the board of Bendix Corporation put him in charge. Agee doubled the company's stock price in six years, but was also the subject of intense rumors about his relationship with a young executive named Mary Cunningham. Mary joined the firm right out of business school, and Agee promoted her to vice president in less than two years. Both were married when she arrived at Bendix, but colleagues almost immediately began speculating about their relationship.

My one prior contact with Mary and Bill, if you want to call it that, had occurred at the height of the gossip. Bendix was located in Detroit, and I had shared the first-class cabin with Mary on a flight that brought me back home after one of my Chrysler missions. After the plane was secured at the gate I followed her down the jetway to see Bill take her into his arms in the waiting area. After I got my car and pulled onto Interstate 94, I noticed they were ahead of me in a chauffeur-driven limo, making out like teenagers in the backseat.

In 1982, after they both divorced, Agee and Cunningham were married and became a team in every way, with Mary seemingly weighing in on all the big decisions Bill made. His last was an ill-fated attempt to takeover Martin Marietta, then one of the world's biggest aerospace companies. Martin Marietta had responded with the so-called Pac-Man defense, trying to gobble up Bendix. By the time that battle was done, Agee had been forced to merge with Allied Corporation and he was out of a job.

Although he seemed to withdraw from the executive ranks, choosing to run his own investment firm, Agee was young and bound to recover. A Boise native, he was a member of the MK board when his fellow directors asked him to become CEO. He quickly expanded a relatively small involvement in railroads to include large-scale manufacturing of rail cars and locomotives, and geared up to dominate construction of new rail lines, which he expected to be funded by federal, state, and local governments. Agee also pursued big international construction jobs, including a subway line in Taiwan and massive bridge projects in Canada and Europe.

Agee may have had good reasons for his big moves, but each and every one of them produced a bad result. MK did not know how to manufacture railroad cars and submitted lowball bids that guaranteed losses. Several of MK's huge construction projects, won on the basis of daring cost estimates, fell behind schedule. For a time Agee was able to cover his losses with investment income and well-tailored accounting reports, but by 1994 certain realities could not be denied, even by the close friends he had ushered onto the company's board of directors.

As bad as things turned out for Agee when it came to performance, he lost even more points on style. He started work by converting the boardroom at headquarters into a massive personal office. He replaced a portrait of founder Harry Morrison with a picture of himself with Mary. While firing six hundred people, he negotiated a much higher pay package than his predecessor's. His company-paid expenses included $7,000 for the Mary/Bill portrait, $16,000 for his wife's legal fees, and another $7,000 for Waterford crystal. It was par for the course in New York, maybe, but deeply offensive in Boise.

At an old company with a culture like MK's, the Agee style didn't go over well. Founded by two guys with horse-drawn scrapers, Morrison Knudsen had grown to build massive, landscape-shaping projects like the Hoover Dam, the San Francisco Bay Bridge, and the Trans-Alaska

Pipeline. MK people wore their hard hats with pride and valued work that produced, quite literally, concrete results. Boise traditionalists resented Agee, and within a few years no one could deny that he faced significant hostility in the ranks. Agee began running the company from his mansion beside a golf course at Pebble Beach. Feeling the hostility at headquarters, he took to wearing a bulletproof vest when he came to Boise. A graffiti artist wrote, "Shoot for the head" in the company washrooms.

By 1992 trust was in short supply in Boise. Executive phones were being tapped (no one ever figured why or by whom), and managers began to delay acting on orders from Bill Agee until the next morning because they expected that after he talked things over with her, Mary would change his mind. So many people were upset about the way things were being run at MK that the 1992 shareholders' meeting was held in Boston, rather than Boise, to limit disruptions. But this didn't stop insiders at company headquarters from writing anonymous letters to board members in which they revealed long-hidden financial problems.

Ironically enough, it was two new board members brought to MK by Agee himself—Zbigniew Brzezinski and William Clark—who finally forced matters to a head. Clark and Brzezinski were old White House hands and knew how to gather and analyze information. They persuaded the rest of the ten-member board, all but one of whom had been recruited by Agee, to let him go. When the decision was announced, Velma Morrison, second wife to one of the founders, told reporters, "Good riddance," and the company's stock price actually rose a bit on the news.

––––––––––

MK SHARES, AND my self-esteem, got another nice boost on April 4, 1995, the day when my appointment as chairman was announced and I flew into Boise to start work. Timing was important that day. I wanted to introduce myself personally to the headquarters staff at a 10:00 a.m. meeting. So when the pilot of the private plane taking me from Oregon to Idaho realized we were going to get to Boise much too early, we decided to stop for coffee at a little airport before going on to Boise.

At MK headquarters, the company's key executives greeted me with a slide show and video presentation on the company's history and current condition. The history, which noted the company's role in building many of the world's great roads, bridges, dams, and tunnels, was truly awe-inspiring. And much of what MK was doing in the present was similarly ambitious. But just like a typical MK project, their problems were also big and impressive. We were having trouble making our payroll and on the verge of defaulting on our bank loans.

During this morning briefing, and later at a general meeting for employees, I made it clear that I was a newcomer and they were the experts. "I don't know anything, so you tell me," I said. I got an earful, as many of the people who raised their hands to speak wanted nothing more than to vent their anger. They blamed Agee personally for wrecking the company by taking it into new areas of business that MK didn't understand. Thirty-year employees said they had been ruined when their retirement program was revamped and concentrated in company stock. Others feared that I, or the people Agee left behind, would somehow scheme to put the company back in his hands.

I did my best to reassure them, even though I knew that in most crises the situation is even worse than it appears at first. In the months to come I would meet regularly with small groups and even invite them to "bark at me" if they need to. As experienced engineers, architects, managers, and construction finance specialists, MK's people were the company's strength. They were the main asset I would try to salvage, and I was eager to keep them in place for the recovery.

On my first day in Boise I was excited to be back at the scene of another emergency, doing my best to save an important company. Here, for the first time, I would get to call the shots in the restructuring campaign and put to use all that I had learned since signing on at Chrysler. Happily, before the sun set we were able to announce something positive. Partly on the basis of the leadership shake-up, our lenders, led by Bank of America, were prepared to approve a sixty-day bridge loan that would keep us from falling into bankruptcy. With this extra time and money, I would get a chance to explore MK's problems more deeply and plot some solutions.

In the meantime I was enough of a ham that I enjoyed being greeted at the company and in the press as a white knight riding to the rescue. When the task you face will require you to deliver plenty of bad news and generate headlines that will upset folks from Wall Street to company headquarters, you might as well savor the positive hype when it comes. I won't deny it. It felt good to read a *Wall Street Journal* headline describing me as "Chrysler Hero" and to see in the *Times* that my appointment would draw "cheers in the market." But I didn't forget that these words were like the toasts made at a wedding. Come morning, when I awoke in the long-stay hotel that would serve as my home in Boise, I would have to make the marriage work.

———————

IN THE CLEAR light of dawn it was plain to see that while MK needed to return to its roots in heavy construction and engineering, this wouldn't happen until we fixed our finances. Major building projects, whether you are talking about highways, bridges, or industrial plants, are so costly and time-consuming that customers won't even consider your bid for a project if they have doubts about your financial strength. This is why most government agencies require you show three straight years of good financial performance to get on the bidders list, and both public and private projects must be backed by surety bonds issued by insurers who guarantee the customer won't be hurt if the builder goes belly-up prior to finishing the work. Of course, the surety companies won't sell you a bond if they have real worries about your ability to perform. You can see how in this system bad news tends to have a snowball effect. MK gets into trouble with new businesses and troubled projects. A huge loss for 1994 shocks the market. Surety companies get nervous, and that means that MK will have trouble qualifying to make bids and buying surety coverage.

To make matters worse, we were getting bad news every day from accountants working the books and engineers working in the field. We were losing huge sums in Taipei, where a big, expensive tunneling machine kept getting stuck in the muck as it bored a hole for a new subway line. (Reports on "progress" noted the machine moved a few feet on a good day.) Similar losses loomed at a bridge linking New Brunswick and Prince Edward Island in Canada. In this case Bill Agee had made MK a partner-owner in the project, delaying current revenue in exchange for a share of every toll paid by a driver until the year

2032. In theory, the partnership would provide a great revenue stream. In practice, MK was not in a position to help finance a massive public works project while waiting for long-term payout.

The losses caused by the bridge and tunnel projects, and by the ill-fated locomotive and rail car divisions, had been obscured by certain accounting choices made under the Agee regime. I use the word "choice" rather than something harsher because, in all fairness, the decisions could be seen as legitimate judgment calls. Take as an illustration a five-year, $100 million bridge contract with an estimated $10 million profit. In the beginning, you might not realize any actual profit, but you could claim one-fifth of the ultimate profit you expect, $2 million, during the first year. The trouble arises only if and when the final accounting is done and your estimate is found to be faulty. Until it's over, all you have is management's optimism that the project will turn out a winner. And Agee was an incurable optimist.

With accounting similar to what I note above, and one-time gains from investments and the sale of certain assets, Agee had managed to make sure that MK's annual reports had shown profits when, in fact, long term prospects were bleak. By the time I arrived, the company's bankers, twenty-eight institutions in all, couldn't be sure we would make payments on loans and credit lines worth roughly $122 million. With more than a little anxiety they had advanced us $50 million more on the promise that we would sell MK Rail, MK Gold Corporation, and other noncore businesses.

Experience with Chrysler's purchase of Gulfstream and other side businesses had taught me that this streamlining was essential. After all, it wasn't our job to give stockholders a diversified investment. They could do that for themselves. Our job was to create a strong construction company that would generate profits and grow over the long term. In other words, we needed to return MK to its traditional role, which it had played for generations, as a reliable builder of great public and private projects.

My confidence in MK's future as a great builder grew whenever I met with the people in Boise who actually did the work. Sometimes these encounters took place in formal meetings. In other cases I did my own independent fact-finding. From my very first day on the job, I made it a habit to go to the company cafeteria at lunchtime, grab a tray, work through the chow line, and then plunk myself down at a table with an empty seat.

Since I was the new guy and many people didn't know me, these chance encounters helped me gauge morale. Later, when everyone seemed to recognize me, the simple fact that I carried my own tray and listened more than I talked gave people permission to speak openly. I learned as much from these lunch hours as I did from most of the reports that landed on my desk. I'll never forget the time an employee showed me a picture he had discovered, showing me with Mary Cunningham at some long-ago event where we had both spoken to a national association of accountants. He wanted to know if I was connected to the Agees in some sort of conspiracy. I assured him I was not.

My habit of meeting with employees had been inspired by Charles Koch, who had become one of the richest men in the world while building his family company, Koch Industries. I visited him at his company headquarters in Wichita during my Chrysler days, when Koch had bought a package of about a hundred Chrysler dealership sites. I can't recall the details of our discussion, but I never forgot that this billionaire took me to lunch in the cafeteria, where everyone else in line seemed quite comfortable chatting with the boss. This was how Koch assured himself of reliable, timely information and avoided the isolation that brings down so many imperial executives. After seeing him in action, I decided to adopt his lunchtime habit if I ever got the chance.

At the start of my tenure at MK, the lunchroom morale was an unusual mix of anger and pride. People were furious at Agee but also fiercely loyal to the company. Morrison Knudsen had once swaggered across the globe, creating marvels so big they could be viewed from spacecraft in orbit. The people I met over sandwiches were desperate for the chance to return the company to glory and make their own mark on the planet.

The same attitudes prevailed at the jobs sites I visited to get a sense of MK's strengths. In Colorado I toured the new Denver International Airport, which we were helping to build, and the Rocky Flats nuclear weapons complex, where we were doing waste cleanup for the feds. (With a nod toward the fancy but troubled baggage system at the new airport, which no one seemed to know how to fix, I suggested that the crew at Rocky Flats load the nuclear waste into suitcases and make it disappear by checking it in at the airport.) In Texas I toured a huge coal-scooping machine that was operated from a control room as big as a tennis court. In Boston I saw the start of a huge public works project, a tunnel and highway masterpiece connecting downtown to the airport. In every location I met people with great expertise, abilities, and experience. All they wanted from me was a fix for the company's finances so that they could continue doing what they did so well.

————

TIME AND MONEY were my two biggest concerns, and we were running out of both. The $50 million bridge loan announced upon my arrival at MK was much too small, and set up a June 1 deadline for our next big payment, which was much too soon. Because I had learned the value of imagery during other negotiations, I looked for a symbol to present to our bankers to help them appreciate our shared predicament. The most appropriate image I could imagine was a melting ice cube bearing the MK logo. It looked solid, and it was. But the longer we waited to save it with secure financing, the smaller it would get until, in the end, it would melt away completely.

While our lenders contemplated the ice cube, I pursued other top agenda items, including the sale of assets to raise cash and halt losses and the pursuit of possible partnerships. Over the years I had seen how with the right matchmaking strategy, a merger or buyout could save the key parts of a troubled company and keep thousands of people employed in productive work. At Chrysler we had actually explored combining with Fiat or Mitsubishi. (While those talks came to nothing, eventually Detroit's number three would team with Daimler-Benz.) Since MK was an Idaho-based company, I guess it made poetic sense that our first suitor appeared to be J. R. Simplot, a titan of agribusinesses also known as "Spud King." Simplot had become a billionaire by selling Idaho potatoes to McDonald's and others. His firm was the state's other great success story, and as our trouble deepened it was inevitable that folks began to suggest him as a savior.

The man most responsible for pushing the Simplot solution was Jack Lemley, a former executive at Morrison Knudsen who had served for a time as head of the consortium building the channel tunnel, or "Chunnel," connecting Great Britain with the European continent. Lemley wanted Simplot to finance the creation of a new firm that would take over MK and run it under the same name. As our former manager of construction he likely had the ability to operate such a venture, and Simplot definitely had the money to pay for it. With these factors in mind I happily made a first-thing-in-the-morning appointment to hear more.

On the morning of May 15 I arrived at the Simplot headquarters just as eighty-six-year-old J.R., wearing his trademark cowboy hat, wheeled into the parking in a big old Lincoln Continental bearing a license plate that read "MR SPUD." I introduced myself as we walked inside, and we chatted as we rode up to his office together in the elevator. By the time we got to the top floor, I was almost certain that Mr. Potato was only mildly interested in saving MK. "Well, that's *his* idea," he said, referring to Lemley. "I'm not so sure about it."

As it turned out, Lemley had become connected to Simplot when he married into the family. A divorce had subsequently severed the relationship, but the two remained on good terms. Simplot had a history of making wise investments outside agricultural businesses. He had provided start-up cash for the wildly successful computer company called Micron Systems. No wonder Lemley thought he would be open to buying a construction company. But in this case I could tell that J.R. was only humoring his would-be partner. We had a nice enough chat, but not so nice that I expected we would ever see each other again.

As I left Simplot I wasn't so much disappointed as amused. He was one of the truly great characters in American business, a high school–educated farm boy who turned himself into a billionaire. I was grateful for the chance to meet him. And besides, I knew there were other potential saviors out there and that some of them were probably working on proposals to merge with MK or acquire the company outright.

Why was I so confident? The reasons were summarized quite nicely by *BusinessWeek* at the time Mr. Spud and I got together. The magazine noted that except for transit, all of our core businesses were "cash flow positive" and that our problems were man-made "and we know who that man was." The implication was obvious. With proper leadership, a pared-down Morrison Knudsen was as attractive as the head cheerleader at prom time. The paring was an ongoing activity. In mid-May we would sell our gold company, which was producing about 10,000 ounces per year, to Leucadia National, raising more than $20 million. Cutbacks at our railroad car plants produced further savings while we continued to look for someone to take them over completely.

These moves and others were followed closely by the local press, which was not surprising given MK's importance in Boise, and also by the national media. The media interest was driven in part by MK's storied history and also by Bill and Mary Agee's notoriety. To my amazement, Bill participated in lengthy interviews for an article that appeared on the cover of *Fortune* magazine just two months after he left MK. Titled "Agee in Exile," the piece reviewed the Agees' chilly relationships with folks in Boise and described Bill's evolution into a "tyrant" at the office. It explained that after a break-in at their home and a box arrived bearing one black rose, Bill hired some bodyguards and Mary took their kids out of school. At its conclusion, the piece allows that Agee wasn't solely to blame for MK's troubles and quotes him saying, "At no time was this a fun job."

Decorated with truly beautiful photos of the couple, the *Fortune* opus was just the most sweeping of the many Agee pieces done by various print and broadcast outlets during my first few months at Morrison Knudsen. The coverage was so extensive that someone who caught only the headlines might have thought that Bill was still running the place, which was not a good thing since we were trying to emphasize new leadership and a new direction for the firm.

————

THE DEADLINE SET when we got our $50 million bridge loan was June 1. As it approached, the banks demanded we hand over more than $30 million we had accumulated from tax refunds and asset sales. Although this demand would have put us into bankruptcy in about thirty days, they presented it as the only option.

A less experienced crisis manager might have been hurt, outraged, and flustered. But after Chrysler and Olympia & York I knew that I was dealing with the sharks that banks put in charge of working out troubled loans, and you can't get angry when a shark tries to devour you. It's what sharks do. But I also knew that I had options. Another $29 million worth of one-time earnings were due in the month of June. Potential buyers were asking for information on our big transit operations, and we were also getting feelers from investors who would be in a position to support a new MK devoted to construction. The bankers should know we were making progress.

Still certain that MK was worth much more as a live, functioning entity than it would be if it was forced into premature bankruptcy, I went to California to wrestle with the wolves. In these meetings I described our progress and won a brief stay of execution, which was followed a month later by a much broader pact that increased our credit by another $30 million and would let us operate well into 1996. The deal required us to shed MK Rail by turning it into an independent company backed by our bonding agents. New shares in MK Rail would be issued to people holding MK stock, and we would no longer be affected by the losses connected with rail car contracts.

To obtain all these benefits, we had to agree to revamp our board of directors and clear up several pending legal problems that threatened our future. One of these was Bill Agee's pension. During his reign, Agee had shifted MK's employment retirement plan to one that depended on company stock. The collapse in the stock's price, which many laid on his leadership, left everyone in the plan hurting. For this reason and many others, the rank and file were against paying the many generous retirement benefits guaranteed in his contract. There was a part of me that agreed with our workers and the view that we shouldn't pay him a dime. But in the end, we needed his signature on some critical documents. To get it, we had to agree to pay him. When this was done I called our employees into the headquarters auditorium and told it to them straight. I knew they'd be angry, but I wanted to deliver the message face-to-face. They understood we had no other choice.

As we worked our way toward a new MK, we experienced almost daily victories and defeats. In the summer of 1995 we had to give up our share of an exciting project to link Denmark and Sweden with a $700 million bridge and tunnel project. But we more than made up for this setback when a Colorado highway authority awarded us a contract to build a toll road portion of a new Denver beltway. We were able to get this work by forming an alliance with another big construction firm, Fluor Daniel of California, which had the financial strength to get a surety bond. This arrangement meant we had to share project profits, but it was far more important for us to put some new work on the books and add to our cash flow.

Through the summer, as we stopped the losses, retooled our finances, and tried to save the essence of Morrison Knudsen by pursuing new work and finding ways to make money on the projects we had under way. I did what I could to rally everyone from the support staff to the board of directors. Some of my moves were inspired by others. For example, I took a page from the Iacocca playbook and had the company buy big advertisements in key newspapers, announcing that "We're rebuilding a great company and thanking all the stakeholders." But I also followed my own instincts, adopting a "fullest possible information" policy in my work with the board of directors.

Over time the MK board had been filled with Bill Agee's friends. I'm not saying the Agee board was underpowered. It was a smart bunch that included Peter Lynch of Boston's Fidelity Investments. But perhaps because they didn't know the peculiarities of construction management and finance, they were blindsided by the huge losses Bill Agee posted for 1994. To reassure them, and signal a new era, I would make sure they were informed of every major development and give them every opportunity to participate in developing strategies.

One key tool we had at our disposal was bankruptcy, and it was a subject we discussed several times. Over the years, attitudes about bankruptcy had changed. The key, it turned out, was a company's customers. If, like an airline, you sold a service to the public and they still bought tickets after you went bankrupt, then you could do it and survive. Suppliers, investors, and even lenders had to accept that while the process might cost them money, the entities that emerged were often strong and reliable. Bankruptcy wasn't the best option, but it was sometimes regarded as a cleansing procedure, a way to salvage something good from a bad situation.

For Morrison Knudsen, which served customers in government and industry, bankruptcy was more problematic. Our customers depended on our ability to complete massively expensive projects. They wouldn't sign with us if they didn't have confidence in our future. For this reason the board and I decided to avoid bankruptcy if at all possible. Our employees, who were sensitive to the stigma of bankruptcy, clearly agreed with this stand. After I worked things out with the banks to keep us rolling into 1996, I met with a couple hundred workers at headquarters and they greeted the news with cheers and applause. Velma Morrison told the local paper, "I just couldn't be happier."

———————

THERE'S A BIG difference between not going bankrupt and being financially strong. Although the press declared "Morrison Knudsen Back from Brink" (Spokane *Spokesman-Review*), we were not yet built for the long run. Bonding was still going to be a problem. The lead contractor on the Denmark-Sweden connector had forced us out of the project even after we set up our new bank deal because they lost confidence in MK. And we would never get back to full strength if we continued to make deals like the one reached with Fluor Daniels on the Denver Beltway. In that case we kept up cash flow but gave away too much profit.

Investors understood our problems. Brokerage house analysts who followed our stock reported that other companies had begun angling for our work and poaching talented employees. A Smith Barney specialist told his firm's clients, "If there are any good brains left at Morrison Knudsen the competition is tapping it." The statement was a bit of an exaggeration. We still had plenty of great people. But some of those who got a chance to move to more secure positions, and were willing to move, did.

The analysts were correct about some of our problems, but they generally overlooked the most serious threat on the horizon. Because they moved very slowly, government bureaucracies had yet to respond to our crisis. Their rules typically required a contractor show three straight years of profitable operation to get on a bid list. MK had been coasting on past performance to meet those requirements. New work would be much harder to get once our 1994 losses were considered. Indeed, as we competed in the latter part of 1995 we ran into increasing resistance. By the start of 1996 we were unable to book new work without partners who could obtain bonding.

It was the fear that we might go bankrupt that eventually pushed us toward that option. By February 1996 we could see that our cash flow wasn't going to meet our near-term obligations, and we had gone back into crisis mode. (So much for my initial plan of working three or four months and handing the company off to Bob Tinstman.) Although we had until September to make the next big loan payment, it was already clear to everyone that we were not likely to have the cash.

Fortunately, events outside my control had given me a whole new cast of creditors to engage in negotiations. Our former banks had sold their loans at bargain basement prices to new lenders. These vultures, as they are called, saw opportunity in our cause. Instead of squeezing the last drop of blood from a presumed dead carcass, the new debt holders had an entrepreneurial approach. I went to them and said, "Cancel our debt and I'll give you stock in a new company that might be worth much more in the long run." This swap—debt for equity—would become the basis of a so-called prepackaged bankruptcy. The way these things work, the parties agree to the terms of reorganization, go to court to declare the old firm bankrupt, and immediately form a new one. In this case our creditors would get stock in the new entity. The arrangement was likely to wipe out investors who held old MK stock, but it would move us toward our main goal, preservation of the core company. With one more element, the "prepack" would create a truly new MK. What was that element? We needed an investor with deep pockets to make a long-term commitment to a company that had been all spiffed up and was worthy of a merger. I had just the fellow in mind.

Months before, I had met with a self-made billionaire named Dennis Washington, who had gotten his start in business as a subcontractor for Morrison Knudsen in his home state of Montana. Almost three decades later his Washington Construction Company was the biggest highway builder in California and was starting work as prime contractor for a new airport runway in Las Vegas. Dennis could recognize an undervalued treasure when he saw one. When others thought the old Anaconda Copper mine was played out, he bought it for $18 million and turned it into a going concern that made $85 million in profit in 1995 alone. Anaconda and other smart acquisitions had made him one of the Forbes 400's wealthiest Americans.

When we first met, Dennis wasn't too enthusiastic about joining our two companies. We weren't very far along in our recovery program, and he couldn't be sure about the size of our losses for the current year. By the time we got together again in the spring of 1996, he was happy to see we were a much more attractive bride. We had completed our refinancing and settled lawsuits threatened by shareholders. As he said, "There had been a tremendous, well-planned attack on the problems."

As an entrepreneur, Dennis had the authority to negotiate quickly and directly, without worrying about pleasing shareholders. He also enjoyed the life that wealth provided. He owned a Gulfstream IV jet, which at the time was the premier private aircraft for executives, as well as an oceangoing tugboat that had been converted into a luxury yacht. At one of his homes, which occupied a private island in British Columbia, he built his very own golf course. His other house, in Palm Desert, was a $15 million masterpiece. Some of our talks on a merger were conducted there.

Dennis appreciated the history of MK and its capabilities. In fact, our merger would be one of those odd situations when a financially robust but smaller company takes over a much bigger but troubled one. Just one-fifth the size of Morrison Knudsen, Washington Construction was primarily a West Coast firm, lacking both MK's reach and broad engineering expertise. But Washington's spotless financial history and capable managers had great value. Without them, MK's future would be in doubt. That's why Dennis would receive roughly 35 percent of the combined entity and become its controlling owner.

Why would Dennis put his hard-earned fortune on the line to save MK? In large measure it was because of the deep romance he had with the company's history and the heavy construction industry. He loved the growl of bulldozers and the spectacle of rock-busting dynamite blasts. As a young man Dennis had actually met Harry Morrison and adopted him as a role model. Later he often lost out to MK in the competition for work. In taking over his old rival, Washington bought himself a chance to honor and preserve his hero's legacy and perhaps exceed him in the industry.

When it came time for us to present the deal to those creditors who had converted their loans to stock, they pressed me about the way shares were to be divvied up. Why should the little guy with a company one-fifth MK's size get more than a one-third share? In response, I asked, "Would you rather own 100 percent of a failed company or 65 percent of a successful one?" The answer was easy.

As so often happens, news that a deal was afoot drove some people to buy old MK stock on a speculative basis. Those who did foolishly ignored our repeated warnings that its value would likely plummet when the company was reorganized. This is exactly what happened at the end of June, when we went into court and declared bankruptcy. According to the conditions of the prepack, a new MK was formed immediately, our creditors received stock in the new firm, and we were able to wipe nearly $400 million in debt off the books. Shares of the old stock were traded for warrants, giving owners the right to buy into the new company on a favored basis. But otherwise, their shares were worthless.

In wasn't the ideal outcome. I felt the stockholders' pain because I was one of them and my losses would be real. But it was the best result available because it kept MK's most productive elements—its people, expertise, and organization—functioning and contributing in very tangible ways to our national economy. Thousands of families, whether in Idaho or distant construction sites worldwide, would continue to be supported by MK jobs, and the vital projects we were building, from roads to factories, would be completed. In the ten years since the deal was closed and I returned to Oregon, the company's annual gross revenues have grown several times over, with similar growth in employment and value. The giant builder that was nearly ruined by an imperial CEO is once again the pride of Boise, being run by Steve Hanks, a longtime friend who endured the dark days of 1995–1996 with me. I left town for Oregon and supposedly returned to retirement, feeling much happier than I did at the end of my stint as a New York banker. With the merger of MK and Washington Construction, a vital American company that supported thousands of families had been saved. And my batting average was up again.

Seven

A LONG, SLOW RECOVERY

Fate didn't give me a chance to claim that I was retired when I left Boise. Before Dennis Washington even took control at Morrison Knudsen I knew I was headed back to Detroit for a new adventure in the auto business. As a member of the board of directors for the Federal-Mogul Corporation, which made parts for cars and trucks, I had watched chief executive officer Dennis Gormley struggle to raise profits with a complex scheme for diversifying. In mid-September 1996 the board decided that Dennis had run out of time and chose me to replace him temporarily and lead the search for a new boss. What I didn't know at the time was that the Federal-Mogul challenge would turn into a long-running saga that would bring me into the role of interim CEO three different times.

The big issue in auto parts, one that Gormley couldn't overcome, revolves around the fact that those who supply manufacturers have a very limited number of customers. These customers—in the Detroit area it was the Big Three—are very demanding. They want you to design and make parts on an exclusive basis, guarantee reliable deliveries so that assembly lines keep moving, and slash prices until your profits are razor thin.

In contrast, companies that make replacement parts for what's called the "aftermarket" can charge much more for the items they ship to car care stores, neighborhood garages, and dealers. But this business requires sophisticated manufacturing, warehousing, and shipping operations so that you can produce and hold a huge variety of products that are purchased one at a time, instead of by the thousands. It is almost like providing products on a made-to-order basis and requires a very different set of skills.

Federal-Mogul had long been focused on serving manufacturers with big shipments of original equipment, especially seals, bearings, and chassis parts. Eager to find new revenues, Gormley bought a replacement parts business from the giant TRW Corporation, and some retail stores in South Africa and Puerto Rico. He wanted us to become an integrated aftermarket company, producing and warehousing products for our own chain of retail stores, which would compete with the likes of AutoZone and the Pep Boys. The problem was, our management team didn't know this side of the business, and several quarters passed without us seeing any benefit from a growing focus on retail.

Bogged down with these acquisitions and eager for improved cash flow, Gormley took a risk. He went to Harold Kuttner, purchasing head for General Motors, and demanded a 15 percent price increase on certain parts by month's end or Gormley would stop shipments. At the time, Kuttner controlled countless billions' worth of purchasing at GM. And while Gormley had some leverage—he would stop GM assembly lines if he halted shipments—Kuttner held the real power. GM (as well as Ford and Chrysler) gave in to Gormley's demand, but then Kuttner called me in Sunriver, as an independent member of the board, to deliver a stinging complaint.

"I want you to know two things," he told me over the phone. "First, we are going to accept the price increase because we need the parts. Second, Federal-Mogul will never, ever get a new business award from GM."

Why such a bitter response? Well, obviously, Gormley had blackmailed GM, and nobody likes that. But it's important, also, to understand that if Federal-Mogul got away unscathed by this tactic, thousands of other suppliers might try this also. GM needed to nip it in the bud.

Inside Federal-Mogul, Gormley might have gotten away with his price-rise gambit if it hadn't come during a period of ragged performance that had already attracted the board's attention. A few months earlier he had abruptly fired our chief financial officer, a reliable former Chrysler financial executive named Marty Welch, who until the moment he was axed, had received nothing but praise from

Dennis. Next we saw a number of key managers quit to go to other companies. Add the soggy earnings reports, and the signs of trouble were too numerous to ignore. And the frosting on the cake was that Gormley had negotiated a deal to sell all of Federal-Mogul's manufacturing assets, our century-old center of expertise, to Dana Corporation, in order to focus on retail, where we had virtually no experience.

The board decided to replace Gormley after a very long meeting that allowed us to air every issue. Another director, Roderick Hills, went with me to see him the next day. It was a difficult mission. Gormley was basically a good guy, and he had spent his entire working life at Federal-Mogul. Dismissing a CEO is never easy, but Rod was so gracious that I think he overdid it. He actually tried to arrange a golf date in the moments after we told Gormley he was through.

There's nothing for a CEO to do once he or she loses the confidence of a board of directors except go, and Dennis Gormley left immediately. Fortunately, his executive assistant, Judy Johnston, was willing to stay and help us keep the company going. It's no secret that executive assistants generally know more about a company's history, culture, and operation than anyone. In Detroit they have a subculture of their own, communicating constantly and keeping relationships within and among companies fluid and functional.

As temporary CEO, I relied on Judy and she never let me down. She was especially helpful during my first days as CEO when I called all of our top customers to introduce myself and reassure them that the transition would be smooth. This duty seemed like a no-brainer. Introduce myself, say some reassuring things, then offer a polite goodbye. But on the very first call I told a purchasing guy, "Don't worry, you're still going to get the same service you have always gotten"—and received a very surprising response.

"Please don't do that," he said, adding that "the same service" would mean late shipments, defective parts, and price increases. I immediately changed my tune. Instead of promising more of the same, I asked for advice on ways to do the job better. Even with this, it would take great effort for us to regain trust in an industry where everyone knows everybody, and everybody talks. I did see signs of improvement, however, when I fired the head of our aftermarket division a week later. The man had alienated so many customers, I really had no choice.

FORTUNATELY, FEDERAL-MOGUL WASN'T in such bad shape
that it required a dramatic rescue effort. It just needed a new leader,
and within months we found one in Richard Snell, at Tenneco Automotive. A capable fellow who won board approval with ease, Snell
thought our entry into the retail business was a mistake. I seconded
his opinion after I saw some of our thirty-two recently acquired retail
stores in Puerto Rico.

The Puerto Rico trip had begun with a visit to a brand-new retail
store that was clean, efficient, and beautifully laid out. It was a show-
place, and if I had stopped there and gone home, I would have reported that this business was very promising and recommended that
we stay in the retail field. But I didn't stop there. I asked to see another shop, one that had been open for business for more than a few
months. I was taken to a rough neighborhood and a store that looked
like Fred Sanford's junk shop. Inside, greasy parts were stacked hap-
hazardly, and nobody seemed in charge. Outside, tires, rims, and hub-
caps were literally hung from the branches of trees. If this was the way
we were doing most of our business abroad, then Snell was right. We
needed to get out.

In his first two years on the job, Snell returned Federal-Mogul to its
traditional business model. He sold the retail stores and distribution
centers we operated overseas and bought a huge British parts supplier
called Turner & Newhall (T&N) for about $2 billion. He cut adminis-
trative costs, eliminated a small number of jobs, and sold some under-
performing facilities. By the end of 1997 the business press noted that
we had gone from a struggling "underachiever" to a "$5.5 billion giant
with a bright future."

What the press didn't take into account, however, were the long-
term trends in the car business. Always intensely cyclical, the industry
was still suffering from the ills that afflicted Chrysler in the 1980s,
only most of them had gotten worse. Global competition was growing.
The cost of wages and benefits, including health care and pensions,
was much too high. At the same time, arcane work rules, established
when the Big Three were rich, made it almost impossible to use labor
efficiently. (One big problem was the so-called jobs bank, which re-

quired manufacturers to pay employees while they just sat around, waiting for actual work to do.) These problems made life tough for the manufacturers but also affected parts companies, which often operated under similar labor agreements. Nearly all of Federal-Mogul's competitors were suffering financial reverses.

To make things worse for Federal-Mogul, there were some time bombs hidden in our acquisition of T&N. One involved potential liability for health problems related to asbestos products made decades earlier by a T&N company. The other had to do with pensions. For years T&N had seen employment decline due to efficiencies and tough global competition. At the same time, old labor contracts guaranteed lifelong pensions for retirees who, thanks to advances in medicine and health, were living longer and longer. The pension plan became an ever-growing, underfunded obligation.

By the mid-1990s T&N had eight thousand active employees and forty thousand pensioners in Britain. Early analyses of this problem suggested the program was in deep trouble. When we found out that our asbestos liability was far greater than the amount our insurance would pay, the pension issue became more critical. Without a dramatic development of some sort, there would never be enough cash, and the retirees would have to hope for help from the British government. The problem was so big that Dick Snell would have trouble protecting Federal-Mogul.

Snell was a terrific leader when things were going well. He gave great pep talks and put up posters that urged everyone to go after the "BHAG" (the Big Hairy Audacious Goal). But when the job required grit, like surviving a liability crisis, Snell was not such a fun guy. He would call in senior people and ask, "How's it going this quarter?" If someone said, "I'm sorry, we're $10 million behind budget," he would say, "If you can't make your numbers, I'll find someone who will." As a result, people tended to cover up problems, pushing them from one quarter to the next, on the theory that it's better to get beat up only once. Of course then when Snell got frustrated, he fired people.

CEOs come in all flavors, and a board of directors will grant a company leader plenty of leeway if the results are good. But throughout the year 2000, we kept seeing signs of poor performance to go with the bad morale. In the summer Snell had to revise a third-quarter earnings estimate, wiping out almost all of the expected profits. Unfortunately it wasn't a big surprise. We had failed to meet earnings forecasts in the five previous quarters and our stock had fallen from $59 per share at the start of 1999 to $6.38. At our September board meeting we worked late into the night and decided that after almost four years, we needed another change at the top.

At the board's request I went back to run the company on a temporary basis. Judy Johnston was still the chief executive's assistant. This time when I went to tell her what had happened, she simply said, "Don't worry. I know the drill." Later I addressed an auditorium full of managers (hundreds more tuned in via teleconference) and explained what was happening. We were not meeting Wall Street's expectations, I said, and our stock price was taking a beating. Snell's growth strategy had made the company much bigger but not healthier. We were going to sell some excess assets and refocus on our strengths. But I didn't know if Federal-Mogul could be saved from bankruptcy.

My uncertainty was caused by the asbestos issue and the liability claims related to it. As most people know by now, lawsuits over lung disease suffered by workers and others involved with asbestos have bankrupted many of the companies that made and utilized this material in the past. By the year 2000, after decades of court proceedings, the matter of just who knew what and when about the danger of asbestos was beside the point. Many companies were paying big money to settle and contain their losses. They figured it was better to manage the risk this way than chance the uncertainty of the courtroom.

Federal-Mogul's lawyers advised us against settling. They noted that many of the thousands of people filing claims weren't even sick and were unlikely to ever get sick. With the help of well-organized legal teams they were suing simply because they had been exposed. We should fight these claims, said our attorneys, because it was the right thing to do and we could win. I tended to agree. "Let's not be a bunch of weenies," I thought. "Let's take 'em on. How bad could it be?"

It was easy for me to say. I didn't have to implement the legal strategy because, once again, we quickly hired two veterans of the parts business to grab the helm at the Federal-Mogul. Frank Macher had run the parts division of Ford Motor. And Chip McClure had worked at Detroit Diesel and Johnson Controls, both big suppliers to the auto companies They took over just before the start of our first big asbestos trial, which took place in Beaumont, Texas.

Years later I would still believe that we had a valid legal argument and that if the outcome depended on the facts and the law, we would win. (For example, the plaintiffs had failed to name us as a defendant on their complaint.) But juries rarely decide liability lawsuits on the basis of mere facts and laws. When a plaintiff enters the courtroom in a wheelchair or hauling a tank of oxygen, he instantly gains the advantage. In our first trial, where we were one of two defendants, twenty-two workers were awarded a total of $35 million.

By the middle of 2001 we faced more than 350,000 plaintiffs and potentially billions in liabilities. (This in addition to billions in obligations from our acquisitions during the 1990s.) In October, after the terrorist attack of September 11, business collapsed, and we had to seek the protection of bankruptcy in both the United States and Great Britain in order to preserve whatever valuable assets remained. As we did this, we joined roughly seventy other corporations forced into bankruptcy by asbestos lawsuits.

Although I could see how some plaintiffs had a right to make claims, the great majority of the people who signed on to these lawsuits were not sick and were unlikely to ever become sick. For this reason it is hard to escape the fact that these suits, driven by very activist lawyers, multiplied the harm done to good companies. The situation is one of the classics cited by those of us who believe we need stricter limits on just who can sue whom and for what. Too many monstrous lawsuits are filed by lawyers seeking big fees by threatening to put companies out of business.

WHETHER I WAS functioning as a director, temporary CEO, or chairman of the board, I found the cause of Federal-Mogul compelling because it was yet another old company that contributed tangible value to our society and supported thousands of families. It was, in its way, a Moore Mill type of operation and deserved to live. Between 2001 and 2005 I would invest a substantial amount of time and effort to this task, even as I took different full-time jobs in other companies.

Although each of my assignments was unique, my approach depended on basic principles that had become essential tools in my kit. Just before New Year's 2001, the *Wall Street Journal* asked me to provide some "Tips from a Turnaround Specialist" for a column they called Boss Talk. The interview gave me a chance to reflect in a formal way on what I had learned at the scene of so many wrecks. In response to reporter Joann S. Lublin I was able to boil it down to some essentials:

1. Tell everyone the truth, especially if the truth hurts.

2. Don't study things to death. Most of the choices you need to make are clear, and decisiveness breeds confidence.

3. Listen to your customers. They know more about what's wrong with your company, and what's right, than anyone.

4. Listen to your people. Consult everyone, from the boiler room at the plant to the executive suite so you become fully informed. Invite everyone to send e-mails, and answer them!

5. Do a wardrobe check. If people proudly wear caps and shirts with the company logo, morale is good. If no one wants to be identified as your employee when they go to the mall, you're in trouble.

6. Practice calm realism. The key here is to stay balanced. Truth-telling can be scary, but if you let people know that there are solutions for most problems, they'll be less discouraged.

7. You don't need all new players to make a team into a winner. Even at companies in crisis you'll find lots of people who know their jobs and do them well. Try to hold on to them.

In the weeks after Federal-Mogul declared bankruptcy, we relied on our good people to improve our performance and gear up for a new $400 million engine-parts contract that called for the first deliveries in 2002. Suppliers continued to send us raw materials, and customers continued to rely on us for deliveries because bankruptcy didn't change a thing when it came to routine business. It did, however, protect us from asbestos lawsuits, which were threatening to drain as much as $500 million a year from the company.

As often happens, bankruptcy allowed us to get so-called debtor-in-possession, or DIP, loans to help us continue operations (in this case it was $675 million). At the same time, the crisis drew the attention of investors who believed they could profit by purchasing our bonds, at a sharp discount, from sellers who had lost faith in the company. One of the most interested of these hopeful scavengers was the famous billionaire Carl Icahn.

Icahn had reason to hope that Federal-Mogul might recover. Federal law allowed a company to be relieved of its asbestos liability if when it restructured it contributed half the stock to a trust for victims of asbestos. Icahn, who bought up a substantial interest in the company, favored this kind of solution if he could wind up being in control. From my perspective, Carl appeared to be a smart guy who could take over and create value. But I also knew he was a very aggressive, very litigious person who could make life miserable for anyone who crossed him.

As time passed, Federal-Mogul CEO Frank Macher worked with our bankers to find new investors who wanted to buy a lot of shares in a new Federal-Mogul. Their presence would have diluted Icahn's power and deprived him of control. When the plan was announced he complained loudly, and the bankruptcy judge stopped it dead. Those of us who were on the board of directors felt unfairly criticized—we had simply wanted a solution that would put Federal-Mogul on sound financial footing. But if the bondholders and asbestos lawyers didn't want the dilution, so be it.

Icahn was uniquely creative in his demands. He was impatient with the board's decisions and would bully us to do things his way. He wanted us to fire our insurance broker and hire his, although there was no particular reason to do so. If he called on the phone and couldn't immediately get what he wanted, he'd get angry. In face-to-face meetings he gave everyone whiplash. One moment he'd bellow, "That's the stupidest goddamn thing I ever heard," and the next he'd put his arm around you. He's effective, I think, because people become so traumatized that they wind up suffering from Stockholm syndrome and will do anything to please him. Gradually he would acquire a commanding interest in the company and become a dominant force in its long, slow march toward emergence from Chapter 11 protection.

Under the court's supervision we continued to operate the company, delivering critical parts to keep manufacturers humming, and we tried to resolve our many scattered and complicated issues. In Britain, for example, we confronted our huge pension liability, which I addressed with both the trustee overseeing our bankruptcy and members of Parliament. It was a treat to visit the House of Commons, walking up the worn steps that led to a committee room and sitting in a cracked green leather chair flanked by dusty heavy drapes.

At the time, Britain had nothing comparable to America's Pension Benefit Guaranty Corporation, which insures that retirees get paid when plans fail. Under their system as it existed, every available penny would be used to pay workers who were already retired, and there might be nothing left for active employees. The Federal-Mogul case grabbed huge headlines in the UK. Most people there saw Carl Icahn and the American asbestos trial lawyers as the evil source of their pension woes.

T&N was a century-old firm, and Tony Blair's government was sensitive to the predicament faced by both its workers and retirees. We kept funding pensions until they created a new Pension Protection Fund that could help with the problem and deal with a host of other retirement "schemes," as they are called over there, that were in similar straits. For years afterward, T&N pensioners received their expected payments as the company operated in bankruptcy.

My involvement with Federal-Mogul would include yet a third short stint as interim CEO from the summer of 2004 until early 2005. In this time one of my main tasks was the hiring of industry veteran Jose Maria Alapont to take over. Alapont is, to put it mildly, a self-confident man. In fact, some critics say he's arrogant and volatile. But I thought Federal-Mogul needed someone very smart and tough as nails to deal face-to-face with Icahn. The two alpha males would get along well enough to gradually pull the company out of bankruptcy. As a turnaround event, Federal-Mogul was an extended relay race, not a sprint. I was glad to carry the baton a few times, but my efforts didn't produce the kind of decisive moments that I find most rewarding. In my long experience I had come to accept that my peak performance comes at the start of a job and that as things drag on I am less and less effective. Maybe I'm a kind of corporate action junkie, or perhaps I have the CEO strain of attention deficit disorder. In the end I don't need to define myself with such precision. As I tell young business-people who come to me for advice, it's enough to know what makes you excited about getting up in the morning. For me it's a fresh chal-lenge that requires lots of quick action.

Fortunately, executives like Alapont and the controversial Icahn have more patience and could grind away in the bankruptcy system to salvage value from a Federal-Mogul in a way that helped great num-bers of people. Yes, by the time it was over the old stockholders lost pretty much all their value. But they had knowingly accepted the risk inherent in stocks. Others with a stake in the company—workers, re-tirees, and asbestos litigants—benefited greatly from the efforts made to keep it functioning. In 2007 more than forty-five thousand people drew Federal-Mogul paychecks, and even greater numbers of pension-ers in Great Britain and the United States could depend on their ben-efits. Even asbestos victims stood to gain, as Icahn paid $750 million to a trust established for their benefit. In return, he received Federal-Mogul shares held by the trust.

The outcome showed how the bankruptcy system can produce a relatively fair result. But it is far from perfect. The process requires that all the key parties hire lawyers and advisers, who are paid almost entirely out of the troubled company's assets. Everyone who works in the turnaround field knows that these experts come from a relative small pool, and you see the same folks whenever there's a big case. These professionals know one another so well that they are all fairly chummy, even though they are supposed to be adversaries in the pro-ceedings. Why wouldn't they be friends? They get to sit on commit-tees and in negotiations, with every minute of their time and every cent of their expenses—travel, hotels, stenographers, etc.—covered by the struggling corporation. In big cases their combined billing tops $100 million per year, and they will be paid before anyone else.

Is there an alternative to the costly process that makes bankruptcy a party for lawyers, accountants, bankers, and advisers? Certainly, it's better to avoid the process if you can or do a "prepackaged" bank-ruptcy that is negotiated fully before a judge is approached. Otherwise you run the risk of paying for every delay, inquiry, and objection, no matter who raises an issue or stands to benefit.

Federal-Mogul paid its dues to the bankruptcy industry and cleared a path for progress. With the asbestos and pension issues resolved, the company could pursue the global parts market, supplying manufactur-ers on every continent. But the industry it served in America still faced fundamental problems. It was a sign of the times that as Federal-Mogul was emerging from bankruptcy, Ford posted its biggest quar-terly loss ever—$5.8 billion—and Toyota seemed poised to overtake ailing General Motors as the biggest vehicle-maker in the world.

What stood between the U.S. auto business and real long-term via-bility were the same issues that gave foreign competitors advantages during the 1980s—health care costs, labor costs, pensions, and inef-ficiencies. These problems were costing American manufacturers thousands of dollars on each car they produced. But the situation wasn't hopeless. In fact, as conditions in Detroit grew more desperate, the players who had resisted real change for decades seemed ready to reconsider. I would be lucky (or crazy) enough to find a role in the middle of it all, but more about that later.

Eight

EXECUTIVES BEHAVING BADLY

There's something that makes big machines—sawmills, ships, earth-movers, trucks—irresistible to many of us. Whether they growl, grumble, whine, or roar, the engines of industry fill us with excitement and maybe even a sense of importance. Big machines shape the land, bend steel, and deliver goods. They also take away the waste and recy-clables produced by a dynamic economic. Yes, I'm talking about gar-bage trucks. And before you dismiss these lowly servants of society, consider for a moment what city life is like during sanitation strikes. In a matter of days sidewalks become impassable, and commerce begins to slow. Civilization requires that someone clean up, and for that reason the garbage business is a vitally important and potentially profitable enterprise all over the world.

The truth about garbage and our need to handle it properly is obvi-ous, and yet even savvy businesspeople were long willing to leave this enterprise to an almost ad hoc system of local governments and thou-sands of small operators. In some older cities we even tolerated the presence of organized crime, in part because so many people thought the job was too dirty to merit their concern.

Then, beginning in the 1960s, a few aggressive operators like Wayne Huizenga and Dean Buntrock began buying hundreds of local carters and stitching them together to create large efficient compa-nies. With the help of stricter environmental regulations the garbage business became "waste management," and the process became far more sophisticated and professional. By the 1990s a handful of multi-billion-dollar companies dominated the business, including Waste Management Incorporated, which was built by Huizenga and Buntrock. In 1990 they renamed the company WMX Technologies. I was asked to join the board of directors in May 1997.

With my experience I was recruited for more board seats than I could handle, and I turned down most offers. But this industry intrigued me because it seemed so vital to community life, the environment, and the economy. It was also a great long-term business. After all, people create a ceaseless stream of garbage that must be handled on a reliable basis. Serving this need produces revenues that are just as reliable, much as a utility does.

However, any time you develop a big new business through acquisitions, the building-up years are the easiest. Each new purchase adds to your revenues and, hopefully, earnings. When this happens year after year, Wall Street analysts and players expect it to continue. But sooner or later you run out of small fish to gobble. When they reached this point, executives at WMX tried to keep things going through diversification, acquiring lawn care and pest control companies. With Buntrock as chief executive officer they also expanded overseas and got into the water and sewer businesses.

By the late 1980s there was little left for Buntrock to buy. Growth stalled and managers put great effort into making quarterly and annual reports look better than the underlying reality. For eight years running, profits reported one year were later wiped out when results were restated to account for "one-time" charges. The stock price sagged despite a great bull market that seemed to lift every other company higher.

Some of the major investors who looked to the company's top management and board of directors for answers became convinced that they were unwilling or unable to make necessary changes. Most frustrated of all, perhaps, was billionaire George Soros. Soros, who had become famous while speculating on the British pound, had invested heavily in WMX when he thought it was a bargain, only to see its battered stock decline further. He blamed the company's troubles on chief executive Philip Rooney, a lifelong employee who had replaced Buntrock in 1996 but changed little in terms of management. Soros forced him out in early 1997. And to signal the company's return to its core business, the name was changed back to Waste Management Incorporated.

Of course when the boss is deposed, it's up to the board of directors to reassure the markets by quickly finding a new leader with impressive credentials. Though I was a newcomer, I was assigned to the search committee along with former CEO Buntrock. Dean, who had a deep emotional investment in the process, was especially particular about the choice and hard to please. We found only one candidate acceptable to both him and to the rest of the committee. His name was Ronald LeMay, and he came, not from the ancient business of garbage disposal but from the glamorous and modern field of telecommunications.

LeMay was president of Sprint, a so-called New Economy company that had real cachet. He was known to be very effective when it came to building new business and forging alliances with other companies. Sprint had recently emerged from a turbulent period to become an industry leader. In fact, it was such an exciting company that LeMay had many reasons to stay put.

In our negotiations LeMay belabored every issue, right down to the make and model of his company car and dues at a prestigious country club. At one point he called me at my house in Sunriver to decline the job. Convinced that our shareholders wanted a new captain for the ship, and fast, I asked, "What would it take to change your mind?" That's how we got to the idea of covering the potential gains he might sacrifice by leaving Sprint.

Besides a $1.5 million base salary, incentive rewards, and options to acquire millions of Waste Management shares, we offered to compensate LeMay for money he would miss out on if shares at his old company, Sprint, soared. The total value of this benefit could be as much as $48 million in five years. It was an extraordinary package. But we wanted to lure Ron away from a go-go company where he had a realistic shot at the top spot, so we did what it took to get him.

We should have read the situation better. When someone is so reluctant to be hired that you have to offer him the sun, the moon, and the stars, the relationship almost never works out. Ron knew next to nothing about the garbage business and was hardly enthusiastic about coming to Chicago. He moved into a hotel near Waste Management headquarters in the suburb of Oak Brook, and though he said his family would soon join him, they never did. At the office, the more he learned about the company, the less he seemed to like it.

The problems at Waste Management were hard for an outsider to recognize because they were obscured for some time by quirky accounting moves. Eager to prop up earnings, previous managers had changed certain assumptions to make the books look better. For example, trucks that were given an estimated life of eight years were suddenly expected to operate for ten or eleven. This change reduced the amount the company needed to set aside for replacement trucks by tens of millions of dollars. Similar adjustments were made to the value of containers, which were suddenly expected to last thirty years and then retain value as scrap metal. The costs at various landfills were stretched out over decades based on new assumptions. None of these changes were necessarily in violation of accounting rules, which allow for variations in judgment. But they represented a level of optimism that many investors would not share.

Investors were also concerned about the company's ragged performance in businesses other than trash hauling. Landfills acquired through a buying binge in the 1980s became money losers when a surplus of these facilities arose in the 1990s. Businesses devoted to recycling and the management of discarded chemicals withered as markets failed to develop.

As LeMay learned, the company's performance had actually been worse than he knew, and its recovery would demand a long, hard slog. He had to recognize that it might take years of cost cutting combined with the sale of many company assets to make things right. And then, three months into the job, his chief financial officer, John Sanford, the one person most directly responsible for straightening out the company's books, quit without warning. When you have accounting problems, the last thing you want is for the CFO to abruptly resign.

––––––––––

IN THOSE DAYS before the famous scandals at Enron, Adelphia, WorldCom, and other companies shook the world, directors were less engaged and certainly didn't have day-to-day involvement in company affairs. Those of us who sat on the Waste Management board knew that LeMay had issues to confront, but we couldn't possibly have been aware that the CFO was about to bolt and that management and accounting problems ran deep into the company's structure. But we were about to find out.

It was Halloween Day and I was in Pittsburgh to meet with a Carnegie Mellon University business school class studying corporate crises when Ron LeMay called my room at a hotel airport. It was a little after noon. He got right to the point.

"I've got two pieces of bad news," he said.

"Okay. What are they?"

"Well, our CFO, John Sanford, just quit amid a deepening accounting mess."

"Okay, it can't get much worse than that. What's the other thing?"

"I'm also resigning."

"How long have we got?"

"I'm going back to Kansas City on the Sprint plane this afternoon."

There was no use trying to talk him out of it. Sprint had always been LeMay's true love, and his time at Waste Management was something like a midlife crisis affair that was ending badly. He was going back to his true love, where he was being welcomed with open arms and the company jet.

The news was going to be bad for Waste Management, but there was nothing I could do about it. The Carnegie Mellon class was starting at two o'clock, and I would never beg off on the promise I had made to be there. I only had time to call the company's chief counsel, Herb Getz. We agreed that we shouldn't let the sun go down without announcing what we were going to do.

The news from LeMay gave the Carnegie Mellon class something exciting to talk about, especially since they were focusing on crisis management. While we were discussing the hypotheticals of the situation, the board, minus me, held a telephone conference. During a class break I went to a pay phone and called Herb again. He jokingly said, "The board has elected you chairman and CEO. That should teach you never to miss a meeting. We've sent the company plane down to Pittsburgh to pick you up and bring you to Chicago for dinner with the senior management. You're in charge as of now!"

As the fourth CEO in a year, I knew Waste Management needed me to act quickly and calmly. They told me that LeMay had them working on a plan to cut out big parts of the corporate bureaucracy to save money and improve efficiency. His goal, called Five Up and Five Down, was a 5 percent increase in revenues paired with a 5 percent decrease in expenses. Within a few days I would direct them to go ahead with LeMay's plan. This decision was based on the fact that LeMay was no dummy and on my belief that we needed to act decisively or risk having the whole company seize up like an engine deprived of oil.

The next morning we conducted a videoconference sent by satellite to conference rooms and offices where all fifty-eight thousand of our worldwide employees could see it. People were shocked, and it made no sense to ignore this fact. I noted that we had thousands of experienced and competent people to run the company and that the one person who knew the least was me. "I am now your leader. That's got to scare the hell out of you," I said with a smile. "I promise to catch up fast. But in the meantime, stay the course and take care of your customers. This is a terrible shock, but if you do your job we will be able to sort through this."

In the early moments of a crisis everyone wants to see that you understand the issues and are serious about fixing things. The market showed its anxiety by driving our stock down 20 percent in a single day. To calm everyone's nerves I called on two friends to join me on the board. Jack Pope, recent president of United Airlines, was a sophisticated financial expert. Roderick Hills had been chairman of the Securities and Exchange Commission in the 1970s and was a leading figure in the accounting world. We made him chairman of our audit committee, a move that guaranteed everyone that there would be a thorough review of accounting and that in the end our books would have credibility.

These quick appointments silenced the critics in the press and our stock price stabilized, but not one of our big shareholders was happy. George Soros's money manager Stanley Druckenmiller arrived in Oak Brook with his complaints a few days after LeMay resigned. He told me the company was bloated and unresponsive and needed cuts in the management ranks and a thorough reorganization. Pension fund managers and others who held big blocks of stock made the same criticisms, and I had to deal with Nell Minow and Robert Monks, self-styled watchdogs for what they called "shareholders' rights," who operated a small money management company. Their Lens Fund was backed with $50 million from Soros, and they used their status as shareholders to badger the managers of struggling companies for improved performance.

In every case I told shareholders that I worked for them and wanted their input. To show them we were listening, the board restructured its committees to put new independent members in charge and formed a CEO search committee made up entirely of new directors.

These moves were reassuring but not enough for the likes of Monks and Minow, who were outspoken critics of the "old boy" style of corporate governance, where a CEO or a company's founder seems to dominate the board of directors. Nell pushed for directors to be more independent and practice more active oversight. In Waste Management's case she was, like other shareholders, especially critical of Dean Buntrock, who had constructed the company but never developed the ability to manage it through hard times. In the current crisis he even seemed to resent perfectly reasonable questions. He'd say, "Why are you looking at me? The CFO and the auditors signed off on everything. They said it was okay."

Leaving is never easy for a founder or CEO who identifies strongly with a company. Like Iacocca at Chrysler, Dean was a visionary who truly dominated a huge corporation. And this was part of the problem. He was such a powerful figure inside and outside of Waste Management that no matter what title he held, people would continue to look to his leadership as long as he was around. This is why it's never a good idea to keep a former CEO on the board.

The two of us talked it over and two weeks after LeMay hopped the Sprint plane to get out of town, Buntrock resigned from the board. On the same day that his departure was announced, Waste Management also made public a restructuring plan that would reduce two hundred and fifty managing units to thirty-two and eliminate twelve hundred jobs. (These moves would save $100 million annually in costs.) More layoffs were in the works, and we were actively looking for yet another CEO to take the chair I was warming on a temporary basis. Little did

I know that this mission would bring me one of the most memorable encounters in my long and varied career.

———————

IT BEGAN AT a daylong meeting in New York, where I had invited people who collectively represented a majority interest in Waste Management stock to tell me their ideas for fixing the company and restoring the value of their investments. At the afternoon session, a shareholder who said he spoke for the majority said they believed they had the answer. "You have a bloated bureaucracy," he explained, "and the right guy to deal with it is Chainsaw Al Dunlap."

Leader of the Sunbeam appliance company, Dunlap was the CEO of the moment, a master of self-promotion whose recently issued book, *Mean Business*, was rising on the bestseller list. His main claim to fame was a turnaround job at Scott Paper, where he sold off parts of the business, slashed the workforce, and cut costs allegedly by ignoring maintenance and repair schedules. In eighteen months the stock rose 160 percent. Dunlap made $100 million for himself. At Sunbeam he was using the same tactics, disrupting the lives of thousands of employees who were suddenly fired to force temporary improvements on the bottom line.

I knew Dunlap only by reputation, but what I knew had been sufficient for me to reassure the people at Waste Management during my day one televised address that "I would not support a Chainsaw Al. This is a great asset," I explained. "We're not going to rip the place apart and destroy things."

I dismissed the chainsaw approach because I believed that indiscriminately slashing costs to meet short-term investor goals hurt companies when it came to their long-term prospects in the global economy. There is nothing wrong with efficiency, but it has to be matched by smart management and investment in the kinds of things that prepare you to offer the best goods or services in the future. Dunlap's "mean business" approach didn't consider these things.

But now, in New York, everyone in the room seemed to think Dunlap was the answer for Waste Management, and as owners they were my bosses. The person most eager to have me approach Dunlap about the CEO position was Nell Minow, the activist shareholder.

Minow told me she had reserved space in the *Wall Street Journal* for an ad describing the members of our board as "long-term liabilities," which she would run if Waste Management didn't shape up. The implication was clear: go see Dunlap or face public humiliation

"Look, I know what you are thinking," Nell told me. "Your personal style is completely different. But your heart is actually similar. At least you should meet him."

Before the day was out, Dunlap and I spoke on the phone and agreed to get together on the coming Sunday at his home in Boca Raton. That morning I read his book on my flight south, discovering a remarkably self-confident fellow—"I'm a superstar in my field"—who graduated from West Point and took a slash-and-burn approach to troubled businesses. He didn't study problems or innovate. He simply issued orders for drastic cost reductions and asset sales and then followed up to make sure they were carried out.

The strategy had worked for investors at Scott Paper and at the moment seemed to be working at Sunbeam, where reports of high Christmas season orders were driving the stock upward. Combine these orders with the cost saving that came after he fired half the company's workers, and you've got a much improved bottom line, at least in the short term. I could see how Dunlap impressed investors looking to reap quick rewards, but I was more interested in building businesses than squeezing them dry.

I confess I wasn't optimistic after reading Dunlap's book, and the car trip to his home made me even more skeptical about the man. He lived in a community that was so exclusive and protected it reeked of paranoia. You had to be admitted at two guardhouses just to get to his driveway, and that was protected by yet another gate. The house itself was a 6,500-square-foot palace with a Spanish tile roof. Two enormous German shepherds snarled behind the door as I waited for someone to answer the bell. Al and his wife, Judy, held them back as the door opened and calmed them with a command that signaled that I was okay.

After we said hello and I had been introduced to his wife, Al led me on a little tour through the house, which was decorated like a shrine to Chainsaw Al. There were more portraits of him than I could count. As we walked he spoke rather loudly, like someone who is a little hard of hearing, and recited a stream of platitudes, many of which I had already read in his book. This reminded me of the one time I met with Ross Perot. He also relied on pithy bromides that he repeated and applied to every situation.

In our more formal conversation, conducted over sandwiches, Dunlap said he would be interested in the job at Waste Management and believed he was very nearly finished with Sunbeam, which he was hoping to sell. I thanked him for his time, and as I left said we would be conducting a full search for the next CEO and would keep him informed of our progress.

The ultimate decision would be left to our directors, of course, but before I even got back to the car I knew I wouldn't recommend him for the job. How could Nell Minow have said we had anything in common? Al reveled in being called a pinstripe Rambo who tore companies apart. I considered myself a careful rebuilder who saved as many jobs and assets as possible. He worshipped share price. I believed that executives should consider the interests of customers, employees, communities, lenders, and others along with shareholders. Quarterly profits are important, but they are not the only measure of a company's worth, value, and potential.

As a Deloitte & Touche survey published at this time showed, eight out of ten executives at major corporations agreed with my view of business. But as my next encounter with major shareholders showed, those who ran public companies could still expect pressure from investors. At a dinner for Waste Management investors hosted by First Boston, Dunlap was again mentioned as a prime candidate for CEO. I dodged the issue by saying no decision had been made. But I let it be known that Dunlap was clearly campaigning for the job. He had told me he was interested and available, and he was talking to major shareholders.

Meetings like the First Boston dinner are generally off-the-record affairs, but no one actually announced that our conversation was private. Days later, one of the First Boston folks issued a report on Waste Management telling investors they should buy our stock, citing my remarks about Dunlap to suggest he might soon take charge. However, instead of boosting our shares as the analysts may have hoped, the report hit Sunbeam's hard. Dunlap was in the middle of a three-year contract, and his work was not yet done. His stockholders weren't pleased to hear that he had his sights set on a new job.

Clearly upset, Dunlap wrote a statement for the press, insisting that he never wanted the CEO chair at Waste Management and attacking me as "a typical, arrogant professional director playing at being an executive." Speculating that I was trying to use his name to boost Waste Management stock, Dunlap denied "pursuing or having any interest" in leading the company.

Even for a hot-tempered sort like Chainsaw Al, this document was remarkably emotional and contradictory. In almost the same breath he denied being interested but then announced, "I clearly am the CEO that [Waste Management] needs." Of course he had to add that he would never come to a company where I was a director. In an interview with the *Wall Street Journal* on the day he issued his statement, Dunlap complained that he had the flu and was going home to bed. He admitted that he was "extremely agitated" but had no regrets about speaking out.

I was taken aback when I heard about Al's complaints and called his office to apologize for misreading the situation. (A staffer said he was unavailable to take my call.) But it was always clear to me that he wanted the job and that he was talking with stockholders about making the jump. Of course, as I told the *Journal*, "I guess now he's taken himself out of the running."

A major biography of Dunlap would later report that he had quickly used the publicity about Waste Management's interest in him to leverage a new contract with Sunbeam that increased his potential gains by tens of millions of dollars. The negotiations over this deal were intense, and the news that followed its completion may explain why. Sunbeam's first quarter results for 1998 came in much lower than expected (a $44 million loss). Chainsaw Al fired his executive vice president for worldwide products, and then, when a key stock analyst issued a negative report, the company's share price plummeted 25 percent in a single day.

The analyst had been following Sunbeam closely and had noticed the company was shipping huge numbers of products and dramatically increasing its accounts receivable. Some of these shipments, like barbecue grills sent out in the late fall, made very little sense. In time everyone would learn that Dunlap was making "bill and hold" deals, shipping merchandise to third-party warehouses, recording the transactions as if they were actual sales, but giving the receivers a right to return the goods and not pay.

Eager to repair the damage done to his stock, Dunlap blamed lower-level executives for "stupid, low margin deals," announced new layoffs, and promised big future earnings. It didn't work. Instead the business press reported that all of Sunbeam's net income for the previous year had been based on special maneuvers to boost profits. The underlying business, it appeared, was actually losing money despite all the cuts in the workforce and other expenses. Prospects for a sale of the company evaporated. Directors began investigating the operation of the company, skirting Dunlap to consult other executives within the firm. In mid-June they let him go. Eventually Dunlap would be charged with fraud by the Securities and Exchange Commission. He would pay a $500,000 fine and be barred from ever again serving as an officer or executive at a public company. Dunlap would also pay $15 million to settle a shareholders lawsuit.

———

I CITE THE Dunlap saga not to affirm my own judgment but to point out that a one-size-fits-all approach does not work with troubled companies, and that the behavior, reputation, and performance of a CEO are critical when it comes to investors, customers, and workers. Chainsaw Al behaved badly, striking others as arrogant, ruthless, and shallow. His style may have worked once, with Scott Paper, but it was no substitute for substance. Similarly, at Waste Management, Buntrock couldn't adjust to new realities and find new techniques to apply to the company's needs. His successor, Rooney showed too little independence, and LeMay, who never made a real commitment to the job, abandoned us.

As temporary leader, my highest priority was finding strong, smart, and flexible people to save the assets of Waste Management. It seemed the best way to do this might be a merger that would bring the company both leaders with experience and a stronger balance sheet. Consolidation in the industry and Waste Management's size meant that there were few potential partners to consider, and I was resigned to searching for a new CEO while we worked to clean up the accounting records.

Nonetheless, I had been called on my first day on the job by Jerry York, my old friend and former colleague from Chrysler days. Jerry was on the board of the third largest and the fastest-growing waste company, USA Waste Services, based in Houston, and he felt that a merger of our two companies would be the best outcome for us and would bring us a highly regarded CEO, John Drury. I first met Drury in a hastily arranged conference room at Houston's Hobby Airport. While he seemed slowed by what he said was a recent sinus operation, I found Drury to be dynamic, confident, and extremely knowledgeable. Though he didn't have a college degree, his family was in the trash hauling business, and he literally came of age working on the back of a truck. His on-the-job training had made him into a financially sophisticated and effective manager, and he had a decade of experience at BFI (Browning-Ferris Industries), the number two in the business. As a result, he knew all of the wild characters who were important in a rough-and tumble-business.

In contrast with Waste Management's centralized bureaucracy, Drury favored greater autonomy for his local divisions, where managers handled everything from the trash pickups to budgeting and billing. He said this made sense because garbage was a very local business, where customers and regulators had very local concerns, and everything from the geography to the weather affected operations. The schedules, equipment, and processes used in a modern Sun Belt city like Phoenix, for example, varied dramatically from the practices required in the mountains of northern New Hampshire. Who was better positioned to know how to get results from these markets, a bureaucrat in Houston or a veteran of the local business?

Although Drury impressed me, the books at Waste Management were such a mess that I told him I couldn't talk to him about a merger until after the end of the year. True to his go-getter reputation he drafted a proposal for joining the companies that arrived at my home in Sunriver on January 1, 1998. As a business matter, his timing was probably perfect. For me, personally, it was a very bad moment. Maggie and I were in the middle of a marital crisis.

For years Maggie had shown signs of serious social anxiety, finding it more and more difficult to travel, attend functions, visit with friends, and even play host to our extended family during the holidays. Sometimes she could rally and follow through on an invitation we had accepted or go on a vacation trip. But in many cases she would get so tense and upset preparing to leave the house that she would simply refuse to go. And when it came to home-based family events like Christmas, her genuinely happy anticipation often turned into terrible anxiety once everyone was together. Convinced she was responsible for everyone's happiness and entertainment, Maggie couldn't be at ease. She would organize activities, cook and serve meals, tidy up after everyone, and then feel terribly overwhelmed.

Between Christmas 1997 and New Year's Day 1998, things at our house got so bad for Maggie that she actually packed a bag and ran away. She had threatened this kind of thing before, saying she just couldn't take it anymore and declaring she would go live in a hovel somewhere and support herself with menial work. But she had never actually left and stayed away. This time she did, and though I checked the parking lot of every motel in the only nearby city of Bend, I couldn't find her vehicle. I tried to reassure everyone, including myself, that she was okay, but I worried.

Maggie finally phoned on New Year's Day, as I was trading calls with John Drury, who happened to be in France on vacation. In a weak voice she said, "We need to talk," and then told me that she was hiding at lonely little highway motel in the tiny community of La Pine, which was in the opposite direction of Bend. (She really didn't want to be found.) I dropped everything and drove down to see her, not knowing what to expect.

Maggie looked tired and upset when she answered the door of her motel room. We sat together inside, and she poured her heart out, delivering both complaints about our marriage and a fearful confession of her own insecurities. It was a confusing conversation. She said she resented that we generally spent only weekends together, but then admitted that she wanted me to work and wasn't interested in traveling to be with me during the week. She said she wanted to be closer, but also insisted that she wasn't the right person for me and that we should get divorced.

"You're doing what you were cut out to do," she said. "But it's not the life I was cut out for. I'm not the kind of wife you deserve."

Maggie then repeated something I had heard her say in similar circumstances. She said that she didn't want anything from me, that she would start over on her own and live in impoverished isolation. "I came into this marriage with nothing," she said. "I'll leave it the same way."

Part of me wanted to tell that Maggie that she was being ridiculous, but I could see she was feeling hurt and that she was earnest about what she was saying. Besides, I was shocked and worried about losing her. I tried to refute her, to make sure she knew that *I* thought she was the one for me and that I loved her. None of this seemed to get through, so when we both ran out of things to say I stood and tried to accept her ultimatum. If she wouldn't come home, I couldn't make her. I left the room and was in my car when she finally ran out and asked me to stay.

"Don't leave," she said. "I'm coming home."

She did come home and was soon acting as if nothing had happened. I didn't know what to make of it all. But I was happy that she had stuck with me, and I didn't press her to talk about what happened because I hoped she would get over it. No sense picking at a scab.

Since we had gone through similar episodes in the past I was obviously doing a bit of wishful thinking. And while she never actually left again, Maggie would struggle with the same issues for the rest of her life, never quite settling them. A friend would one day note that Maggie's childhood had been very insecure. Her father, an alcoholic retired navy officer, had often been absent and died young. Perhaps Maggie's biggest fear in life was returning to the loneliness and struggle of her childhood. She had never talked about this issue in a direct and open way, never dealt with the terrible sadness she had felt as a little girl. It's possible that when she felt stress as an adult, she was reminded of those lonely times, and something in her subconscious drove her to confront her fears by recreating them.

Of course at the time I couldn't even guess about what was going on in Maggie's psyche, and we were not the kind of people to seek professional help or try to analyze ourselves. I confess that my moods were linked to Maggie's, and when she felt better I was able to forget our troubles. On this day, as soon as I got back to Sunriver I had to resume my discussions with John Drury, who was eager to make the deal that I hoped would solve Waste Management's problems.

———————

THE PROPOSAL THAT Drury sent on that turbulent New Year's Day became the starting point for a merger. In subsequent meetings with my board and key investors, Drury and his second-in-command, Rodney Proto, performed flawlessly. The board and the investors were persuaded that these fellows knew what they were doing, which is essential because even though Waste Management was four times the size of USA Waste, Drury and Proto would run the combined company. When the transaction was completed, we got a 12 percent premium on our stock, which went to our investors, who also got half the seats on the new board of directors. The company would also keep the name Waste Management, and everyone would benefit from savings realized through efficiencies. We estimated the total savings to be roughly $800 million annually. When the deal was announced, a few outside experts said that he might save much more than that.

For Drury the alliance meant he was finally king of the trash heap, the most powerful person in a business that was fiercely competitive. He moved quickly to consolidate and impose his decentralized management scheme on the combined entities. Instead of a two-thousand-person headquarters staff in Oak Brook, he would have just three hundred running things from Houston. Instead of a big room full of mainframe computers managing data at headquarters he ordered field offices to run things from their desktop PCs.

Much of what Drury did was intended to focus Waste Management on its immediate need to cut expenses. For example, he shut down the company research lab, which Buntrock had funded to develop techniques for everything from incineration to compacting to metal extraction. These innovations had made us an industry leader and helped us set standards that gave us a competitive advantage. But Drury didn't want to spend money to be the industry leader. He wanted to do waste collection and handling as efficiently as possible. Drury also closed the massive billing center in Oak Brook, where Waste Management processed thousands of customer checks each day, choosing, instead, to have our local offices send out invoices and make collections.

Everyone applauded Drury's moves, believing he had brought modern management to a business that needed some updating. I supported him but was a bit wary, especially when he closed the billing center. It was an impressive operation, automated and yet flexible. If someone sent a payment that was $10 short with a note saying we failed to make a trash pickup, we were able to handle it without upsetting the flow. The setup may have been costly, but more than a billion dollars in revenue flowed smoothly through the place every month, keeping the company alive.

Having never run a big waste company I went along with John's plan and retreated to Sunriver. Though I remained chairman of the board, I was supposed to hand the gavel over to John the next summer. He clearly didn't need me, or so I thought, as the merger and his initial actions inspired investors to double our share price before the year was over.

———————

IN EARLY 1999, word reached the board that John Drury was sick. When I heard he had brain cancer I was reminded of the day we met in Houston and he was recovering from what he said was a sinus operation. Did he know then that he had cancer? I wondered.

Though the diagnosis sounded very serious, Drury's doctor spoke with the board of directors and described a treatment plan that would help him recover completely. He sounded very optimistic and warned us against asking him to step down. Doing so, he said, might endanger John's health. What a dilemma—if we replaced Drury, we might kill him! We did nothing, and at a late winter board meeting held in Phoenix, Drury seemed fine. I noticed, however, that he ran out of gas by midafternoon and bowed out of the dinner, which is typically a highlight of the board's day.

Nothing in the company's performance suggested we had to worry about Drury's leadership. In the first quarter, earnings per share missed his target by just a penny, which was close enough to make Wall Street happy. In May I converted some of my own stock options to shares, selling just enough to cover all the costs, including taxes. I could have done this at any time, but I waited until the first quarter report was issued so that I would be acting on the same information available to the public.

With summer approaching I was looking forward to stepping down from the chairman's post at the company's annual meeting. Drury had proved himself by making the merger work and deserved to be re-warded with the added title. I went to the meeting expecting a cele-bration, but when our CEO was missing from the informal board dinner the night before I knew something was wrong. The next day, shareholders gathered in a hotel ballroom, and Rod Proto delivered the important reports.

As Rod finished, John finally entered the hall in a wheelchair pushed by his driver, Jim Horn. The audience was absolutely silent as Jim helped John to stand at a podium. He was recognized as taking over as chairman and then turned to a one-page statement that he hoped to deliver. He stumbled through it, almost incoherent, and then was helped back to his chair. I began to wonder just who it was I had handed over the gavel to.

Few annual meetings have featured such drama. The members of Waste Management's board knew Drury was sick, but none were aware of just how bad things had gotten. Fortunately, Proto was an able second, and while Drury took a leave of absence—still insisting he'd come back—we had confidence that Proto would keep things moving in a good direction. That confidence would soon be de-stroyed.

In reports issued shortly after the time of the annual meeting, man-agement restated profits for the first quarter, setting them far below the projections made in the spring and announced a $250 million drop in earnings for the year to date. In between these admissions came a story in the business press about big stock sales made in May by Proto, who netted $16.6 million, and fourteen other executives, in-cluding chief financial officer Earl DeFrates. At the time they sold, when the news about Waste Management was all positive, the stock was worth about $55 a share. Two months later, when the figures were restated, share price fell to $34.

It wouldn't take a team of forensic accountants to conclude some-thing potentially unethical, if not illegal, was taking place. It only took a *Wall Street Journal* reporter named Jeff Bailey, who spoke to Maggie in Sunriver before reaching me in Cleveland, where I was attending a Morrison Knudsen board meeting. Maggie told Jeff that I had con-verted some options to stock but taken out no cash. He saw nothing untoward in this, but did want to talk with me about the huge sums taken in stock sales by others and the problems building at the company.

Until this moment, I had little reason to believe that Drury and his team weren't making great progress. But in fact they had all but lost control of the big new entity created in the merger. In closing Waste Management's Oak Brook computing and billing centers they had cut the flow of information and dollars that made the operation work. At regional and local offices people did not know how to run the special software used by USA Waste, and they had never been asked to keep track of accounts. In many places months went by without bills being issued and receipts coming in. Payments that were received weren't even processed and deposited.

It was probably the most extreme crisis I had ever seen at a company. Drawn back into the fray by this emergency, I again became temporary CEO and worked feverishly with a board member named Ralph Whitworth (who became chairman) to see if we could stop the train before all the cars jumped the track. We went to see Drury at his apartment at the Ritz-Carlton in Houston and found him so debilitated that he could hardly talk and barely recognized us. At headquarters CFO Earl DeFrates and general counsel Gregory Sangalis both resigned, and we announced a massive review of the books. In the weeks to come, Rodney Proto would also leave, and we hired over a thousand accountanting professionals who fanned out across the globe to interview both managers and workers, examine records, and try to construct a true picture of the corporation's condition. The place was almost totally in chaos.

It was hard to believe that once again top management was not up to the job, and worse in this case, the trouble was not just incompetence but perhaps fraud. But in fact, that was what we faced.

I felt miserable. The merger of which I had been so proud had become an unmitigated disaster. I would come to regard it as my biggest ever corporate belly flop. Although John Drury would die before things were resolved, both the New York Stock Exchange and the Securities and Exchange Commission launched immediate investigations into insider trading by Proto and the others. Between the government's efforts and shareholder lawsuits, the culpable execs would wind up returning many millions' worth of option gains. While neither admitting nor denying the charges against them, Proto and DeFrates would pay a combined $4.2 million to settle the case brought against them.

The damage done to the company by the charges against its executives was far worse than any of Waste Management's genuine business problems. Corporations are, in the end, only as good as the people who run them, and the best ones are open about their management moves, their mistakes, their personal finances, and their health. If you don't practice this kind of honesty, it won't matter whether the public thinks you're a genius or a chainsaw-wielding tough guy. The truth always comes out eventually, and you hurt everyone.

———————

MY FINAL EFFORT to help find a true leader for Waste Management, a job that was now infinitely more difficult than before, led to a pair of solid candidates. Dave Cote was a hotshot at the best-run corporation in the world, General Electric. No company is a better training ground for executive talent, and everyone knew that a GE vice president was a prize catch. Our other candidate was a more rumpled, workaday CEO named Maurice "Maury" Myers of the Yellow Corporation, a big trucking concern, who had also worked at Ford and for several airlines. Myers was down-to-earth and likeable. Once, during our extended deliberations I asked him to be patient, and he said, "Don't worry about it. I know you're just keeping me warm while you check out your other options. Call me when you decide."

Younger than Myers, David Cote was brilliant and polished, and as head of appliances for GE, he knew how to work with union labor, having once been an hourly worker himself. He was intrigued by the challenge at Waste Management, but we sensed that he had reservations about the trash business and moving to Houston. He was from the Northeast and asked us about moving headquarters in that direction.

Slightly intoxicated by the notion of capturing a GE superstar, we actually entertained the idea of moving the company headquarters for the second time in as many years to make Cote happy. We offered him the job, and he took some time to think about it. I went home to Sunriver, where I had a long conversation with my most reliable adviser,

Maggie Miller. When I told her what we were doing, she had to restrain herself from physically shaking some sense into me.

"You've got one guy who's down-to-earth and enthusiastic about the job. He's worked in airlines and trucking and understands what Waste Management does. He doesn't want a gold-plated contract, and he doesn't want to move the headquarters. The other guy is not in love with the job, and he doesn't want to go to his next cocktail party and explain that he works for a garbage company. He is never going to be comfortable at Waste Management."

She was right, and after consulting with the board, I called Cote and withdrew our offer. He was stunned, as if the idea of us turning him down was beyond his comprehension. Maury Myers, on the other hand, was calmly pleased when we offered the post to him. He moved to Houston and dug into the job with both hands. Past sins were confessed, and besides relinquishing their stock sale proceeds, the executives responsible were appropriately sactioned. Arthur Andersen paid many millions of dollars to cover their share of the blame, and strict controls were imposed on accounting processes. Before he retired in 2004, Maury Myers had Waste Management completely stabilized.

In retrospect you can see that Waste Management first got into trouble in the late 1980s when the growth-through-acquisition strategy stalled. The executives turned to creative accounting to make things look better than they were. Years passed and just like the fines on an overdue library book, the price of not dealing with problems in an open straightforward way grew and grew.

Remarkably, the company didn't have to go into bankruptcy and was strong enough to survive the turmoil at the top. And while worse debacles of the era—Enron, Tyco, WorldCom—got more attention, the problems at Waste Management contributed to improvements in the way the boards of public companies operate across industries. The days when directors practiced quiet oversight and depended solely on a CEO for input were ending. Independence, skepticism, and strength were the qualities that would make for effective directors in the future. As a result, things were going to get tougher for both executives and board members.

Besides highlighting the need for sharp oversight, Waste Management taught me invaluable lessons about relating to CEOs as a director. Eventually they would evolve into a list of warning signs that signal when a top dog might be going astray. They include:

- Repeatedly missing quarterly forecasts.

- Impatience with subordinates bearing bad news.

- Lack of candor or a penchant for rosy scenarios.

- Abrupt firings of executives previously praised.

- Total agreement in the ranks. (No healthy internal debates.)

These are just signals and not absolute proof that an executive is behaving badly. And since I remain an optimist, when they flash on I don't immediately search for a replacement. Instead I consider the signals a call to look more closely and open a dialogue. There's always a chance, you know, that a CEO needs some help and you can provide it before a problem become a crisis.

Nine

WHO'S IN CHARGE HERE?

Before we judge short-serving executives too harshly, we must consider that there are times when the shoe just won't fit. This may have been Ronald LeMay's problem at Waste Management. He accepted the job in good faith, but he just couldn't adjust to a challenge that was bigger than he expected and to life in suburban Chicago. Also, he wasn't the short-term, rescue mission type, which was demonstrated by the fact that when he returned to Sprint he stayed for six years.

Most turnaround specialists share certain qualities. Among them are the ability to focus intently in a crisis and a relatively short attention span. Although we can leave it to the experts to determine for certain if this is a kind of attention deficit disorder, the special qualities shared by corporate firefighters do echo the traits of gifted students with ADD. We are easily bored by a routine flight in a cloudless sky but thrilled to take the controls when crosswinds blow and the engines start to fail. Of course, we can't bring the plane in for a landing if someone bigger and stronger refuses to let go of the controls.

Reliance Group Holdings was already in a tailspin when its chairman, CEO, and major stockholder, Saul Steinberg, called for help at the end of 1999. An insurance and investment firm, the company was losing more than $1 million per day and faced $700 million debt load without the resources to pay it. Several years earlier Steinberg had suffered a stroke and was recovering slowly. He still had a fundamental financial wisdom, but not the stamina to work long hours or focus on details. The future looked bleak. Rating agency A. M. Best was about to downgrade the company's rating, which would make customers flee; the most important thing when you are buying insurance is the confidence the insurance company will be there when you have a claim. And of all ironies, Reliance's largest customer, Waste Management, saw the handwriting on the wall and took their business elsewhere shortly after my arrival at Reliance.

Insurance isn't an exciting industry, but the Waste Management crisis was over, and Reliance *was* in Maggie's favorite city, New York. Steinberg was a charming man who seemed very open about his company's troubles and very eager to have me come help. But his board said no when I was first offered the job as president at a multimillion-dollar salary. Months later he came back with a more modest offer, which was fine with me—I was interested in the challenge, not making a killing. Even then I had to cool my heels more than an hour outside the boardroom, as the board debated whether I'd be worth it.

I assumed I would have real power inside the company since I'd report directly to Steinberg and carry the lofty title of president. Maggie and I also looked forward to a lovely way of life based in a company-paid hotel suite on Park Avenue, which was, for Maggie, about as close to heaven on earth as she could get.

Steinberg had been a boy genius in the 1960s and a financial tiger in the 1970s and1980s, using the cash flow generated by Reliance insurance premium payments to play the markets. In one of his most famous deals, he mounted a bid to control Disney but then accepted a sweetened, $60 million offer for his holdings from the wealthy Bass family on the condition that he turn his attention elsewhere. At the time it was described as one of the biggest "greenmail" episodes in history. It also cemented Steinberg's reputation as an aggressive investor.

For a time Saul occupied a place near the top of the financial world. He bought $50 million worth of art, much of which went into his 17,000-square-foot Park Avenue apartment and an oceanfront mansion in the Hamptons. That beach house was the site of Saul's $1 million fiftieth birthday party, in 1989, which would be remembered as one of the great parties of the century. A decade later it was the scene of a wedding that paired Saul's son Jonathan with the famous financial newscaster Maria Bartiromo.

The wedding, which took place in August 1999, turned out to be the Steinberg family's social swan song. By the time I arrived in December, the press was filled with reports of the empire's collapse. Although he was recovering from his illness, Saul was still too weak to spend more than a couple of hours per day at work. Meanwhile, disappointing investments and big losses in the firm's workers' compensation program were draining cash at an alarming rate. Angry investors who were losing money on their Reliance shares and lenders who feared they would never be repaid were bellowing about the lavish salaries taken by top executives.

Given a chance, I might have been able to help salvage something at Reliance, but the chance never came. Although Saul wanted my aid, it was almost as if he tried to perform a heart transplant but the body rejected it. Some of the directors he sent me to consult praised the very executives I thought should be replaced, while others kept canceling appointments until I understood that they didn't want to deal with me.

The board excluded me from executive sessions, where the important decisions were made. Equally important, the organization chart was structured so that no one other than my secretary actually reported to me. I was so out of the loop that the major decision-makers excluded me from working lunches. When a reporter from the newspaper in Portland, Oregon, came to write about me as a hometown boy made good, I actually pretended to have a meeting to attend outside the office just so I would seem to be busily engaged. His article noted how clean my desk was and how well organized and calm I was—actually, I had almost nothing to do.

The chill at Reliance was so deep that I would serve for just three months. In that time I developed what I termed a plan B rescue strategy, which called for cutting costs by replacing the existing high-priced executive team with more aggressive lower-cost young Turks, moving to much cheaper offices, and finding someone new to take over Saul's leadership position. Although no guarantees were made, I also talked with the CEO at one of the world's largest insurance companies who was ready to invest in Reliance if this kind of reorganization were done.

The board rejected my ideas, and I was kept almost completely isolated in my short time at the company. With that rebuke, I felt I was not doing any good by hanging around. I voluntarily resigned and waived any contractual rights to compensation or any severance whatsoever.

———————

ABOUT A YEAR after I left, Reliance would be sunk by its losses, and every officer and member of the board of directors—except for me—would face charges of wrongdoing from insurance regulators who assumed control of the company in order to protect policyholders. I'm glad I left when I did.

Reliance was one of the least happy stations in my journey through corporate life, but the negatives were balanced by Maggie's happiness over our time together in New York, where we soaked in the lights and wonders of the holiday season and hit every museum and concert hall. She loved roaming the city by bus and subway and reveled in our hotel's neighborhood, which was the heart of Midtown.

It was fun for me, too, to see celebrities like Larry King next to me each morning on the treadmill in the hotel health club, and to visit with longtime friends in the finance and legal communities. New York at the start of the new millennium was a cleaner, brighter, safer place than it had been the first time we lived in the city. As we packed our bags to leave I felt a little wistful about never getting a chance to do the Reliance job right and about taking Maggie back to the Oregon woods.

Somewhere between boxing up some personal papers and emptying the sock drawer, the hotel phone rang. It was the financier William Donaldson, one of the founders of Donaldson, Lufkin & Jenrette and a director for Aetna, an insurance giant suffering from a yearlong slide in its stock price. He wanted me to stop packing and call the front desk to say I was staying at least for the few days it would take to consult with him about helping him out with the crisis at Aetna. I did what he said and started doing a little research.

Begun in 1850 as a general insurance company, Aetna had recently acquired a company called U.S. Healthcare and refocused its business to become the top health insurer in America. The marriage had been rough as several old and trusted managers were replaced by aggressive execs from the new division. Thousands of employees were laid off, and regional offices were closed. But instead of cutting costs, the result was confusion that drove them higher and caused problems for customers. The combination of mismanagement and a heavy-handed, combative approach to reimbursements for doctors and patients made U.S. Healthcare a symbol of all the problems the public associated with health maintenance organizations (HMOs) and so-called managed care.

The anger that patients and doctors expressed toward U.S. Healthcare had peaked in recent months as several hospitals and hundreds of doctors—including many top specialists—severed relationships with the company. The biggest blow came when a California jury ordered the company to pay $116 million to the widow of a man who died of cancer after the HMO refused to pay for an experimental treatment. After the verdict, Aetna CEO Richard Huber, who had already got in trouble by calling doctors lazy, made things worse when he told the press, "This is a travesty of justice. You had a skillful ambulance-chasing lawyer, a politically motivated judge, and a weeping widow."

Where had this guy been? Just a year earlier Helen Hunt and Jack Nicholson had both won Academy Awards for their roles in a movie called *As Good As It Gets*, which featured a big bad HMO in the villain's role. Audiences applauded spontaneously when Hunt's character condemned those "Fucking HMO bastard pieces of shit!" for getting between her sick son and his doctor. Nobody liked HMOs, and U.S. Healthcare had an especially bad image problem that was interfering with its business prospects.

By the time Donaldson called me, Aetna's stock had lost half its value in a little more than eight months, and troubles related to the recent acquisition of Prudential's health care unit loomed on the horizon. The board had just fired Huber, and Donaldson was stepping in as CEO. Donaldson said the challenges at the company were even bigger than they appeared. After we talked, he offered me no officer's title, just the label "consultant" and his personal assurance that I would be taken seriously.

Why did I accept? The answer was twofold. First, I respected Donaldson and was eager to work with him. Second, Aetna was in a vital activity—health care—that represented one of the most critical challenges to the continued success of the American economy. For as long as I could remember, the cost of care, driven by new technologies and

an aging population, had increased at a rate much greater than inflation. With most of the insured getting policies through their employers as a benefit, U.S. corporations faced huge costs and a great
disadvantage in the competition with companies in countries where
the government paid for health care. (Car manufacturers estimated
that health care added roughly $1,500 to the price of an American-
made vehicle.) As the largest health care insurer, Aetna was in a position to help with these problems for the good of its shareholders and
the nation. This was my kind of job. And Maggie would be delighted
to remain in New York while I commuted daily by helicopter to either
Aetna headquarters in Hartford or to the U.S. Healthcare main office
in the Philadelphia suburb of Blue Bell.

———————

IN HARTFORD, AETNA occupied a sprawling redbrick structure
considered to be the largest colonial-style building in the country.
With its vaulted copper roof, aging with a green patina, it had the look
and feel of a capitol building in some northeastern state and was fur-
nished with enough antiques to outfit an entire eighteenth-century
town. Although I was just a consultant, I was given former CEO Huber's big office, while Donaldson occupied the only other office on the
spacious top floor. This spot, combined with the way Donaldson introduced me to the staff, made everyone treat me as if I was in charge. It
was a strange and somewhat delightful situation. And it was an amaz-
ing contrast to the situation I had left at Reliance. There I'd had a
fancy title but no authority whatsoever. At Aetna, I wasn't even an employee, but the staff gave me the same respect they would give a
CEO.

The shareholders had demanded Huber's exit, so at the moment
when the directors announced that Donaldson and I had arrived, they
also made Huber's departure official. Though clearly very bright,
Huber had had no previous experience in health care and was a confrontational and openly aggressive executive. He was not the right guy
to run a troubled company engaged in a business as sensitive as health
care. And the only commentator who told the press he would be
missed was a consumer activist who said Huber had been "the best
weapon we had to bolster the case for patients' rights."

My grandfather, D. H. Miller, at a logging operation in 1948. I learned from him the lessons of honesty, hard work, risk taking, and respect for the workers. *Photo courtesy of the author.*

A 1949 photograph of the Moore Mill at Bandon, Oregon, where I spent much of my youth. *Photo courtesy of the author.*

Me and my grandfather at the little house by the mill in 1949. *Photo courtesy of the author.*

My father, Robert S. Miller, a highly successful corporate lawyer in Oregon. *Photo courtesy of the author.*

In 1962, I learned the tough physical demands of working in the logging camps. *Photo courtesy of the author.*

Maggie, the woman to whom I was married nearly forty years, and Chris in Hawaii in 1964, a year before we met.
Photo courtesy of the author.

Maggie in her twenties.
Photo courtesy of the author.

In June 1980, I signed ten thousand documents for the Chrysler loan guarantees.
Photo courtesy of Bowne & Co.

Celebrating with Gerry Greenwald (*left*), Lee Iacocca (*center*), and Fred Zuckerman (*right*) the payoff of Chrysler's guaranteed loans in 1983, seven years ahead of schedule. *Photo courtesy of Chrysler LLC.*

Once we secured the loan guarantees, I called Maggie to tell her the good news. *Photo courtesy of the author.*

With American Motors President Joe Cappy, signing the deal that transferred the Jeep brand to Chrysler in 1986. Perhaps the best deal I ever made! *Photo courtesy of Chrysler LLC.*

Photographed with my brother Randy (*left*), who was a leader in the Oregon legislature for twenty years; my sister Barbara (*center*), who has always been active in community volunteer services; and my brother David (*right*), who has been the president of Moore Mill (now a timberland management company) for more than twenty years. *Photo courtesy of the author.*

With Maggie at the 1988 black-tie season opener of the Detroit Symphony Orchestra (DSO), which may have been my best turnaround ever. *Photo courtesy of the* Detroit News.

Proudly posing with the team I hired to revive the DSO: world-renowned conductor Neeme Jarvi and executive director Deborah Borda. *Photo courtesy of Detroit Symphony Orchestra.*

Sitting in the hot tub in Sunriver in 1994, enjoying life between turnarounds. *Photo courtesy of the author.*

Investment banking partner Jim Wolfenson, later president of the World Bank, stands next to me in 1995 as I express a somewhat exaggerated view of my turnaround capabilities. *Photo courtesy of the author.*

Speaking at the October 2005 press conference in which I announced Delphi's bankruptcy. My misunderstood remarks about paying $65 per hour for mowing the lawn at one of our plants enraged the United Autoworkers union. *Photo © 2007 The Associated Press. All rights reserved.*

The resulting firestorm could not be contained even with my gesture of cutting my salary and bonus to one dollar a year at the beginning of 2006. *Photo courtesy of the* Detroit News.

My three sons gathered for Maggie's sixtieth birthday in 1997. Robin, a lawyer on the Oregon Coast; Alexander, an oboist with the Grand Rapids Symphony; and Chris, who runs a high-tech company in Oregon. *Photo courtesy of the author.*

Addressing thirty thousand people at a 2002 steelworkers rally to support steel tariffs in Washington. Union president Leo Gerard holds the sign that exhorts the crowd responses. *Photo courtesy of the author.*

As the Delphi case was wrapping up, I began a new chapter in my life and married Jill Jablonski in September 2007. *Photo courtesy of Judy Elias/Studio 925.*

Huber's style, which was transmitted down the ranks to shape the entire corporate culture, had demoralized the rank and file. I discovered this on my early visits to various offices, where people confessed that they were reluctant to tell their neighbors what company they worked for because almost everyone had something negative to say about Aetna. This low morale stood in stark contrast to the old, pre-HMO days, when Aetna was a highly regarded, even beloved institution.

Physicians I met had nothing but complaints about the company. They resented U.S. Healthcare's gatekeepers, who required substantial documentation before approving treatments, and they were incensed over declining compensation and increasing workloads.

Doctors said that the U.S. Healthcare reviewers kept them on the phone for forty-five minutes, gathering data on routine procedures, and too often tried to overrule them on decisions that really should be handled by caregivers and patients.

The U.S. Healthcare policies that made doctors so unhappy were intended to curb costs and improve the bottom line. The strategy worked but had other consequences. Doctors and patients both grew to dislike the company and refused to renew policies and service contracts. Employers got an earful from workers who were unhappy with their health coverage. With enough complaints they might kick us off the list of HMO and insurance options, making it impossible for us to offer coverage to their employees.

As you can see, it is entirely possible for an HMO to make itself so difficult to deal with that paying customers turn away in droves. U.S. Healthcare, which accounted for 70 percent of Aetna's business, was on the way to accomplishing this sad feat. The solution, as it so often is with troubled companies, would require time, money, and a change of management culture.

The first two elements of the solution, time and money, could be had with a single counterintuitive move: selling the parts of Aetna— foreign operations, financial services, and other business—that were profitable. This may sound strange since those businesses were generating cash, but those revenues were what made them attractive to potential buyers. Nobody wanted to buy an HMO network that was on the rocks. But by selling the other units we could focus on the sick business of health care and prepare it to succeed. Considering the aging of the baby boomer generation and the growing population, health care had the greatest potential for long-term growth. Prospects were further improved by higher demand for more expensive policies with greater flexibility and benefits. If U.S. Healthcare could offer these products, in addition to more cost-conscious options, there was profit to be had.

In a short time, weeks really, a deal was fashioned to sell Aetna's businesses other than U.S. Healthcare to the Dutch bank ING, which was eager to get into the U.S. market for financial services. Out of proceeds of about $8 billion, Aetna's stockholders received a special one-time dividend of $35 cash per share. The remaining shares were worth about half that, but it was a pure play on the turnaround of the health business.

Fixing the culture at U.S. Healthcare would take a little more time. In Hartford we organized groups of midlevel executives to study our problems and suggest solutions. I told the participants that I didn't want to hear them report on ideas from their bosses. I wanted them to give me their perspective as managers in the trenches.

At U.S. Healthcare's operations center in Blue Bell we discovered a demoralized workforce dominated by managers who had created the in-your-face cost control system that put heavy pressure on health care providers and patients. These were the people who by the year 2000 had made physicians and customers so angry that no one wanted to do business with them. As we began to remake the company, these superaggressive types were let go, and we replaced them with more flexible and responsive managers who were customer oriented.

News of the firings in Blue Bell signaled a change of direction that impressed the corporate benefits managers who controlled whether we could offer our plans to workers at hundreds of companies. We helped our image further by settling lawsuits in several states and adopting new policies to give doctors and patients more power over treatment decisions. Rules requiring referrals before patients could see specialists were eased, and the system for paying physicians was changed so that they could be compensated for each visit with a U.S. Healthcare participant. Previously they were paid a flat monthly fee per patient, who could make unlimited numbers of appointments.

Guess what happened? Many patients doubled their annual visits, coming in for every little sniffle and sneeze, and the docs were overwhelmed.

Overworked as they may have been, physicians did educate themselves about the world of managed care and became almost as keen as investors when it came to assessing big moves at our corporate headquarters. For this reason we moved very carefully as we pursued a CEO to replace Huber and free both Donaldson and me of our temporary duties. We tried at first to woo Leonard Schaeffer at a California-based health care company called Wellpoint Health Networks, which *Fortune* called one of the fifty best companies in the country. Schaffer was an ideal candidate for U.S. Healthcare, but he was so emotionally attached to the work he was doing at WellPoint that there was no way we could lure him to Hartford.

The next person on our list was a physician with a specialty in geriatrics who was author of the leading medical textbook in his field and CEO of the Mount Sinai-NYU Hospitals/Health System in New York City. John W. Rowe had orchestrated the merger of the system's two big components—NYU Medical Center and Mount Sinai Medical Center—and got them to work together efficiently and productively. He was that rare creature we needed, a doctor with business sense, but before he would join us we had to persuade him that we would respect his colleagues, the ones who were healers.

"Aetna?" said Rowe the first time we spoke. "Why would I want to come to Aetna? I'm *suing* Aetna."

In fact, Rowe was involved in a suit filed by twenty-four New York–area hospitals accusing Aetna of deceptive practices, delaying payments in violation of state law, and violating contracts. The complaints all predated my arrival, and I told Rowe that the problems were a legacy of the old Aetna, the one run by the guys who tried to deny every claim. As we talked further he came to appreciate that we were changing for the better and that we offered him a big role in addressing the nation's health care issues. Troubled as the company was, Aetna's health care programs served twenty million people, more than any other private operator in the country. If our industry was going to be part of the solution for health care, Aetna would have to lead the way.

Once he understood the opportunity and was certain we were sincere, Dr. Rowe took the leap. On the day his hiring was announced he told the press, "We can deal with doctors and hospitals in an environment of respect. Trying to just make money on the backs of them is stupid."

In this case the shoe fit perfectly. With his empathy for doctors and patients, Rowe would say and do all the right things to repair our relationships with providers and customers. No longer charged with policing every prescription and bandage issued to patients, our management centers were able to streamline their operations, which led to both cost savings and better medical care. As the company's reputation improved, more people would opt for Aetna coverage during their annual health insurance review. And in a little more than five years, with Rowe at the helm all the way, the company's stock would increase almost 400 percent in value. Good medicine would turn out to be good business.

————

THANKS TO WILLIAM Donaldson, my nine months at Aetna would stand out as one of the most satisfying if brief episodes in my career. Donaldson wisely recognized that with a history going back to before the Civil War, the company was filled with proud and capable people who just needed support to fix what was wrong. By September 2000, when Dr. Rowe took office and I departed, the direction was already set. Aetna was going to recover, and everyone in the private health care triad—doctors, patients, and the insurer—would benefit.

Coming after Reliance, the experience at Aetna reinforced my confidence in the ideal of business done honestly with the interests of all—owners, managers, workers, customers, and community—taken into consideration. Also, the extra nine months in New York, where Maggie and I soaked up culture and had the kind of social life that was not available anywhere else was also a great reward. The two of us would remember this time as one of the best in our lives.

But unfortunately, my look behind the scenes at health care in America didn't reveal any immediate solutions for the problems of rising costs, which overburden companies, and the forty million people who have no health insurance at all. The uninsured pose several problems. They often fail to get care early in the course of an illness and as a result, need much more expensive treatment once they do seek help. This problem can bankrupt families and drain money from hospitals that are required by law to provide care.

In time, the challenge of the uninsured would prove exceedingly stubborn. Middle-class families would be strained by insurance premiums, and major industries, like the Big Three in Detroit, would be staggered by the cost of providing coverage for current employees and retirees. Health insurance added roughly $1,500 to the cost of each car they made, which was more than the amount paid for the steel used in the same vehicle. Since no other industrialized nation in the world burdened business with this cost, manufacturers abroad had a distinct advantage whether they were making cars, computers, or toys.

At Aetna we possessed one of the most developed systems in the country for delivering health care, and we knew something about how better management and cooperative relationships reduced costs and improved patient health. But it seemed clear to me that much more creative thinking would have to be applied to the big issues around our industry. As a nation we couldn't keep relying on corporations to pay ever-higher costs, and as human beings we had to be concerned about those, especially children, who fell outside the current system.

People across the country had been talking about the health care crisis for more than a decade. The outlines of the problem are clear enough. Health care delivery depended heavily on information, but our systems were hamstrung by excessive concerns about confidentiality, making it very difficult to manage data efficiently. Lawsuits and the threat of lawsuits forced health care providers to make high malpractice insurance payments and practice expensive defensive medicine, ordering every test under the sun to protect themselves from second-guessers. Too many people lacked access to basic preventive care that could forestall much more costly illnesses later. And both the aging of the population and the constant development of pricey new treatments were driving greater demand for services.

Among business leaders, politicians, and experts, the consensus about the nature of the challenge in health care was broad, and most seemed to agree that something had to be done. But here the conversation always seemed to get bogged down. We hadn't yet reached the moment when economic and political conditions would force a decision. Soon enough, however, I would get a chance to see, close up, the ultimate price we could pay for waiting too long.

Ten

STEEL DRIVING MAN

Nature offers many universal lessons. Consider the basic truth about destructive weather systems. By the time you see the clouds on the horizon, you can be certain that the storm has already ravaged someone else. Things work the same way in our economy. Structural problems generally sweep slowly through businesses and industries, affecting vulnerable sectors first but eventually reaching stronger ones. This was certainly how the health care challenge worked. In the 1980s and 1990s alarms sounded everywhere, but the problem was most serious for shaky companies and poorer individuals. It was easy for many to believe that the reckoning could be put off until tomorrow.

Tomorrow arrived for an icon of the venerable American steel industry in the fall of 2001, a year after I had left Aetna. At that moment Bethlehem Steel was being driven toward bankruptcy by, among other things, a health care bill for 130,000 dependents—mostly retired employees and spouses—that exceeded $280 million per year. This expense, combined with pensions, high-cost labor contracts, and intense competition at home and abroad had produced huge losses. Then, with the terrorist attacks of September 11, the entire economy went into a stall. Steel orders dried up, and the directors of Bethlehem had to acknowledge that the company faced a life-or-death crisis for which the incumbent management was not well equipped. One of their board members, a New York lawyer named Lew Kaden, tracked me down in Salt Lake City, where Maggie and I were attending a model train show and doing a bit of genealogy work (her growing passion) at the famous Mormon Family History Library.

By this time I seemed to be on everyone's short list for corporate crisis jobs. I was fully comfortable in these roles, even though others avoided them because they feared failure. What they didn't seem to grasp, however, was the tremendous freedom that comes with these assignments. It's like being the backup quarterback called into a game in the fourth quarter when it seems that all is lost. Ever notice how many times a replacement player who is given carte blanche to take chances, throw passes, and call plays actually wins the game? It happens more often that you might expect. And nobody blames him if the game is lost instead.

In the case of Bethlehem Steel I got the call about a week after 9/11, when everyone in America felt a strong sense of duty and the urge to do something for their country. Few corporations had played such a critical role in America's growth as an industrial and military power, and Bethlehem was still a functioning, strategically important national asset. They had produced six million tons of steel since the start of the year and were an important source for some vital material. For example, Bethlehem had provided the armor plate that was used to repair the USS *Cole* after it was attacked by Al Qaeda in 2000. No other company was capable of making the stuff.

Once America's post-9/11 skies were opened again to commercial flights, I kissed Maggie good-bye at the Salt Lake City airport and flew to New York for dinner with Bethlehem's directors. I said, "You guys probably don't know how bad it is. It's usually worse than you might think." We talked about ethics and business principles. I told them to drop any concerns they might have about my salary. "The job sounds interesting. You need my help. I'll take it with enthusiasm. You can decide later what to pay me—I will just assure you that compensation will not be an issue." Leaving the pay issue up to them seemed the right thing to do. I trusted they would be fair, and I wasn't interested in a laborious negotiation that might delay starting the work.

––––––––––

BETHLEHEM STEEL—FOUNDED BY Charles M. Schwab in 1904—helped power America through two world wars and to the top of the global economy. Its gradual decline, matched by the decline of the entire industry, was practically a case study on the effects of rigid union contracts, globalization, and technological change. The contract issues were similar to the ones affecting the auto business. When times were good Big Steel and the United Steelworkers had loaded all sorts of benefits for both workers and retirees into their contracts. Then global competition (much of it from companies subsidized by foreign governments) and new technology in the form of small mills that turned scrap into new product brought low-priced steel into America. As their market share declined, the fully integrated companies that made virgin steel from iron ore kept cutting back until there was too little income and too few active employees to support benefits for a vast number of retirees.

As so often happens when you're talking about a slow-motion crisis, most people don't act fast enough, or with enough creativity, to fix the problem before it gets very bad. In the American steel industry the exception was the United States Steel Corporation, which had expanded overseas and further protected itself with the acquisition of Marathon Oil. Virtually all the other big American companies had failed to find a similarly successful strategy and continued to slide toward oblivion.

A book could be written (actually, many *have* been written) on the rise and fall of Big Steel. Fortunately, my task in September 2001 didn't require that I learn everything that had brought us to the brink of disaster. Instead I needed to assess the company's prospects based on a reliable inventory of its assets and liabilities and get a good read on the people—executives, union leaders, etc.—who held key positions.

For a very sick company, Bethlehem operated some very impressive and productive facilities, including huge blast furnaces and mills near Baltimore and Chicago. The company made everything from railroad rails and bridge girders to flexible and resilient sheet metal for cars. Bethlehem also operated several short-line railroads to move materials at its mills. Although our roster couldn't compare with the three hundred thousand employees who worked for Bethlehem during the production boom demanded by World War II, the company still employed thirteen thousand, and just about all of them earned much more than a typical industrial worker.

The steelworkers who remained on the payroll were, by and large, very skilled or brave or both, as my tour of the sprawling complex at

Sparrows Point, near Baltimore, revealed. Dominated by a huge blast furnace, it is a place where molten iron flows from suspended "ladles" big enough to hold a couple of cars. The heat is so great that even men wearing fireproof clothing can work no more than a few minutes in the most hazardous spots before retreating.

Along with the blast furnace, Sparrows Point operated slab-making machinery to create massive blocks of steel and several different plants for reheating, pounding, stretching, and shaping this basic material into different sizes and weights. Between the noise, heat, smoke, and fire, it was the closest thing to hell on earth I had ever seen. The place was also magnificent, a monument to American industry, and far more lively than the scene in the company's hometown of Bethlehem, Pennsylvania.

Once home to facilities that rivaled Sparrows Point, Bethlehem had ceased to produce any steel at all in the mid-1990s. The massive buildings, smokestacks, and piping at the hometown mill remained, however, looming over the city like an army of giant alien robot monsters. These hulking and decaying facilities, which were visible from the office tower where top managers still worked, were constant reminders of the company's better days. Indeed, wherever you went in Bethlehem you got the feeling that you were in a once prosperous, even mighty place that was in rapid decline. Grand old Victorian houses that once were homes for middle-class families had become run-down makeshift apartment buildings. Sturdy row houses built in the prewar era for the families of men who walked to the mills for work went begging for tenants despite some of the lowest rents on the East Coast.

The scenery in Bethlehem was depressing. The mood was worse inside the company's twenty-three-story headquarters building—called Martin Tower—where I found the most discouraged team I have ever encountered in a troubled corporation. This once-great company had been struggling against negative trends and bad news for more than a generation. But somehow people still clung to the memory of the good old days and couldn't really accept that they were over. I imagine this is what it felt like during the fall of the Roman Empire, when everyone accepted that the glory days were finished, except the Romans themselves.

In its waning days, Rome was administered by a figurehead who lacked many essential skills, and so it was at Bethlehem Steel, where a terrific salesman named Duane Dunham had been put in charge even though he possessed few of the qualities required to lead a huge industrial company in a financial crisis. He would soon retire. In the ranks below were many managers who ran the company as if it still had three hundred thousand workers. They lacked the energy, creativity, and candor we needed. This was brought home to me when I came into the office on a Sunday and discovered a whole crowd of folks in a conference room, laboring with the chief financial officer over some commentary to go on a chart they were to present to me the next day. What a monumental waste of everyone's time.

As I soon learned, the CFO was so afraid of the bankruptcy bogeyman that he had soft-pedaled signs of trouble for months prior to my arrival. In fact, his head-in-the-sand forecasts seemed designed to avoid even talking about the bankruptcy option. This seemed absurd given that the company pension plan was $2 billion short and the pending bill for health care was another $3 billion. These so-called legacy costs added about $60 to the $300 price of a ton of steel.

Within a week, I replaced the CFO with one of his key men, a younger executive named Len Anthony, who proved to be the ideal person for the tough job we faced. We found others within the company to promote into key positions as we took out one entire layer of management as part of our effort to make ourselves leaner and more efficient. Len and several others would emerge as allies in the struggle to salvage this iconic company and its people. Another important partner would be a Canadian-born steelworker named Leo Gerard, who had just become president of the United Steelworkers union. I went to visit him my first week on the job.

Having dealt with rather hidebound and closed-minded union leaders in Detroit, I was wary about what I'd encounter when I went to visit the main offices of the United Steelworkers of America, in Pittsburgh. The union, born in militancy during the Great Depression, had long passed its heyday, when wages, benefits, and membership were certain to remain sky high. Now it faced inevitable declines in membership as steel required fewer and fewer man-hours. Wages and benefits were destined to come down, and retired members could not assume their pensions and health insurance were going to last, even though I wanted to protect them.

Despite having much to fear and resent, the union leaders I met, especially Gerard and his behind-the-scenes strategist Ron Bloom, were remarkably practical and focused on the present problem. A smart guy who knew more about the business than I did, Gerard had thought through the problems and accepted that change was coming. Of course the solution he suggested, bankruptcy, was a trauma that Bethlehem's management had been trying to avoid. "But you can get the creditors off your back," he argued, "and our union knows how to deal with bankruptcies." He didn't have to say that under the bankruptcy laws Bethlehem's responsibilities under the union contract would take priority over most other obligations. For this reason, bankruptcy was the best option for the union workers.

To his credit, Gerard was considering more than the immediate relief that bankruptcy offered. He also was thinking about the long-term health of steelmaking in all of North America, and wanted to force a restructuring of the industry that might create a small number of bigger companies capable of competing around the world. As a stimulus for consolidation, bankruptcy might help someone to gather up the best parts of Bethlehem, perhaps add some other good pieces, and create a high-functioning modern steel company. This new firm would need fewer workers, but their jobs would be secure.

Gerard and I both knew that the game clock was running down and the moment for decisive action had arrived. With the post-9/11 business crisis drying up our orders, it took weeks, not months, for bankruptcy to emerge as the only option. Finance specialists came around to offer debtor-in-possession loans that would let up keep operating. The best offer, by $100 million, came from GE Capital. General Electric didn't become the most successful company in the world by playing soft. As lenders, they were as tough as the mafia and had a reputation for punishing borrowers who slipped in the slightest way. Wary of this, I called Jeffrey Immelt, who had become the CEO of GE, succeeding the legendary Jack Welch on September 7.

Fortunately, Bethlehem Steel was still a big-name company, and as the CEO I could get a guy like Immelt, whom I'd never met, on the phone. I told him we really appreciated GE's offer, which would make

$450 million available to us right away. "But I've got to know one thing," I said. "If we get into a rough patch will you work with us, or will you pull my fingernails out?"

"We'll work with you," he said.

That was all the reassurance I needed. We signed the DIP loan with GE, giving them a favored position among our creditors, and then went to federal bankruptcy court in New York to file for protection under the law known as Chapter 11. The news wasn't unexpected in the company's hometown, where for many decades they had mourned the incremental shutdown of the mill complex along the Lehigh River. Still it was covered on the front page in the local paper, the *Morning Call*, which did a pretty good job describing the goals we would pursue, which included reducing cost, seeking government help on cheap imports, and possible consolidation in the industry. In the meantime we were going to keep making steel, as always, and deliver it to our customers. The last thing we wanted to do was let our furnaces go cold, because once you let that happen, they virtually self-destruct, and it can be hugely expensive to fire them up again.

———

THE BOOK OF news clippings distributed throughout headquarters by our public relations office on the day after our Chapter 11 filing was about an inch thick. Anyone who glanced through it would have thought that I must be completely overwhelmed with demands for my time and attention. This was partly true. We were all scrambling. But experience had taught me the steps we needed to take, and I was ready to make the necessary moves in a calm and steady way. I had already started talking with Thomas Usher, CEO of U.S. Steel, about a merger. We were also working with industry and union leaders to get relief from Washington on unfair imports. And strange as it may seem, I never feel more at ease than when I'm dealing with a large number of troublesome issues at the start of a big mission.

Though Bethlehem Steel had entered new territory, things really were under control and there was no reason why we couldn't operate in a normal manner. (This was another reason why I thought that the CFO's Sunday work session simply to massage a report for me was kind of dumb.) Maggie came east to share a pleasant little apartment I had taken a few miles out of downtown Bethlehem in an area of rolling hills and horse farms. The place was close enough to New York that we could spend the day or an evening in Manhattan and still be back in Bethlehem at night. It was also smack in the middle of a region with enough historic places—Gettysburg, Philadelphia, Valley Forge, Washington—to satisfy anyone like Maggie who has a passion for the past.

Beginning with our visits to historic sites as tourists and then her own amateur archaeology in Mexico, Maggie had shown a true devotion to history. But in the mid-1990s it became a more personal thing. I had gone shopping during a break from business in San Francisco and stumbled upon a computer program for genealogy. I bought it for Maggie, and one day, when she had the time, she loaded it into her computer and began filling in some data. Genealogy can be like a never-ending crossword puzzle, with fascinating stories connected to all the answers. Maggie was hooked. She often spent eighteen hours a day online, made connections with others doing similar work, and tracked down leads like a true detective. Ultimately, her database included fifty thousand of our closest relatives.

Although she did trace several generations in my family, Maggie was mainly interested in her lineage, and Bethlehem was a great base for research on the extended Kyger (also known as Geiger) clan. Many had first settled in America in nearby Pennsylvania "Dutch" (really Swiss and German) communities. On excursions from our Bethlehem apartment we found records of their lives in courthouses, graveyards, and archives. (The Lancaster County Historical Society was an especially valuable source.). We eventually traced Kygers to the Shenandoah Valley and found some who fought for the Confederacy during the Civil War.

Maggie's research led her to contact distant relatives who sometimes held valuable papers and artifacts. One, the diary of a relative who took part in the Oklahoma land rush, described how she and her husband had staked out a claim in the new territory and endured incredible hardships. Maggie got a particular kick out of peeling back the glossy veneer that people pasted onto accounts of their lives to find things they had tried to hide. In one instance she even discovered an out-of-wedlock child that a certain ancestor had been determined to wipe from the records.

Together we enjoyed both the trips to the countryside and scouring dusty old records. Of course this work was confined mainly to weekends, since I was otherwise busy with Bethlehem Steel. When I wasn't available, Maggie continued her work online and by telephone, but she chose not to make outings on her own, even though valuable records might lie in some archive or library. At the time I didn't think too much of her decision, but later I would recall that her confidence and spatial abilities—finding her way around, reading a map—took a nosedive in this period. Even in Manhattan, where she once navigated easily on streets that are mainly laid out in a numbered grid, Maggie had trouble orienting herself. Though I blamed it on age—she was sixty-four—in time I would have to wonder if these difficulties were early signs of the brain cancer that would too soon take her away.

———————

THROUGH THE FALL and early winter, executives at U.S. Steel and Bethlehem continued to discuss the idea of a merger and even explored adding two or three more big producers to create a megacompany with the capacity to ship thirty million tons of steel annually. This would be almost twice the volume that U.S. Steel could produce on its own, but it wouldn't come close to matching the output envisioned by a European group that was working on an even bigger deal for a fifty-million-ton company.

This scale was a necessity in a market where producers the world over competed with the advantage of much lower wages and aid from local governments. But a megamerger was not the only option. In bankruptcy we could also sell Bethlehem in its entirety to a new entity or break it up and sell the pieces. Either way, the postbankruptcy operators would have the great advantage of getting out from under the burden of supporting health care and pensions for all those retirees.

At the same time, the entire U.S. industry would benefit if federal tariffs were imposed on steel being shipped from certain countries—China, Japan, South Korea, and others—that seemed to be dumping artificially low-priced metal on the U.S. market. Of course as a capitalist and free trader, I generally oppose government efforts to protect industries or limit competition. But when a large, strategically vital industry needs temporary assistance, I can see that protections may be needed, especially if other countries seem to be up to some mischief.

This was the argument I made on periodic visits to Washington to meet with Secretary of Commerce Donald Evans and trade ambassador Robert Zoellick. (Sometimes Leo Gerard and I went together to make the case in person.) Both seemed receptive, and the United States International Trade Commission had found the industry was eligible for protections. However, there were many in the Bush administration who opposed tariffs as a matter of principle. They were joined by certain business leaders who shared this philosophy and others who wanted steel at the lowest possible price, regardless of where it was made. I spoke with a few of them, including car guys I once worked with in Detroit. Their position was logical, and in their place I might have made the same argument (Give me my supplies at the lowest market price!). But while they might have loved cheap steel, it was not the basis for a long-term business plan because if they allowed the American industry to be destroyed, they might one day be at the mercy of foreign suppliers who could control both price and availability. Think about it: who would get a Korean steel mill's output first when supplies were short, Ford or Hyundai?

On the tariff issue, Bethlehem and the union had a common objective, which put me in the odd position of joining thirty thousand steelworkers and their allies for a rally near the White House on the last day of February 2002. I proudly wore my union jacket (a gift from their leadership) and carried a sign with a message about unfair imports. The rally was an emotionally powerful mix of patriotism (it began with the *Star-Spangled Banner*), demagoguery, and the occasional reasoned argument. A whole parade of senators and representatives stirred the passions of the crowd. I gave a short speech that allowed me to play call-and-response with the crowd, which roared with the cry, "Unfair imports!" each time I asked them to tell the world why their industry needed help. It was an exhilarating *Norma Rae* kind of moment, and it helped me understand the powerful emotional attachment some people feel toward their union experience.

What a long way I had come. By nature and education, I was a free marketeer who favored Darwinian competition on a global scale. But just as I had been willing to bend to seek government help for Chrysler, I was again making a special plea to the Feds for an ailing giant.

The difference this time, however, was that we were seeking relief from foreign subsidies that were well documented, and we were looking only for temporary shelter, not a huge long-term loan.

Fortunately, the administration came through just days after the rally, imposing tariffs ranging from 8 to 30 percent on foreign shipments from the countries where local producers got unfair help from their governments. Politics played a role in the details, with the highest tariffs placed on products that competed with stuff made in West Virginia, where the president had made a campaign pledge to protect a big mill in Weirton. And foreign policy considerations led to exemptions for Canada, Mexico, and a few others. Overall, the tariffs, while hurting some big steel customers like automakers, would help us keep our mills going. However, the tariffs did not move us any closer to a massive restructuring of our industry or a long-term scheme for keeping thousands of steelworkers employed. And fear of the future still hung over Bethlehem.

IT WOULD BE easy to look at a company with $1 billion worth of assets and $7 billion in unfunded obligations to retired workers and conclude there's nothing worth salvaging. But in fact, many of the plants that Bethlehem operated were fairly up-to-date and placed in strategic locations, either near key customers or with access to national and international shipping routes. The Sparrows Point facility, recently refurbished at a cost of hundreds of millions of dollars, was one of the best blast furnace complexes in the world. If these facilities could be kept in operation under competitive pay and benefit schemes, they would employ thousands of workers and contribute billions of dollars annually to the U.S. economy.

Sparrows Point seemed a perfect fit for a major Brazilian steelmaker called CSN, which operated a similar blast furnace complex about a hundred miles away from Rio de Janeiro. I brought a union delegation with me to visit CSN and tour their mine at Casa de Pedra, which was one of the biggest open-pit iron mines in the world. (As an aside, it's informative to note that I had to fight Bethlehem Steel's bureaucracy to get business class air tickets for these union representatives. I wasn't about to ask them to travel less comfortably than me.) The

CSN blast furnace and mills were comparable to ours, but the mine was like nothing I had seen before. It was as big as the Grand Canyon, and it was run with great efficiency. Big earth-scooping machines dug and poured ore into railroad cars that went to a highly automated port facility. It was plain to see that the Brazilians could easily increase their production of this low cost/high quality ore, send it straight to Sparrows Point, and produce steel at a very competitive price.

We saw similar advantages for a European company called Arcelor in a takeover of Bethlehem's integrated steel plant at Burns Harbor, Indiana, which supplied U.S. automakers. Located right on the shoreline of Lake Michigan, the big facility at Burns Harbor was one of the most efficient steelmaking complexes in the country and could be served by deep-water vessels capable of delivering its products worldwide. In acquiring the sprawling Indiana complex, Arcelor, a recently formed behemoth with no production in the United States, would instantly become a major force in North America. After visits to their headquarters in Luxembourg and plants in France and Belgium, it was clear to me the Arcelor had the strength to manage a big acquisition in the States, and they did seem eager to do business with U.S. auto companies.

The mating dances we had to perform over selling pieces of Bethlehem were extremely complex. Given the company's importance in Bethlehem, local reporters covered each step. I reassured them that I was trying to find "the best, strongest, most logical partner" for each plant. And they took hope when the Brazilians toured Sparrows Point in March 2002. They probably didn't know that CSN was contemplating another huge deal—merging with the British company Corus—and that might distract them from the Sparrows Point proposal.

Also, since any new owner would still have to negotiate with the steelworkers union, the outcome of any sale would depend on them as a third party. And in the end, Leo Gerard did not want to follow our lead. He believed that a breakup, with facilities in different communities going to separate buyers, wouldn't create the kind of strong global competitor that would preserve jobs in America. "I'm looking for the next Andrew Carnegie," he said. This meant that he hoped that a single entity, perhaps even a solitary wealthy man, would come along to consolidate the American steel industry and make it boom as Carnegie did in the late nineteenth century.

A VERY BALD, very plain-looking man, Wilbur Ross lacked Andrew Carnegie's strong chin, thick white hair, dancing eyes, and dapper style. But from an early age he had shown Carnegie-like energy and ambition. (As a teen he commuted two hours each way to attend a special high school.) After a hugely successful career in finance, where he cleaned up after bankruptcies and other debacles, he began building his own businesses with $400 million from investors who knew his capabilities. But while others chased esoteric new technologies and financial schemes, he sought to make investments in basic industries like steel.

In early 2002 Ross bought most of the assets of the bankrupt LTV Corporation in a deal that allowed him to avoid the old operator's legacy costs and forge a new relationship with the union. His International Steel Group (ISG) would establish new work rules, and pay arrangements gave managers greater flexibility to use union employees in various roles and eliminated old retirement benefits. At the same time, ISG's hourly workers would get many opportunities to earn bonuses based on their own productivity. In short, if they made more quality steel in fewer hours, their paychecks would get fatter.

The mini mills and ISG model represented the future for steel in America, and I said as much in a letter to Leo. "They kill us on hours per ton," I noted, and though most were not capable of producing key products like sheet metal for cars, "our exclusive turf gets smaller every day." I also told him that in my opinion Bethlehem was "hopelessly bankrupt" and that we needed to work quickly if we were to salvage any of the working plants and the jobs they provided.

Leo responded well, opening sincere negotiations with Ross and his associates. Soft-spoken like your wisest uncle, Wilbur had a way of getting along with union leaders and would work with Leo to set up a new kind of contract that would allow him to run the old Bethlehem mills competitively.

I was grateful that Leo and Wilbur could work well together because in the fall of the year I was diagnosed with prostate cancer and had to take some time out for surgery and recovery. Others have written at length about this all-too-common type of cancer, its treatment, and the necessity of regular screening tests. Like most patients, I checked out the many options for treatment, eventually choosing to have surgery done by Patrick Walsh, a specialist at Johns Hopkins who literally wrote the book on prostate cancer.

With Maggie's support and great care at the hospital, I sailed through surgery. (It was done under local anesthesia, and I was so alert I could hear the doctors talking baseball.) I did hit a squall in the recovery room, however, when my heart actually stopped for a short time and I passed out. From what I was told, all sorts of excitement ensued as I was revived, but I was unaware until it was over and I woke up. If that's what death is like, I thought, it's pretty boring.

Recovery was quicker than I expected, and I returned to work on a light schedule after about three weeks, but it would take months for my body to adjust to the new plumbing configuration. In the meantime I learned there are plenty of men out there willing to offer support and encouragement. I got a chance to compare notes with Senator John Kerry when I ran into him at the Philadelphia train station. He had been operated on by the same surgeon a week after me. As a crowd gathered around us, he asked me the most intimate questions about postoperative incontinence and impotence. All things considered, I'd have preferred to talk policy with him, rather than acknowledge we were both part of the postsurgery brotherhood, but being a cancer survivor sure beats the alternative.

Thanks to good luck, and a good team at Martin Tower, none of the business problems I was dealing with as I entered the hospital blew up before I returned to my office. Wilbur Ross had used the time to put the finishing touches on a $1.5 billion bid to fold Bethlehem into ISG. Because ISG was a completely new entity, it wouldn't be liable for the old retirement benefits. Further savings would be achieved by closing Bethlehem's headquarters and consolidating sales and other professional staff.

The deal was about the best anyone could hope for. I believed I could get my board of directors to approve, and Leo Gerard was fairly certain he would be able to sell it to union members. In general they trusted him, but that doesn't mean that everyone understood his strategy. During the long negotiations with Wilbur Ross, some steelworkers had distributed leaflets suggesting that food be stockpiled to support a sit-down strike. "Once we are inside we weld the door shut from the inside and dare them to come get us," they wrote. But these militants didn't gain much support, and when Leo eventually explained the deal to the rank and file, they accepted it because it meant the union would survive to participate in a new and more competitive industry.

THE RESULT WAS mixed. I was unhappy with the result on pensions and health care benefits for retirees. In every previous crisis I had managed, we had saved the pension system and kept health care in place for everyone. The last thing I wanted to do was stick the federal government with a $3.5 billion obligation for the pension plan and watch health care for retirees simply evaporate. But if the new operators were going to succeed and contribute to the future wealth of the country, they needed to be freed from these burdens. The PBGC would have to step in, and in the process the rest of the nation would be alerted to the larger problem of old-fashioned pension plans, which were no longer sustainable.

Some younger retirees opposed the LTV-style solution. Given that they would lose their health insurance and still not be old enough for Medicare, it was no wonder that a handful peacefully picketed headquarters with placards reading, "Don't Let Bethlehem Steel Our Benefits." But while they had a right to complain, these people would retain at least some of their monthly incomes, thanks to the PBGC. Shareholders were going to be wiped out, and thousands of others workers, most of them nonunion employees, were going to lose their jobs and benefits and be forced to start over completely. The best I could do for some of them was to insist that Wilbur Ross fund a severance plan. He resisted at first, but after a caucus with advisers agreed to it.

Ideally, we would have had more than one suitor, and members of the Bethlehem board certainly hoped for some competition to up the ante. But as I reported to them in periodic letters, Ross was the only investor with the resources, vision, and money to carry out the kind of transaction that would transform the Bethlehem plants into a functional steelmaking operation. Equally important, he had the confidence of Leo Gerard and the ability to implement the LTV-type labor agreement at Bethlehem's facilities. By the start of 2003 the board accepted this in principle and Ross submitted a formal proposal. The business press was on top of the story. In a nod to the risk that Ross was taking, the headline in the *New York Times* noted, "A Contrarian Bets That Steel Has a Future."

The *Times* was correct, at least for those burdened with conventional wisdom about the steel business. But anyone who studied the landscape as thoroughly as he did would agree with Wilbur about the future of steelmaking under the new rules he had fashioned with Leo Gerard. If the deal was consummated, Ross's company would become the largest producer in America—with a capacity of more than sixteen million tons per year—positioned to compete well with overseas mills and with the nimble "mini mills" that transformed scrap into new product.

To make the deal happen, Ross and I went to Washington to lobby the PBGC, where we got a fair hearing and a request for a big stack of documents. (They needed facts and figures before they could declare our pension plan insolvent and take it over.) We also saw key officials in the Bush administration and Congress, all of whom seemed to understand that Ross was making the one and only offer that might yield something positive from Bethlehem's bankruptcy. Weeks would pass before all the pieces came together. In the meantime, others began to recognize that the time was right for consolidation. U.S. Steel, for example, offered nearly $1 billion for National Steel, an acquisition that would allow them to raise their domestic market share.

In mid-February 2003, Bethlehem's board approved the sale, closing the cover on the story of a once-great company that was one year shy of its hundredth birthday. For everyone involved, and most especially the local community, it was a sober moment. Over time, perhaps a million people had worked for Bethlehem Steel, possibly more. "The Steel," as so many called the company, had been a source of wealth, pride, and even identity, and now it had gone the way of all living things. But they could take solace in what they had accomplished. In a very real and tangible way they had built modern America, and many of their contributions—bridges, skyscrapers, railroads, and more—would stand for generations to come.

There was comfort for me, too, in the outcome of the Bethlehem story. Yes, employees and retirees and creditors and stockholders had been forced to accept losses. But I had also contributed, along with Wilbur Ross and Leo Gerard and many others, to the transformation and preservation of the American steel industry. At year's end, as President Bush lifted tariffs and declared they had "done their job," all six of the major steelmaking complexes that were part of Bethlehem Steel when I arrived were running strong and producing steel with significantly fewer man-hours per ton. Labor and management were working together as never before. Imports were down. America was again exporting steel to other countries. And we may have even set an example for other major industries bearing huge legacy costs and needing dramatic reforms in order to face the future.

Eleven

MOTOWN MAELSTROM

Old dogs may have trouble learning new tricks, but there's something to be said for a hound who has been around. Experience, especially in a landscape that is strange and frightening, inspires confidence and improves the odds. A corporate meltdown with bankruptcy looming will spook anyone who hasn't been through a similar crisis. But as I became familiar with this territory, I actually felt drawn to its most forbidding corners. In the Delphi case I hoped to use everything I had learned to lead one the world's largest corporations—number sixty-three on the Fortune 500—through the wilderness.

The call from Delphi—a story told at the start of this book— brought Maggie and me back to Detroit, where we had started the adventure of our long married life. We may have been a little creaky and less energetic than we had been during our first tour of duty in Motor City, but there was a depth and a level of understanding in our relationship that was much greater. And on the professional front, I never felt more prepared and motivated to help a company losing close to $1 billion every quarter.

Long service with Ford and Chrysler had given me perspective on the auto industry, while my stints at Federal-Mogul and Bethlehem had taught me about the high-pressure business of supplying auto manufacturers. I knew many of the important people and all of the key issues—foreign competition, outdated union contracts, health care, etc.—because they had been boiling since the 1970s. Some might say that better people than me had tried to resolve them. But I hoped that I had some advantages.

First, I was parachuting in from the outside, with little excess baggage. This was especially important considering that the Delphi crisis included a widely reported accounting scandal going back to the year 2000. Earnings had been overstated by about $80 million. No one directly profited personally and the numbers were corrected, but the federal investigation cast a shadow over the old management team.

Second, I wasn't concerned about future employment. I was thoroughly committed to my life as an itinerant fix-it man and didn't have to worry about my long-term security. I could speak my mind without fear.

And third, my experience with the steelworkers showed I could work well with an entrenched, heavyweight, industrial union. The steelworkers' tradition of solidarity and hard-nosed negotiations was legendary, yet together we found a way to transform a major part of that industry.

All of my experience led me to find hope in a situation others considered hopeless. Although it wasn't something I discussed in great detail, I even let myself dream that at Delphi we could set some precedents that might solve similar problems that threatened the entire Detroit-based auto industry. It was a lofty goal, especially when you consider that we also hoped to save thousands of Delphi jobs and do right by creditors and stockholders. But when would I ever have this kind of opportunity again? When would there be a better time to attempt the ideal corporate rescue?

ALTHOUGH EVERY CRISIS is unique—that's the first rule of managing them—a few general truths will confront anyone who lands in the top spot at a company careening toward bankruptcy. Among them are:

- Bankruptcy is a process, not a solution. It can buy you time, give you access to new financing, and help you reorganize. But it doesn't relieve you of the wrenching decisions required to reshape a failing company.

- It will take longer than you think. As negotiations drag on and you are distracted from normal business, your company's value may decline. Think of kids fighting over an ice cream cone as it melts.

- It's expensive to go broke. Nearly all the fees paid to lawyers and other advisers, regardless of which side they represent, will come out of your hide before it's all over. For a Fortune 500–size company, figure $100 million-plus per year. And by the way, all those professionals are part of a clan. You'll be the outsider squirming uncomfortably while they plan lunch together.

- If you decide to file, timing, preparation, and communication are essential. You don't want to wait too long to seek protection, or there will be too little left to save. Once you do go to court, everyone must be assured that you will "stay in business during renovation." Put a strong public relations team in place to answer questions from the press, customers, suppliers, and government officials.

- There are ponies in there somewhere. Remember the joke about a barn full of manure and the optimistic kid who starts looking for the pony? Troubled companies typically harbor lots of competent people frustrated by poor leadership and organization. Find these ponies and use them to rebuild.

These observations, and a few more, were in my mind when I started at Delphi, and they motivated me to build a strong team and seek a solution that wouldn't force us into the bankruptcy process. Unfortunately, the circumstances that made Delphi's situation unique limited our options. Federal bankruptcy laws were set to change on October 17, 2005. No one knew for certain how that would affect our case, but none of us wanted to be guinea pigs under the new law. Also, the solution to our major problems depended more on the actions of the United Auto Workers (UAW) and General Motors than on anything we could do. The union would have to give us concessions to move forward. GM would have to accept it was responsible for billions of dollars owed for pensions, health care, and guaranteed union jobs.

Why was GM on the hook? The short and true answer is that when they spun off Delphi as an independent parts company (burdened with labor costs comparable to a car manufacturer), they guaranteed the UAW that in the event of a financial meltdown at Delphi they would cover retiree pensions and health care. Also, they had to know back in 1999, when the split took place, that Delphi couldn't compete while burdened with a contract requiring that it pay workers more than double the national average for domestic parts makers and many times the going rate in low cost countries. To make matters worse, the precipitous decline of GM market share shrank orders for Delphi parts after the breakup, while at the same time GM was insisting on parts price reductions.

In the three-way negotiation that would determine Delphi's future, GM was the man in the middle. The union could, and likely would, refuse to concede anything until General Motors acknowledged its responsibility. At the same time, they could strike Delphi, an option they mentioned frequently, and thereby force an almost immediate halt in production at GM plants.

The facts presented a pick-your-poison choice for General Motors. Which would be more damaging, a crippling strike that could go on for months and bankrupt GM, or paying for an expensive but manageable restructuring at Delphi? Considering that the second choice might also set some precedents for bringing common sense to the wage structure in the entire industry, the answer seemed obvious to me.

This was the great opportunity hidden in the Delphi crisis. We could, through our restructuring, start to deal with some of the irrational labor practices that were slowly killing the Big Three. Under old-fashioned contracts, Detroit's automakers paid every cent of pensions and family health care costs (even for retirees), carried far more workers than were needed, and thousands of workers were paid for sitting idle when things were slow. Add some bizarre work rules—for example, having to call an electrician to change a light bulb—and you've got a system rigged to fail. In fact, competitors like Toyota and Hyundai, who also made cars in the United States, paid wages comparable to Detroit's, but their benefit costs were much lower, and the absence of work rules helped them be far more efficient. The differential, most of it caused by health care expenses, cost GM more than $1,000 per car.

These problems were well-known, but in the through-the-looking-glass world that was Detroit, people were unable to address them. Union leaders seemed entranced by the fantasy that the gravy train could chug along forever through a land where high school graduates got high-paying jobs, pensions and health care were free, and you could retire after thirty years with an income that went on forever. (Where else in the world can a forty-eight-year-old do that?) For their part, executives were so terrified of strikes or incurring the wrath of the union that they feared speaking forcefully. Instead they worked at the edges of the problem, pushing off a true reckoning into the hazy future. With little to lose, I broke with tradition and began making some blunt statements.

"This town is in deep trouble," I told the influential columnist Daniel Howes of the *Detroit News*. I added that under current labor contracts U.S. plants were "wildly uncompetitive" and that the UAW would have to prepare to give concessions that "go against the grain of what they have achieved over the years."

Wherever I went, I talked about Delphi's unworkable labor arrangement. I also took to displaying a starkly drawn chart, with bars representing Delphi's labor costs and those of our competitors, many of which were union shops. No one argued with the data in this document. The facts proved that we were paying as much as triple the going price for an hour of work in the U.S. In a few cases, where the labor was highly skilled or the products logistically cumbersome to ship, we might retain work in America under a better contract. But we could no longer make small, uncomplicated parts that overseas manufacturers produced at a fraction of our cost.

Auto execs welcomed this kind of talk, but the cooperation I hoped to receive from union leaders never materialized. Not that we didn't try. On a number of occasions I went to UAW headquarters, called Solidarity House, and met with their vice president Richard Shoemaker and newly elected president, Ronald Gettelfinger. The meetings typically lasted over an hour and were civilized and constructive. And I considered it a victory that I wasn't tossed out the second-story window into the Detroit River. At first I was scrambling to avoid the need to go into bankruptcy, and that would need some combination of union concessions and GM support.

———————

I THOUGHT WE might have to severely cut wages and benefits to make things work. We told the UAW we would have to work toward new wage and benefit levels, closer to $20 an hour rather than the current $75. Later, however, we gave the union plans for reducing our workforce through buyouts, in which workers would get big settlement checks to leave their jobs. We would close or sell plants that were no longer competitive, and replace the high-cost workers with new hires at substantially lower wages at those plants that remained.

The UAW had previously acknowledged global conditions in contracts that allowed certain new hires to come in at lower rates. But Delphi's business had been shrinking so fast, we couldn't ever take advantage of it. Since there was an existing contract in place, the union didn't have to act on anything we presented. Instead, they could just wait for us to reach some kind of arrangement with General Motors, and they seemed prepared to do nothing, even if it meant bankruptcy.

Meanwhile, GM was a long way from accepting the magnitude of its obligation to Delphi and its workers. In August their chief financial officer, John Devine, came to my office to review the problem. In the months to come we would meet many times, alternating between the seventy-three-story-high Renaissance Center downtown, where GM was headquartered, and Delphi's home office in suburban Troy. One thing I always liked about the princes of Detroit was the flair they brought to architecture. Ford headquarters was a landmark of postwar modernism, and the Chrysler building in Manhattan is a true icon. While not quite so important, Delphi's seven-story building was a futuristic, silvery, football-shaped structure topped by a black disk (think giant hockey puck) emblazoned with the company name. Nestled in the rolling hills, it suggested that it was high tech, stable, and efficient.

My space on the top floor was decorated simply, with a few of my model trains, automotive picture books, and mementos. I wanted to keep the mood calm and welcoming for visitors who might arrive feeling a bit apprehensive. A sixtysomething guy who came up through Ford, Devine was a Detroit-style executive unaccustomed to surprises.

He seemed absolutely floored when I told him I thought it could cost GM as much as $12 billion to fix Delphi if things went badly. He said that the figure should be closer to $1 billion and if I was asking GM to pay much more, he had a ready answer, "No!"

Devine should not have been so shocked. Low-level talks between our two companies had been going on for some time, and Devine's people had to know that our numbers were pretty solid. I could only say we should work together to cut the cost. We agreed to put together a group to work on the issues, but I worried that Devine was unaware of the seriousness of our mutual problem.

With October 17 fast approaching, I tried harder to wake up Detroit. With all the signs pointing toward possible future bankruptcy for GM, Ford, and Chrysler, I couldn't understand why no one talked about it. When I addressed a big industry conference, people actually applauded when I declared that "our labor contracts are simply unaffordable." I also received more than a few "attaboy, go get 'em" phone calls, but no one came forward to echo my words publicly. Decades of strike threats and fears of shut-down factories had silenced everyone.

I spoke just as bluntly when I met with UAW officials. And I was just as direct with Delphi employees, whom I often encountered as I pushed a tray down the line at the company cafeteria and looked for an empty seat at a lively table. Every worker who received a Delphi paycheck was no doubt anxious about the future. I advised them to work hard to add value for our customers, as the best way to secure their own futures. Nonetheless, many of our American plants couldn't compete in the global marketplace, and the time for closing them had arrived. Others could operate under new arrangements, including lower wages and benefits and, perhaps, new owners. I cared about what might happen to the workers, but they should prepare for big changes.

Despite what some union agitators would say about my evil intentions, I did have their welfare in mind. But I also faced an array of other issues. Delphi had an obligation to deliver parts to manufacturers around the world, but to do this we had to reassure nervous suppliers of raw materials that they would be paid. At the same time, we needed to stay on top of our customers, making sure we got timely payment for the goods we shipped. And quality remained key. The

main thing Delphi had going for it was a reputation for delivering superior stuff on time. Fortunately, I had a terrific president and COO in
Rodney O'Neal. He would keep our core business humming throughout the crisis. Rodney also served as a good adviser as I began to meet
with another significant cast of characters in the Delphi drama—potential buyers, merger candidates, and investors.

Whenever a company flirts with bankruptcy, outside parties start to
salivate over the possibility of acquiring the whole thing at a discount
or picking off juicy bits that fit their business plans. Although still
small compared with the universe of public companies, the private
equity business had been growing robustly for years. These investors,
who can operate without all the scrutiny, rules, and paperwork demanded of public firms, thrive by placing big bets on troubled corporations that they then transform into leaner and more focused entities.
Sometimes they break companies into pieces that are sold for a profit.
In other cases they return to the market with a stock offering. In the
best cases the result is a gain for the investors and continued life for
the business at the center of a deal. Wilbur Ross pulled this off with
Bethlehem Steel.

Investors were well-informed about Delphi because the company's
woes were the subject of constant press coverage. As a result, the
whole world knew we hadn't moved GM or the UAW and that the
October 17 deadline for bankruptcy loomed. But the new law wasn't
the only factor we considered as we contemplated filing papers. We
also looked at our financial position and realized that we shouldn't
wait until we had spent all of our available cash. Another parts supplier, Collins & Aikman, had taken this route to bankruptcy and had a
very difficult time meeting their obligations to supply manufacturers
who depended on them for key components. Their customers had
been forced to fork over $300 million just to keep the parts supply
flowing. Their case was an embarrassment to everyone, but fears that
we would repeat that example made life much more difficult for
Delphi. We decided to come in for a landing while we still had enough
gas in our tanks to take off again once the repair job was done.

And so, on Saturday, October 8, 2005, Delphi declared bankruptcy
in a federal court in New York, noting we hoped to emerge by the
middle of 2007 with most of our U.S. manufacturing operations

closed or sold off. In round numbers we reported assets of $17 billion and liabilities of $22 billion, not including $4.5 billion unfunded pension costs and a global workforce of 185,000. We had more than $4 billion in credit, so we would continue operating normally. But the filing would allow us to reorganize the company and, if necessary, seek the court's permission to reduce wages and benefits unilaterally. Of course the union, which represented about twenty-four thousand workers in America, retained the strike option and would repeatedly threaten to use it and thereby bring GM to its knees.

The news of Delphi's bankruptcy rumbled through Detroit and the country, making enough noise to frighten Main Street and Wall Street. General Motors' stock lost 9 percent, and the Dow Jones Industrial Average fell fifty-three points on the first day of trading after the announcement. And in towns where Delphi operated plants, local papers sent reporters out to gather stories of fear and anxiety. Typical was a piece titled, "Shell-Shocked Workers Fear for Future." In a matter of days the word "shell-shocked" would be replaced by "furious."

IT'S NOT EASY to command a ship that's taking on water. Crew members tend to jump off, and without them, who will operate the pumps? That was a problem we faced even before bankruptcy, as headhunters swirled around our best managers, trying to lure them away with offers of better pay and more secure futures. Our top people were underpaid by industry standards, and yet we were demanding more of them so we could fulfill contracts for parts and rally around the cause of revitalizing the company. To keep them, we devised a plan to reward key people if they stuck with us, improved the company's performance, and helped us emerge from bankruptcy.

A severance plan was included, which would cost Delphi absolutely zero unless we began firing all our managers, which of course would never happen. And the subsequent incentive pay plan would cost money only if the profitability performance was improved by many times the potential added compensation cost. Of course, we were required to lay it all out for the bankruptcy court to consider and for the public to see. You can imagine the complaints that came from the UAW when they heard about it. Ron Gettelfinger, who until this moment had been somewhat muted, called the plan "obscene" and "outrageous," and his vice president, Dick Shoemaker, talked about the possibility of strikes. Michigan governor Jennifer Granholm, a Democrat who depended on labor's support, issued a highly critical statement that said we wanted workers to "to accept brutal, draconian pay cuts while upper management is being offered golden parachutes."

The complaints were emotionally effective. They worked even in my own home, where Maggie told me that she agreed with the critics who said it was the wrong time to increase incentives for management. Never one to be shy with her opinions, especially when she was assessing my performance, she said that at the very least I had made a bad public relations move. I disagreed. I had come to Detroit determined to tell the truth and make the right business moves and accept the consequences. I wasn't going to back down from a policy I thought was right. Instead I began a little public relations campaign of my own, meeting with the press in Detroit and then around the country to answer every question they might have about our bankruptcy.

On the Monday after our filing we went to New York and met with journalists at the *Financial Times* bureau, the *New York Times*, *BusinessWeek*, the *Wall Street Journal*, and the Bloomberg news service. They gave us a chance to send a message to the world that we were still in business and fully intended to meet our obligations. It was especially important for our employees, suppliers, and customers overseas to hear this because they were not familiar with American-style bankruptcy. They hear the "B-word" and fear the doors are closed and locked. I also tried to express some empathy for our UAW folks. More than once I noted that Ron Gettelfinger had the toughest job in Detroit because he would have to lead his members into a new era. As the *Times* reported in an article the following day, he was "in the hot seat."

For the most part the national press got the story right. The *Wall Street Journal* even noted that we planned to save our pension plan without federal help and that workers would be compensated in meaningful ways once job cuts and wage reductions—inevitable due to market conditions—occurred. Back in Detroit we hosted a question-and-answer session for the press at Delphi headquarters, where I shared the stage with Rodney O'Neal and our bankruptcy lawyer, Jack Butler. The meeting was described as "tense" by writers from the *Detroit News,* who said I made a "fiery defense" of the bankruptcy decision. If it was tense, it was because the governor and union had taken the rhetoric to a new, harsher level and we were not ready to back down.

With the whole auto industry listening, we delivered basic truths that people didn't want to hear. We said that everything workers had hoped to retain, including pensions and health care, would simply go down the drain if we couldn't restructure. And without Delphi and its parts, there was a serious risk that GM could wind up bankrupt. Critics didn't understand the forces that required we pay more for managers and less for unskilled labor, but we were only responding to the market. "Philosophers can speculate about fairness," I said, "but we have to deal with reality." Then I offered some examples of the unrealistic practices in our business, including contract language that required us to pay top rates even for unskilled, seasonal chores. "Paying $65 an hour for someone mowing the lawn at one of our plants," I concluded, "is not going to cut it in industrial America for very long."

I may have gone a little too far.

The next day I went to Ann Arbor to attend the grand opening of an automotive research facility built, ironically enough, by Hyundai and ran into the governor. She asked me for a private meeting, and as we went off to talk I couldn't help noticing that a few reporters were watching. I suspected that she had received more pressure from union leaders, and when we were alone she told me she hoped I would reconsider the executive compensation plan. The decision was ours to make, of course, and the governor would try to help Delphi in any way she could. But she thought we looked bad, asking for blue-collar sacrifice while planning boosts for management. Worse, she said, union members were grumbling about strikes. "Steve," she said, "this issue could destroy the industrial fabric of Michigan. You've got to do something."

Leaving the Hyundai technical center—for a flight to a big industry conference at the Greenbrier resort in West Virginia—I marveled over how this issue, out of all the possible concerns that might arise from a major bankruptcy, had bubbled to the top. In countless ways the marketplace was telling us we were making the right moves. In fact, our much-battered stock rose more than 50 percent during the week as one of the nation's smartest hedge fund managers, David Tepper of Appaloosa Management, bought more than fifty million shares. If that wasn't a vote of confidence, I don't know what would be.

Still, the furor was a distraction. I called my closest adviser, Maggie, and told her, "The governor thinks we need to do something. I'm thinking of taking a pay cut and having the top management group take a cut, too." She seemed warm to the idea, especially as a symbol. Of course this was before I told her the details.

What I had in mind was Iacocca's $1-a-year announcement during the big Chrysler crisis. With great flourish Lee had announced that he would accept just a $1 salary in 1979. At the same time, his fellow execs took pay reductions of 10 percent. The move generated enormous goodwill for the man and the company (even though he eventually got back all the pay he gave up) and made a lasting impression on me. Why wouldn't it work the same way now for Delphi?

After giving my speech to the conference at the Greenbrier, I found Rodney O'Neal and told him what I was planning. He was blunt, telling me, "That's stupid. It's going to buy you five minutes of peace, and they'll be right back at you." But he could tell that I had made up my mind and agreed that the whole top management team could also accept pay reductions.

————

OUR TALKS ON slashing and in one case (mine!) eliminating executive pay continued when we returned to Detroit. I drove to Solidarity House and talked to Dick Shoemaker and Ron Gettelfinger about our plans. They said it was a step in the right direction and in the interest of better relations agreed that we should keep public bickering to a minimum.

But the very next morning the suburban *Oakland Press* quoted both of them throwing some pretty strong words around. Shoemaker said his side would prefer to avoid strikes, but it "would be presumptuous" to assume that walkouts weren't imminent. Gettelfinger said our management incentive plan was not only "outrageous" but amounted to "pay for failure," as if we could have found a way to succeed while paying labor costs more than double the going rate. The union had built up a $1 billion strike fund, which it seemed prepared to use, and hired lawyers to fight our plan in court.

The rhetoric was mostly boilerplate until Gettelfinger got personal, trying to make me the bad guy. I was heading for "the checkout line," he said, implying that I was eager to make short work of dismantling Delphi and enjoy a big payday. "We could put [anyone] over at Delphi to go and tear it down with no regard for people or the impact on communities," he told the local paper. "He appears to be doing nothing more than résumé building for his next job." I understood that Gettelfinger was in a bad position, presiding over the decline of his union, but making me the bogeyman was just unnecessary and, I thought, beneath him.

A $1 per year salary ought to stop that kind of talk, or at least that's what I thought. On the day after Gettelfinger's outburst we announced my decision to take a little less than two cents per week pay and an across-the-board reduction of 10 percent for top management. Rodney announced that as president he would double that figure, taking a 20 percent hit. Speaking to the Detroit *Free Press* I explained that I just couldn't look our workers in the eye and ask for wage and benefit cuts while taking my million-dollar salary.

The move got us great press, for a single day. Soon it was eclipsed by news that the UAW had agreed that retirees should share the cost of their health care. The next day also brought word of an intensified effort to cut twenty-five thousand GM jobs and the possible sale of its financing division, GMAC, which would yield cash to offset some of the billions the company was losing annually. Events were unfolding so quickly in the car industry that even the keenest observers had trouble keeping up. Most were left with just vague impressions as the details created a picture of inevitable change.

In the end, the only two people who cared much or really remembered my grand gesture were Maggie and me. And when she found out—this was one of those rare major decisions I made without her—Maggie was not pleased. Despite our many years together and my regular reminders that we were partners in every sense, Maggie never shook the fears of poverty and abandonment she knew as a child. She was angry that I acted without consulting her and began planning ways to cut household expenses. Despite the bitter cold, snow, and rain that are always part of Detroit winters, she wanted to give up an indoor parking space at our apartment to save $50 a month. She began washing and ironing my dress shirts, instead of taking them to the cleaners. And we stopped going out for dinners to save a few bucks. This was painful for me because we had sufficient savings to live well if we wanted to. But she was scared.

———————

OUR INTENTIONALLY ASSERTIVE approach to the public and media had succeeded in telling the world why we were in crisis and how we were going to work our way out of it. But we had also stimulated a backlash, with the UAW trying to make me the poster boy for every problem in the industry. Ron Gettelfinger never stopped the sniping, on the grounds that "you got a two-month head start on me." I don't believe I ever said anything disrespectful of our workforce or the union leadership, but by the time Ron had misquoted and twisted my statements, everyone thought I was a union basher. If nothing else, the UAW are masters at media manipulation.

Of all rescue missions I have tackled, Delphi was the most difficult when it came to working with labor. I'm not talking about rank-and-file workers. For the most part I think they understood the company's troubles, and many even appreciated what I was trying to accomplish. (Without their cooperation, Rodney O'Neal wouldn't have been able to improve operations so dramatically.) Some, indeed, privately expressed fears that the overheated rhetoric and confrontational approach might cost them their jobs. But at the very top of the UAW, we encountered a much different attitude. Instead of calm leadership, we got frequent vitriolic verbal attacks on management.

Soon after we filed bankruptcy, UAW President Ron Gettelfinger organized the six Delphi unions into a 'Mobilization Against Delphi' (MAD), accompanied by a press conference where he blasted me personally yet again. Other union leaders passed the word to my team that they didn't really support this approach, but politically they could not refuse to attend. I understood, and kept my cool. And as time passed, only the UAW maintained a hostile attitude towards us.

Besides accusing me of 'destroying the middle class in America' and having no respect for the worker, Gettelfinger said that I had engineered a 'mechanical (unnecessary) bankruptcy'. With all the bank-ruptcy speculation, we were experiencing a 'run on the bank' in late 2005, and had no choice but to file for Chapter 11 relief before the money ran out. It is true that a bankruptcy might have been averted had both the UAW and GM gotten realistic in the fall of 2005, but my alarms weren't heard in time for that.

Another of Gettelfinger's favorite themes was that bankruptcy was an abusive device used by capitalists to unfairly crush labor and de-stroy pension entitlements. But as the Delphi case so clearly demon-strates, labor is actually a preferred creditor in a bankruptcy. Before you can void a labor contract and you have to show the court that torching the bondholders and other creditors isn't enough for the busi-ness to survive. Similarly, pension entitlements are sacrosanct, except in the most dire circumstances. The only case I was involved in where labor contracts got thrown out was United Airlines (I am a director). The stockholders got zippo, and creditors a few pennies on the dollar. So much for the capitalists making out at the expense of labor. And even there the subsequent labor contracts were negotiated, not unilat-erally imposed.

I am sure Gettlefinger understood the rules of bankruptcy, but in his remarks he ignored the details in favor of transferring blame. One benefit of being a labor leader is that you are not subject to securities laws that limit what an executive can say. The UAW chief could say almost anything, whether misleading or not. On one day, Gettelfinger made a public statement at noon that 'he was not having any discus-sions with Delphi', and then at 5 pm we put out a coordinated press statement with the UAW that the temporary workers we had hired would be made permanent. Only Reuters seemed to catch the utter incongruity of those two events. No CEO could ever have gotten away with such inconsistent, simultaneous statements.

Gettelfinger's disdain of Delphi was not confined to me, and it started long before I arrived on the scene. He simply couldn't get along with anyone at Delphi—not anyone on our Board or senior man-agement, nor our principal labor negotiator, Kevin Butler. If he could have his way, he'd probably have us all run out of town with tar and feathers. At one economic conference in Mackinac, Michigan in 2007, when asked whether he would modify his earlier statement that the Delphi executives were all 'pigs at the trough', he withdrew it and said instead, we were all 'swine at the dining table.'

In point of fact, in the last half year of negotiations, Gettelfinger refused to meet personally with anyone from Delphi. Messages were passed through his subordinates, or through the GM executives. I will always wonder what added costs were imposed on all sides by the delays and miscommunications that inevitably flowed from Gettelfinger's behavior. There were crucial moments in the case where we were advised to stand aside for a few days while Ron got over his latest temper tantrum. I was flabbergasted. With the fate of the world's largest industrial employer, GM, hanging delicately in the balance, we had to wait days for Gettelfinger to calm down.

The acrimony made me nostalgic for the almost daily conversations that I had with Leo Gerard of the United Steelworkers in the Bethlehem case. Despite having a steel industry that was in even worse shape than the auto industry ever has been, Gerard always attacked the problem at hand, not the people involved. While we might have sharp differences of view, there was never a hint of personal acrimony. We were able to speak directly and whatever the content, he tried to be constructive. At Delphi, while I tried to calm the waters and repeated the message that we sought a 'consensual resolution', Gettelfinger kept wanting to yell the 'strike' word. In part I think he welcomed conflict so he could punish Delphi, but he also needed to show backbone to his more dissident troops. Unfortunately, our Asian customers looked at this in dismay. "How can your own workers be so anxious to harm their employer?" they would ask. And I suspect we lost a lot of potential business from customers who did not want to step into the middle of a fistfight.

By the time we were nearing the end of our bankruptcy case, everyone who was listening to Gettelfinger might have thought the hourly workers had made huge concessions. In fact, no hourly worker represented by the UAW at Delphi had given up a penny of pay or benefits. Instead, the traditional workers had by and large taken voluntary buyouts, and the new workers, at Tier Two contract levels, had experienced huge increases compared to whatever paying jobs they came from. The only people at Delphi I am aware of who took a pay cut were the executives. But try and read that in any of the press coverage.

Compared with strong, confident labor leader I had known in Leo Gerard, Gettelfinger was a big disappointment. To his credit, Gettelfinger was in a much tougher job than mine, and I never doubted his passionate commitment to helping his membership. But an industry in crisis needs leaders who can rise above the tactics of intimidation that may have worked decades earlier.

I will give Gettelfinger credit as a very effective politician. Among the hurtful results of his campaign to discredit me were two I recall. One was a friend of my son Alexander in Grand Rapids, Michigan, who asked him, "How were you able to stand it growing up with such an awful father?" And way out in Oregon, my son Robin got an email stating, "It is a shame that such a young, motivated attorney carries the same name as a union bashing, community wrecking, non-American individual. I hope there is no relationship." A demagogue who can spread his venom from Grand Rapids to Bandon knows what he's doing.

In any event, once we had said our piece about the causes and objectives of Delphi's bankruptcy in October of 2005, our team began to talk about "going silent" and developed a report suggesting an approach they titled Project Nerka, after the submarine in the classic movie *Run Silent, Run Deep*. In this paper they argued that while my outreach had worked, I now risked becoming "the personification of bankruptcy and everything else organized labor sees wrong with big business."

The problem was the emotional dynamic building around Delphi as thousands of workers were coming to face the end of an old, sheltered era. Prodded by Gettelfinger and others, they looked for someone to blame, and even though I had just arrived on the scene, they picked me. It's sort of like the family that fights with the emergency room physician who says Dad needs bypass surgery after fifty years of a couch potato lifestyle. It's not the doc's fault, but he cannot escape the blame.

To counteract this problem my communications staff recommended we stop talking, except to say we would work closely with GM and the UAW to bring Delphi out of bankruptcy with the least pain and disruption possible. The approach was decidedly adult. It noted that everyone was feeling pressured, the union probably needed to vent, and the best we could do is listen to others and work hard. Somewhat re-luctantly—because it was ingrained in me to speak out with candor—I agreed to go quiet.

Even as we "ran silent" we didn't escape conflict entirely. I had one ultimately good-natured encounter with the union's displeasure when I visited a Delphi plant in Lockport, New York. On my way into the factory I saw a little shop that sold UAW merchandise. I plunked down a few dollars for a UAW cap and put it on as a way of showing respect. The UAW leadership were offended by it, however. (How dare I put on their cap?) The workers then outdid me in the symbol game, however. On the shop floor I saw a sea of green—thousands of workers wearing customized green T-shirts decorated with the name of a fictitious company, "Miller's Lawn Care Service," and the motto "Mowing Down Wages." The smiles were mixed with flashes of re-sentment as a few union members told me they were offended by my $65-an-hour lawn-mowing quip. I told them I hadn't intended to mock them—it was about seasonal maintenance labor, not production work—and that I would never equate their skilled labor with pushing a mower.

The other uncomfortable incident—or rather incidents—of the Project Nerka period involved a TV news "gotcha" artist who followed me around for a while—even sneaking into private gatherings—trying to get video footage for a hatchet job. The distortions that finally aired on a station in Detroit included the suggestion that I was somehow in line for a payout of nearly $37 million at the end of the Delphi job, which was flat-out wrong. The report also charged that I was wasting company resources by "crossing the Atlantic in a private jet." He also charged that I was deliberately thumbing my nose at Detroit's auto-workers by having a chauffer pick me up after landing in a (horrors) BMW.

The $37 million figure was simply outrageous. Although my original contract included bonus features, I had waived all entitlements beyond the $1 salary, and no such big number ever had my name on it. The private plane ride was aboard a jet that was owned by another company and occupied by several major figures in the auto industry who had attended the annual World Economic Forum in Davos, Swit-zerland, where I had been a speaker. I was scheduled to fly home commercial until I was asked if I wanted to hitch a ride. I got more work done in those seven hours than I could have accomplished in a week and saved Delphi the price of a return ticket. As for the BMW and the driver—BMW is a big Delphi client, so there was no shame in using their cars. And though I almost always drive myself everywhere in a GM car, I had left it at a different airport and I was needed at work. The driver happened to pick the BMW out of the garage pool that day.

Fortunately, the reporter who chased me around with the intention of making me look like Gordon Gecko was alone in his approach. The rest of the press backed off. A dissident union organization called Soldiers of Solidarity would regularly picket Delphi (their signs included the witty "Miller Isn't Worth a Buck") and rail against me on the Internet, where I became "Mad Man Miller" and the "Grinch who stole Christmas." But otherwise we were left to work in peace on the task of recreating Delphi.

My job gradually evolved into a Teddy Roosevelt kind of role, as I used the bully pulpit of the CEO's position to rally the key parties—the union, GM, and investors—toward a solution. I argued for sensible choices, based on what was best for the people and businesses involved, but understood that there were limits to my leverage. I could threaten to ask the bankruptcy judge in New York to let us break our labor agreement, but there was no guarantee he would allow it, and if he did, the union would be free to strike, and the media response to such a move would make the executive incentive fight look like a garden party.

Where GM was concerned, my best hope lay in persuading Rick Wagoner, who had become their CEO in 2003. Having played basketball at Duke, where he discovered that six foot four ain't *that* tall, Wagoner had great competitive instincts to go with his Harvard MBA. They had carried him through a lifelong climb up the General Motors ladder, a journey that coincided with the rise of the global car and truck marketplace, where huge, supercompetitive companies like Toyota would thrive. He was aware of GM's problems and of the strengths that came with its size and experience. "The big and the fast beat the small and the fast," he once said. "If you check out the NBA today, they're big and fast."

GM was big, and Rick still had time to make it fast. Although 2005 was shaping up as one of the worst years in company history, with losses approaching $9 billion, he had more than twice that much cash in hand. GM's factories were becoming more efficient. He was getting better prices for his products, and he had stemmed the rise in health care costs. Although he carried far too many workers, roughly half would be eligible to retire by 2007. With the right combination of buy-outs, retirements, and plant closings he might just produce the big and fast company that could keep America in the car business.

Amid all these challenges, Rick still had to deal with Delphi because GM had agreed, at the time of the spinoff, to backstop our legacy costs and to allow union workers we laid off to "flow back" to GM plants. Remember, these workers had belonged to General Motors in the first place and were originally employed under a high-priced auto manufacturing labor agreement. Many still fabricated GM components and thought of themselves as GMers, and in a sense they were.

Wagoner and I met on the day before Thanksgiving, on a morning when the *New York Times* described the stalemate in discussions with the union and floated the idea that I might be somehow angling for Rick's job. The suggestion gave us both a laugh, and Rick expressed some gratitude for my outspokenness, which had taken some of the heat off him. When the talk turned serious I gave Rick the same assessment John Devine had rejected—that GM could end up paying as much as $12 billion to help fix Delphi, and the cost would be greater if delays and acrimony led to a strike or work slowdowns that would deprive GM of parts. Between brakes, heating and cooling units, fuel systems, steering columns, electronic systems, and other equipment, Delphi supplied about a third of what went into each GM car.

At the time, GM was due to receive $146 million in price reductions from Delphi for the coming year. I told Rick that to avoid a collapse at Delphi, we would have to charge him *more* for essential parts, not less. Given higher raw material prices and uncertainty in our labor cost, we might have to add several billion dollars to their bill in the coming year. In short, Delphi could not address its labor issues in an orderly way unless GM gave us financial assistance.

Rick countered that his group had been searching the globe for alternate suppliers and "you'd be surprised" by how well GM might cope without Delphi. This seemed unlikely to me, given that it can take months or even a couple of years to change parts suppliers. In the end we agreed to waive the scheduled price cuts, which was in effect a $146 million improvement for Delphi. We made the agreement public, and it signaled, at long last, that GM was willing to put serious money into a soft landing for our company and our people.

Wagoner also reported that John Devine was scheduled to retire and would be replaced by Frederick "Fritz" Henderson. Fritz would turn out to be a more flexible and engaged partner.

Nonetheless, it took more than a year to work out the details of the Delphi/GM deal. In part, this was due to the mind-numbing complexity of the matter. But we were also hampered by GM's culture of operating in functional silos. GM purchasing would pull in one direction, GM labor relations staff in another, and GM finance and legal staff in yet another direction. It took a long time until GM was able to tackle the Delphi situation as an integrated strategic issue for them.

———

THE MAD WHIRL of activity that thrilled me in the early going at Delphi had required so many business trips, late evenings, and early mornings that Maggie saw far too little of me. Because she was less and less confident about doing things on her own, especially if it involved driving and the possibility of getting lost, my absence made her a little housebound, as well. College football, long a passion, no longer held her interest so fully. She turned on the games, but her attention drifted. Add these changes to her usual holiday anxiety, and Thanksgiving at our apartment was not a Norman Rockwell experience. Calls from our children, where she tried to solve problems that really didn't exist, left her frustrated and angry, and before we could even enjoy the turkey dinner we had made together, she fled the table, slammed the door, and hid herself away.

In time I would suspect that Maggie was already affected by the brain tumor that would take her from me in less than a year. But at the end of 2005 it was easy to assume it was just a passing storm. When she felt better and started smiling again, I did, too. She seemed to accept more readily the barrage of criticism coming from the UAW. As the holiday season ended we settled back into a routine. When I traveled she stayed close to home. When I was around, we exercised together in the morning on the treadmill and the stationary bike while watching bits of old movies, and at night we sometimes visited our favorite local restaurants. She may have been quieter than usual, and she may have had some trouble focusing on conversations. I'm not sure.

Was I too busy to notice Maggie was failing? I'll never know. What I can say is that no one else seemed to detect anything unusual in her behavior or appearance. She remained my best sounding board and was mother to our three grown sons. And until the moment she was diagnosed she seemed to grasp all of the moving parts of the Delphi project. This included the proposals traded between us and the union, GM's various issues, the growing interest of investors, and proceedings before the bankruptcy court in New York.

In bankruptcies, federal judges must referee among a host of interested parties, including creditors, stockholders, management, and unions. In most cases, ours included, judges approve the formation of various committees that represent the interested parties. Creditors, for example, would form a group to watch the proceedings and advocate for fair treatment. The cost of these groups, including advisers, lawyers, and expenses, ultimately comes out of the estate of the bankrupt company, which makes this activity a nice moneymaker for those who are in the bankruptcy business.

In Delphi's case, all this activity was overseen by a fiercely intelligent judge named Robert Drain, who operated out of Courtroom 610 in a federal courthouse created out of the century-old U.S. Customs House in New York City. Located near the very tip of Manhattan, the historic building was cramped, stuffy, and completely inadequate for hearings that attracted hundreds of people. But it did have that certain charm that comes with age.

Our concerns were generally handled by attorneys from the firm of Skadden, Arps, who were led by Jack Butler. They worked like an efficient army, even deploying special helpers whose duties included showing up early to save seats in the courtroom. Generally, Jack would need to have a Delphi executive on hand, and we would fly in whoever was summoned for a day or two of testimony. Some of the roughest going had to do with executive compensation, but we wound up getting most of what we needed to keep our key managers.

For me a court session involved hours of waiting around, seques-
tered from other witnesses, before I could testify. During one such
hearing I was sent to the judge's modest chambers so I wouldn't hear
what others had to say. Hours later he found me asleep (I hope not
snoring) in his chair. Judge Drain was good-natured about my napping
through most of the proceedings. A former bankruptcy lawyer, he
knew the territory and asked the best questions. You could tell he was
impatient when he put his elbows down and rested his chin on his
folded hands. But he was never distracted, and ultimately calm and
fair in a setting that often has the mood of a battlefield.

IF JUDGE DRAIN'S courtroom represented a major front in the war
over Delphi, a second was occupied by people who were willing to
place big bets on the company's postbankruptcy future. The first general on the scene was David Tepper, the private equity investor whose
firm, Appaloosa Management, spent just $16 million to tie up almost
10 percent of Delphi's stock when it was priced around thirty-two
cents per share. Tepper also invested in bonds and preferred shares.

Having quite literally purchased a big interest in Delphi's bankruptcy, Tepper began pushing for the formation of an equity committee to represent shareholders in the bankruptcy court. Normally, in a
case like ours you would expect shareholders, who are pretty much
last in line when it comes to recovering losses, to be left holding an
empty bag at the end of the proceedings. When we started, we certainly thought that they would be wiped out. But Tepper plays hardball. He organized a drive to create an equity committee. We opposed
it, on the grounds that it would pull money out of Delphi while producing little benefit, but the judge approved the idea (although the
newly formed equity committee would exclude Tepper). The equity
committee then threatened General Motors with a huge lawsuit alleg-
ing that GM had committed fraud by setting up Delphi to fail from
the very beginning. The committee estimated the damage done at $26
billion and suggested the damages number might triple, to $78 billion,
if federal racketeering statutes could also be applied.

As a dominant force by virtue of his Delphi stock and bond holdings, Tepper was in a position to block approval of any bankruptcy

plan. This kind of blocking vote could threaten resolution of the case. Add the threatened lawsuit against GM, which could drag on for years, and you start to see the leverage Tepper and the old shareholders were putting to work. Others might see this as a marauder's approach, a kind of hostage taking, but it is also simply how the game is played by the most aggressive risk-taking capitalists.

At forty-nine, Tepper was one of the great characters in American business, and his fund had enjoyed more spectacularly profitable years than down ones. In 2004 he had donated $55 million to rename the business school at Carnegie Mellon the David A. Tepper School of Business and in 2005 hired Ashlee Simpson to sing at his daughter's bat mitzvah. In the months after he bought his shares of the bankrupt Delphi he gathered funding commitments from other investors to buy stock in the company. That money, combined with contributions from GM and cash from other sources, could be used to cover pension and health care obligations and to make creditors whole.

In early 2006 Tepper wrote to complain that we had rushed into bankruptcy and to demand a general meeting where shareholders could vote on a slate of directors he wanted to nominate. Of course we were already under court supervision, so Tepper's call was more bark than bite. But he did get our attention, and I went to see him at his office, which was in a nondescript building in the small town of Chatham, New Jersey.

A little overweight and balding, Tepper was dressed casually and spoke forcefully, lacing his arguments with the occasional curse. But as blunt as Tepper was, the really hard guy at Appaloosa was his right-hand man, Ronnie Goldstein, who was an avid body builder with a narrow waist and such enormous shoulders I had to wonder where he bought his shirts. Ronnie will call you an idiot, and worse, if he's trying to make and point or a buck for Appaloosa.

Ronnie and David wanted us to sue General Motors, play hardball with the UAW, and simply walk away from health care and pension obligations. Like many of the requests made by Appaloosa, these demands were nonstarters. There would have been a firestorm had we tried to walk away from our obligations for pensions and other benefits, even if the court let us, and we felt similarly committed to working things out with GM and the union in a fair way.

They had to know how we would respond, so it's likely that the Appaloosa fellows were just trying to increase the pressure on GM and the UAW. Along the way, however, they raised some hackles with union leaders like Gettelfinger, who would brand them as heartless "bankruptcy vultures" who didn't care about working men and women.

As time went on, however, I developed a profound respect for Tepper. Not only was he extremely smart, but he proved to be flexible to meet changing conditions. Most important, if he gave you his word about something, you could count on it.

———

DELPHI'S CHAPTER 11 filing had motivated the UAW and General Motors to take a more urgent attitude toward the problems in our company and to start facing the larger auto industry crisis. The days when high-school-educated laborers could rely on plentiful factory jobs to support a family at the middle-class level were coming to a close. Both GM and the UAW folks understood this, I believe, and had been trying to find ways to ease the coming pain of job losses and wage and benefit cuts.

The breakthrough came as GM developed a buyout and early retirement offer for workers employed in their own manufacturing facilities. The entire industry was restructuring, spending billions in the short term to save even more over time. Ford had already announced a plan to cut thirty thousand jobs in a cost reduction campaign. Workers who participated would receive lump sums of up to $100,000 plus generous education grants. The GM plan, when it was finally announced, raised the ante to $140,000.

The deal was generous from a cash standpoint, and in its details offered ways for people without much seniority to get a new start in life elsewhere. Workers with nearly thirty years of service could elect to take a retirement bonus, and wouldn't have to give up anything.

More important for Delphi was the decision to include our workforce in the plan. In fact, thirty thousand of our workers would be able to choose the buyout, retirement, or a third option, which allowed them to "flow back" into a GM manufacturing job. When all was said and done, this arrangement would make it possible for Delphi to hire workers at the so-called Tier Two pay structure for whatever facilities remained after bankruptcy at much more reasonable costs. Hourly rates would start around $14. Benefits might bring the total price for an hour of work to $25 or so, not yet competitive with other suppliers, but a lot less than the traditional workforce.

It almost goes without saying that the new deal was far less generous than the one workers enjoyed for decades at Delphi plants. But if you compared the new package of pay and benefits with offers other companies make to workers with similar skills, it begins to seem quite generous. Where else in America could someone come out of high school and get over $14 an hour to start and full benefits? It sure beat Wal-Mart and Starbucks.

Proof that the offer was better than market prevailing rates came quickly as thousands of workers signed up in the first few weeks. In a few months the list was twenty thousand names long. At first I was worried that our production would falter with such massive turnover of the workorce. But things went smoothly, as the newly-hired workers seemed highly motivated and grateful to have good jobs.

With the fog around our future clearing at year-end 2006, Appaloosa and Cerberus joined with a small group of other investors to propose putting a total of $3.4 billion into Delphi as it left bankruptcy. And as the private equity people got together, GM finally agreed in December 2006 to provide between $6 billion and $7.5 billion to fund Delphi's restructuring. Negotiators for our two companies had been working on the deal for months in periodic meetings at the offices of Skadden, Arps in Manhattan. Their success would contribute to a better outcome than I could have imagined when we started work in the months before bankruptcy. In brief, the plan we were preparing to present to Judge Drain for ending bankruptcy included:

Full funding of pension obligations.

Full recovery by creditors.

Value for stockholders, who would get shares in the new company.

Consensual resolution of our labor cost issue.

Uninterrupted parts supply for our customers.

Looking across the landscape, the new Delphi would operate about eight plants in America, employing ten thousand people making car parts that were either technically very sophisticated or difficult to ship from other countries. Our U.S. operations would become, therefore, a small fraction of the Delphi global operations. This included fuel systems, electronics, and the heating and cooling equipment made by the folks at Lockport, where I was greeted by all those Miller's Lawn Care Service T-shirts. Additional factories were likely to be sold to new operators, who would continue to employ thousands of people. However, a number of plants would be shuttered for good. These facilities produced items that could no longer be made by Delphi or anyone else in America at a profit.

On January 11, 2007, I appeared before Judge Drain to defend our proposal from objections lodged by various parties. I spoke as executive chairman, because a few weeks earlier Rodney O'Neal had been named my successor as chief executive officer. His reward was well deserved. During bankruptcy Rodney had led our operations to record levels in quality, efficiency, and productivity, and in winning new business for the future. He and his team had surpassed every goal set for them, adding value to the company and proving they deserved the incentives we offered. No one was better positioned to lead the new Delphi.

At the hearing I told the judge that "if we get bogged down" with more studies, the value of Delphi could be eroded. I reminded him that our settlement was "a labor transformation deal first and foremost" and that a substantial delay might sidetrack the arrangement with the UAW, which also faced negotiations on a new contract with the Big Three come September. Something in our arguments must have made sense, because Judge Drain ruled in our favor the very next day. Declaring the plan "a watershed event" for American industry, he gave us the go-ahead to finalize things.

A great deal of haggling was yet to come, with the union and the investors arguing over jobs at specific factories, the timing of plant closings, and even the status of specific facilities. Progress slowed once when the union refused to drop its demand that Delphi keep some jobs in the city of Flint, Michigan, where the product mix made it all but impossible to be competitive. However, Flint was where the UAW got its first contract with GM, in 1937, after a long bloody strike. Keeping jobs in Flint was an absolute requirement of the UAW. If ever Delphi was going to emerge from bankruptcy, the company would have to bend to this demand.

As I write this, the last pieces of Delphi's reorganization are being fitted into the puzzle. Management and labor seem to be inching toward better work rules, which would bring common sense to the shop floor. In the meantime, Delphi's extensive foreign operations, which supply parts to the global industry, remain highly successful. My only regret is that the cost of our transformation was so high for GM. But the UAW had given us no choice.

As I prepare to leave for yet another attempt at retirement (even I don't know if I can do it), the results are, in some ways, better than I could have hoped for in 2005. In an e-mail that popped into my computer near the end of my term at Delphi, a colleague I had never met assessed the situation. Here's what he wrote, with some of the more embarrassing superlatives edited:

> *Dear Steve Miller,*
>
> *Today is my last day at Delphi. I am not being let go, I am leaving on my own terms to start an engineering consulting company. Don't worry, this is not going to be a flaming goodbye, quite the opposite in fact.*
>
> *When your name was announced to lead Delphi, I was ready to hate you. Perhaps I did hate you. You were this greedy guy who was going to rape the company and the retirement fund for fun and profit . . . and well, it wasn't right.*
>
> *How wrong I was . . . People can complain about the rules of bankruptcy and the weather and the price of tea in China, but you had nothing to do with those things. You came in to play a lousy hand that others had dealt. And . . . I cannot believe how successful you have been. I was sure you'd have to walk away from the pension liability. I was sure you'd have a strike. I was sure you'd get no help from GM. I was sure DPH stockholders would get 0 cents on the dollar. I was wrong on all counts . . . People hate you, I am sure, but that is not your fault. You have done a whale of a job doing your job.*
>
> > *So, good luck to you. I wish you well. Keep up the good work.*

This guy was not part of management. He wasn't an investor or a stockholder. He was a staff engineer who had watched the Delphi drama with intense skepticism and concern. His assessment and understanding meant more to me than any praise I might get from board members or the business press. And I have to believe that if he "got it," so did many others. We had managed to keep Delphi's commitments. It remained a valuable industrial asset and survived to serve customers, stockholders, creditors, workers, and communities all over the globe. It was an outcome that showed how both the bankruptcy system and the free market can preserve value, even when a giant corporation stumbles.

And what about the larger problems in Detroit? Well, the Delphi reorganization could serve as a template for the Big Three, but as of this writing it's too early to see whether labor and a management will follow it. Ford and GM were investing billions to pursue long-term cuts in costs, and the Chrysler part of DaimlerChrysler was being sold to Cerberus. Some suggest that the domestic makers might be reduced to smaller market shares and fewer brand names. No one doubted that the survivors would have to scramble to catch up to international pacesetter Toyota.

———————

I WOULD LEAVE Delphi feeling optimistic about the industry's future and inspired by the resilience of the people and institutions that will move it forward. I would also leave without Maggie by my side. The shock of her death, described earlier, was gradually replaced by the long-term ache we all feel after such a profound loss. For a long time I would still call out to her in the next room or pause to phone her with some important item, only to quickly realize that she was gone.

I was not the only one who felt her absence. All through the last stage of the Delphi project I received heartfelt notes from many people who knew Maggie well, and from a few who had met her just once and were so impressed that they had to say something about her passing. Maggie was the kind of person who made an impression. If she tested you and you passed, you felt honored. Sometimes this required a little jousting. This is how Lionel Margolick, my close friend, came to love Maggie. He wasn't afraid to match wits with her, and she loved him for it.

Together Lionel and I hosted a memorial celebration of Maggie's life that just happened to be scheduled for the period when Delphi's fate was assured and it seemed clear that the job she encouraged me to take was going to work out well. In early March 2007, close family and friends shared dinner and viewed a video I had made, showing Maggie and the people and places she loved. There were no dry eyes. The next day close to three hundred people came to Orchestra Hall, in downtown Detroit, for a somewhat more elaborate celebration and remembrance of her life.

At Orchestra Hall a champagne reception was followed by brunch in a room that had been transformed into "Maggie's Garden," where fountains gurgled, flowers bloomed, and life-size photos of our grand-children grew among the ferns and evergreens. Every member of the Miller clan attended, as did some of the big-time execs who once found themselves puffing cigars with Maggie after a corporate dinner and answering her pointed questions. I sat at a table with administra-tive assistants from the many companies I had served, each of whom knew Maggie quite well and understood our unique relationship.

After brunch we all moved to the main theater, where members of the family took the stage to perform a program titled *Of Maggie, Music and Motown*. Our son Alexander, the professional oboist, played a piece he first heard while riding in the car with his mother in Venezu-ela. She loved it so much that she had pulled over to hear it all the way through. While she lived he had never dared play it for her, but he did on this morning. Afterward he confessed to a few slips, caused by the emotion of the moment, but all anyone in the hall heard was a beautiful sound and the love it expressed.

Alexander was followed by ten-year-old grandson Logan's beautiful rendition of a Mozart sonata on the grand piano and then seven-year-old grandson Lachlan, dressed as a midcentury Irish boy, sang and danced "Dublin Saunter," accompanied by his mother, Geneva. Alex-ander returned with five more musicians, including his wife, Mary Jane, who performed his remarkable original composition "Memory Box," which was inspired by the items he found when he opened Maggie's box of mementos, gathered during a lifetime. Haunting and yet hopeful, the piece was played entirely on percussion instruments and would have filled his mother with pride.

Finally, after a few folks offered spontaneous recollections, it was time for me to speak and struggle against the feelings that rose in my throat. I described our life together and Maggie's strong character, noting that while I had been a boss for hundreds of thousands of people, "I never was, for thirty seconds, the boss of Maggie." I talked about how she savored and helped me sort out the complex dramas in my business life, and recalled that on the day she died, union workers were picketing, Delphi was engaged in heated negotiations, and I was racing the clock to reach her bedside from New York. I was crestfallen to arrive too late, but I suspect Maggie would have loved the excitement.

At the end of my remarks, Lionel and I would unveil, together, a big poster announcing we had endowed a Maggie Miller Chair for an oboist in the Detroit Symphony Orchestra. The gift was a fitting way to honor Maggie and ensure her spirit would live on. But before we pulled the covering off the display, I quoted our son Chris, who was there when I met Maggie, there when we married, and there holding her hand when she died. He said, "I miss her wisdom, her values, her lectures, and her opinionated stubbornness. She was one tough broad with an attitude."

If I ever answer another call to serve a company in crisis, I will seize the challenge with the same enthusiasm I felt when she was with me. We both believed in the value of hard work, the contributions that healthy companies make to communities, and our obligation to help when we can. I still hold those beliefs and will be guided by them. But I will miss her wisdom, values, lectures, and stubborn opinions. And most of all, I'll miss the tough broad with an attitude.

———

AT THE TIME of Maggie's death, I was certain that romance would never again be part of my life. Between business adventures, hobbies, and time with kids and grandkids, I thought I would be fully occupied through my sunset years. It was Maggie who, on her death bed, not only predicted that I would meet "someone wonderful," but also encouraged and blessed it. I told her that I could not imagine such a thing. Once more, her insight was better than mine.

Several months after her death, I was once again at the Greenbrier Conference, perhaps the most important annual gathering of all the top leaders of the auto industry, and the forum where I had a year earlier first laid out the truth of Delphi's situation. And it was there that I was introduced to Jill Jablonski, the executive director of Detroit's Society of Automotive Engineers (that's the SAE viscosity rating on your oil can), which was the host of the conference. She was beautiful, vivacious, and incredibly competent in handling the eight hundred or so people and scores of speakers who participated in this multiday annual event.

Then in December 2006, I was at an industry Christmas party in Detroit. Surrounded by news reporters and business executives, my eye kept wandering across the room to this gorgeous creature. My heart skipped a few beats. And when Jill put on her coat to leave and shake hands good-bye, I leaned over and said, "Don't leave." To my astonishment, she took off her coat and stayed. I just wanted to talk to her, but I ended up asking her out to dinner a few weeks hence: my first attempt at a date in forty years. I didn't know what had gotten into me. And who was I to think she'd have any interest in me? But she said "yes" as she drove off into the night.

There followed a whirlwind romance. By late spring of 2007 we were engaged to be married. Our wedding took place in September at the spectacular Henry Ford Museum in Dearborn, Michigan, amid hundreds of our friends, family, and business associates. The setting was most appropriate for the two of us, tying together Detroit, the auto industry, and history.

Jill's arrival has added a whole new dimension to my life. I have a partner to share love as well as to recount the events of each day.

One more time, it has proven that I should never try to guess what the future holds for me. I have been wrong every time, and most often pleasantly surprised.

POSTSCRIPT

In general I like to leave politics—and therefore national policy—to those elected to lead us. Unlike some prominent businesspeople, I don't believe everyone wants to know, or needs to know, my opinion on every issue. In fact, I don't think that any one person has a lock on wisdom. As you have seen in these pages, I prefer to explore all the angles of a problem and find realistic solutions that call on a variety of ideas and players. A union chief was one of my most valuable allies when I worked at Bethlehem Steel. A physician became the key executive at Aetna. In every case I have sought the best solution, not one that fit my personal politics.

But while experience has taught me to be flexible and avoid pontificating on political issues, my work with major corporations in crisis has given me a unique perspective. As friends and colleagues tell me, I have spent decades wrestling with certain big problems—health care, pensions, energy—that continue to vex the nation and have so far defied solution. While I cannot pretend to be an expert on any of these Big Three issues, I am a concerned citizen with an unusual, insider's point of view. And as I look to my own future, I hope to contribute to the debate over these three challenges, which will only become more pressing.

PENSIONS

In every corporate crisis I have attended, longtime employees have been intently and vocally concerned about their security in retirement. This is easy to understand. Whether you are a seven-figure executive or an hourly worker with twenty years on the assembly line, you worry about the years when you may not be able to work. We all wonder, will that time be full of fear and struggle, or could it be a chance to enjoy some rewards for a lifetime of productive and responsible effort? Will I outlive the money available for my support?

In days gone by, traditional pension plans worked because our lives were shorter and our expectations were lower. Today we are living longer, hope to retire younger, and expect to live as well as we did while actively working. These are huge changes that fundamentally shift the economics of a pension system. It requires massive savings set aside from the fruits of our labor in our working years to fund perhaps as many years of life beyond retirement. Most of us know the outline of the problem created by these factors, but it helps to review:

- The number of workers contributing to Social Security in order to fund each retiree has dropped from ten to two, putting the system under considerable long-term risk.

- State and local governments are swamped with the obligations to retired teachers, police, and other government staffers.

- Large employers with defined benefit pension programs are being overwhelmed, in part because their retirees are living many years longer than anyone expected when plans were devised.

The legacy of unfunded pensions threatens the survival of major companies that provide the jobs and the business activity that keep our economy humming. In their struggle to survive, those that can have turned to defined contribution, 401(k) type of programs. Newer companies adopt these plans at the start. No more legacy liability issues for the newer sectors of our economy!

I think the move away from defined benefits is a very healthy development, for three reasons. One, an employer-based pension is the ultimate in concentration of risk for the worker. Not only is his or her job at risk if the employer goes bust, but quite often the expected pension entitlement is destroyed as well. In a defined contribution plan, the money is yours, and nobody can take it away from you. Two, employer-based pensions are not portable. You are locked into a job that may not suit you anymore, but you can't afford to leave. In a defined contribution plan, you can take it with you. In today's mobile society, that's a better design. And three, defined contributions are an annual event set by prevailing economic conditions at the company. No more huge uncontrollable liabilities that can sink an otherwise seaworthy enterprise.

While this is a welcome and inexorable trend, traditional old-line companies with defined benefit programs are tipping into bankruptcy at an alarming rate, thrusting their pension liabilities into the hands of the Pension Benefit Guaranty Corporation (PBGC). Congress has been wrestling with this issue for a long time. The big question surrounds the dilemma: Do you tighten the funding rules and risk tipping more employers into bankruptcy and terminating their pension plans? Or do you loosen the rules to provide temporary relief, only to find the problem continuing to grow worse and with more companies getting into trouble later?

Where I fundamentally disagree with current policy is the notion that one-size-fits-all solutions are appropriate. In a nutshell, I would tighten, not loosen, the rules, but at the same time give the PBGC the flexibility, with approval authority vested in its board, to cut tailor-made repayment plans that reflect the needs of a particular company. And I would give the PBGC what I call conventional weapons, including the right to negotiate covenants, collateral, benefit freezes, and other mechanisms, to protect the interests of the PBGC from catastrophic failures.

Consider the analogy of the FDIC. When a private banking institution wants a federal guarantee for its private contract with a depositor customer, it has to submit to frequent quarterly reviews of its fiscal integrity. Required adjustments are swiftly imposed when trouble looms. Hence, you don't read much about bank failures anymore.

Contrast that with pension plans. Again, it is a private contract between an employer and its workers, backstopped by a federal agency. The funding requirements are very loose for two reasons. Point one: Our accounting system permits a near fantasy in the assumptions about the earning power of plan assets versus the present value of the plan liabilities. Let me play with the interest rates, and I can always show you how a one-dollar investment can cover a two-dollar problem. I believe corporate America chronically underestimates the real economic shortfall in the funding of most plans.

Point two is that there is incredible lag time in addressing any shortfall. A stock market decline affecting the value of plan assets occurring in January of year one does not even get addressed by the contribution rules until September of the year following, and then the recovery requirement is spread over a bunch of future years. By the time the rules catch up with you, you may be hopelessly behind. Sure, there are other things companies would rather spend money on than shoring up the pension plan. But it was not the intent of the system to provide easy credit to employers at the expense of the PBGC. I would do a mark-to-market exercise quarterly, rather than annually, and require recovery plans to be worked out with the PBGC promptly.

To repeat my suggestion: Tighten the rules. Let the PBGC deal with individual situations.

HEALTH CARE—TIME FOR A NATIONAL PLAN?

Well, if you think the pension situation is bad, what about health care? This is unquestionably our country's number one domestic issue. Nothing meaningful can get done until the next presidential administration, but the political debate will dominate the headlines well into 2009.

Unlike pensions, which are prefunded to some extent, employer health care promises by and large are completely unfunded and without any federal backstop except the partial coverage of Medicare for those over sixty-five. The numbers are staggering. At General Motors, our largest industrial employer, the unfunded liability for future health care costs for its retirees (probably understated) vastly exceeds the automaker's total investment in plants and equipment to actually make cars and trucks.

The mess we're in is the result of decisions made decades ago, when the country decided to make employers the main provider for health insurance. As a result, ever-higher expenses are handed to corporations that must build these costs into the prices they charge for goods and services. With these higher costs, they lose out to competitors based in countries where no one expects the boss to pay for health care. Lost market share leads to job cuts and struggle for American workers. (Too many find themselves without any health insurance and risk financial ruin if they get sick.) As U.S. companies search for savings, they build plants in other countries. In fact, the single biggest factor driving a decision to put new investment offshore is the punitive effect of health care costs on job creation in America.

I can't offer a single, sweeping solution to the health care dilemma. However, I have seen the problems from the inside—as an employer and as an insurance executive—and I know there are several imperatives that we must face.

First, we need to provide basic health care coverage to all our citizens. There is no good reason that anyone in a country with America's resources should be left without reasonable access to care. In fact, most people can actually get care, but it is typically in emergency room situations that are more costly and inefficient for our system than regular access might be.

Second, we need to reduce the cost of health care. I would focus on improved information technology to determine why some providers (doctors and hospitals) have much better outcomes than others or which therapies are more likely to succeed. This technology can also reduce paperwork and bureaucracy, and it can stimulate competition. How? By providing patients with better information about these choices and forcing providers to compete more openly.

Third, we need to get control of lawsuits. Despite the howls from the trial bar that we need to give an occasional malpractice victim a day in court, the costs imposed on all the rest of us by the frivolous lawsuits and the unnecessary tests and procedures carried out "just in case," are an onerous burden.

Fourth, and most controversially, I'd suggest we admit we have to ration health care. Based on ever-longer lifetimes and advancing medical technologies (both good things), we are gradually getting to the point where we would be theoretically capable of spending our entire GNP on health care! That can't happen—people want food and shelter as well. And frankly, we are going to encounter increasing intergenerational friction as young people resent having their wages reduced and taxed away to pay for health care for their grandparents. At some point, we will have to decide not to spend a million dollars extending the life of a comatose nonagenarian; even though it is medically feasible, it just isn't financially feasible. This will raise a host of ethical and religious debates challenging a centuries-old value system, but the time has come. When my time is up, pull the plug!

When all this is done, it still won't stop the growth in health care expenditure; at best it will slow it down. We do need to stop sending the bill to our job-creating industries in America, although that will create protests about "windfalls for business." Financing health care through consumption taxes, ugly as they are politically, may be the best answer.

Altogether, the challenges will drive us a lot closer to national health care, a bugaboo if ever there was one. But the current system is rapidly destroying our economy and needs to be changed. I am ready to consider all options.

ENERGY POLICY—RAISE GAS TAXES?

Our nation is increasingly concerned with energy policy, and for good reason. The need to import petroleum products is a serious drain on our national treasure, and the environmental impact of our consumption patterns threatens our quality of life. Global warming is real. Greenhouse gases are the source. And we share the responsibility to reduce them.

Many politicians want to fix the problem through bold regulatory decrees, the leading example of which is the debate over CAFE, or corporate average fuel economy. These rules require that automakers achieve a certain level of miles per gallon on the average vehicle sold.

It is hard to imagine a less elegant way to address the problem. For one thing, it puts the manufacturer at war with consumers. We have long had an energy policy based on cheap gas, which in turn creates demand for large and powerful fuel-thirsty vehicles. It has been analogized to addressing national obesity by requiring clothing manufacturers to reduce the size of the suits they sell, while cutting prices at the fast food chains.

CAFE rules also require that a lot of time and money be spent on lobbying the regulators. When Chrysler introduced the minivan in the

1980s, it was crucial that the vehicle be designated a truck, not a car so that the easier standard would apply. Getting this designation required countless hours of lobbying, negotiating, and schmoozing. What nonsense!

As another example, Delphi has the technology to make air conditioners for cars that save a lot on fuel consumption. But the automakers aren't buying it. Why? Because the CAFE calculation rules are based on mileage with the air conditioning turned off! More nonsense.

The rest of the world has a far better answer: fuel taxes. Our politicians pat themselves on the back that the CAFE laws somehow force manufacturers to produce higher-mileage vehicles and that this is a free gift to the consumer. Sorry. The laws of physics trump the laws of Congress. You can get better mileage only by making a smaller or lighter or more expensive vehicle, which involves tradeoffs. In Europe, the average fuel economy of the fleet is much better than in the United States (and Europe extensively uses diesel, which is better yet), not because of CAFE laws or smarter auto engineers, but because fuel costs more than $5 a gallon.

Unpopular as it is, if I were czar, I would add a dollar or two to the price of gas in the United States, perhaps ramped up over several years to ease the way. There would be several important benefits. One, fuel consumption would be reduced. At the margin, people would make choices in the short term to take fewer unnecessary trips. They would opt for car pools or public transport in larger numbers. And they would shop for a more fuel-efficient car next time. Two, the environmental impact would be favorable. Three, the impact on our balance of trade would be favorable. And four, the federal government would raise about a billion dollars a year per penny of tax raised. By their nature, fuel taxes are the simplest taxes to administer. (Compare it to the cost to society of administering an income tax.)

So what's the problem? Voting for a one-penny gas tax is a political death warrant. At least for now. Nobody wants to pay more taxes. But a fuel tax increase can displace other less efficient means by which government raises necessary revenues. I hope that one day soon we can get serious and get the market working in favor of energy efficiency, instead of fighting it. Fuel taxes are a crucial part of the solution.

Pensions, health care, and energy are three things I understand through long and challenging experience. I hope that the stories I have told in this book have demonstrated that very big and complex problems can be resolved when people share a goal, work hard, and let their better nature come to the fore. Honesty, integrity, empathy, and mutual respect played a role in finding resolutions to the crises I confronted. If there's one takeaway lesson to be gleaned from my journey, it is that they are the essential ingredients we need as a society to move forward. They worked for my grandfather in Bandon, for my father in Portland, and for me around the world. They will help us all as we confront the Big Three, and other major issues as they arise.

ACKNOWLEDGMENTS

Over the years, I have been approached a number of times by people saying, "Steve, you should write a book!" I have often described my business adventures in luncheon speeches, but I never considered that there was enough material to make a book.

Then in late 2005, a mutual friend introduced me to HarperCollins, and I became intrigued by the idea. My wife, Maggie, was highly enthused by the idea, but she didn't want to be mentioned in the book. Nonetheless, she immediately went out and bought a fancy hat at Neiman Marcus to wear on the "book tour."

Part of the deal was to have a collaborator—someone who would listen to me spew out all my memories and get them in writing in my vernacular. I selected Michael D'Antonio for this task, based in part on his track record as an author. More importantly, I was impressed by his answer to my question "How will you capture the importance of my upbringing in Oregon?" He said, "I will go with you to Oregon and walk with you following your childhood footsteps." Clearly, he wanted to look at the world through my eyes, and that would make this book more genuine. Michael and I spent numerous weekends together, poring over old newspapers and diaries, and probing the far reaches of my memory banks.

Others who have volunteered to help include Karen Healy, the vice president of communications (and other stuff) at Delphi, and Bev Roberts, my tireless administrative assistant at Delphi. Together, they provided the inspiration and the perspiration to finish the book.

To the many others who helped, I am grateful.

Steve Miller
2007

INDEX

ABOUT THE AUTHOR

Robert S. Miller, better known as Steve, was recruited by Lee Iacocca to work on the Chrysler turnaround in 1979. He led the financial negotiations with four hundred banks and the federal government that led to the bailout that saved Chrysler. He eventually became the vice chairman and CFO of Chrysler. In 1992 he began a succession of restructuring efforts. Working first on real estate conglomerate Olympia & York's $20 billion of debts, he eventually served in a top leadership role at Morris Knudsen (construction), Federal-Mogul (auto parts), Waste Management (environmental services), Reliance Group (insurance), Aetna (health care), Bethlehem Steel, and Delphi (auto parts). Following the death in 2006 of Maggie Kyger, his wife of forty years, Miller was happily remarried in September 2007 to Jill Jablonski. They reside in Michigan.